Modern Waterfowling Guns & Gunning

Don Zutz

Stoeger Publishing Company

Published by Stoeger Publishing Company
55 Ruta Court
South Hackensack, New Jersey 07606

ISBN 0-88317-133-3

Library of Congress Catalog Card No.: 85-051161

Manufactured in the United States of America

Distributed to the book trade and to the sporting goods
trade by Stoeger Industries, 55 Ruta Court,
South Hackensack, New Jersey 07606

In Canada, distributed to the book trade and to
the sporting goods trade by Stoeger Canada Ltd.,
169 Idema Road, Markham, Ontario L3R 1A9

Contents

Preface

Decoys so big that hunters can hide inside them; magnum loads so heavy that the 12-gauge Magnum now throws as much shot as the Magnum 10 did until just a few years ago; a 10-gauge, gas-operated autoloader that fires three quick shots without kicking a hunter out of his duck skiff; steel shot as opposed to lead shot; custom-made duck and goose calls; the finest outdoor clothing to keep one warm and dry in the stormiest weather; decoys that fly like kites; concentrations of weekend hunters surrounding refuges, skyblasting continuously to drive the flights progressively higher; new guns designed and finished specifically for the waterfowl hunter; gunsmithing advances that can significantly improve the long-range patterning qualities of shotguns; and highly sophisticated and refined commercial and hand-loaded ammunition — such are the changes taking place in modern waterfowl hunting.

About the only things that haven't changed are the birds themselves. They may be somewhat warier because of the increased hunting pressure, but, physically speaking, they haven't changed. They are no faster or slower, bigger or smaller, tougher or weaker than they were when market hunters raked the Chesapeake Bay or the great wingshots established their reputations in Illinois and Arkansas.

It is the purpose of this book to match the technological changes in modern guns and ammunition with the field uses to which they will be put. Essentially, it is a semi-technical look at the potency and potentiality of our waterfowl guns and loads, written with the hope that this mildly scientific and analytical approach will prompt hunters to take a more critical look at their equipment and its capabilities for the betterment of our sport by shooting within effective ranges and by dropping birds cleanly.

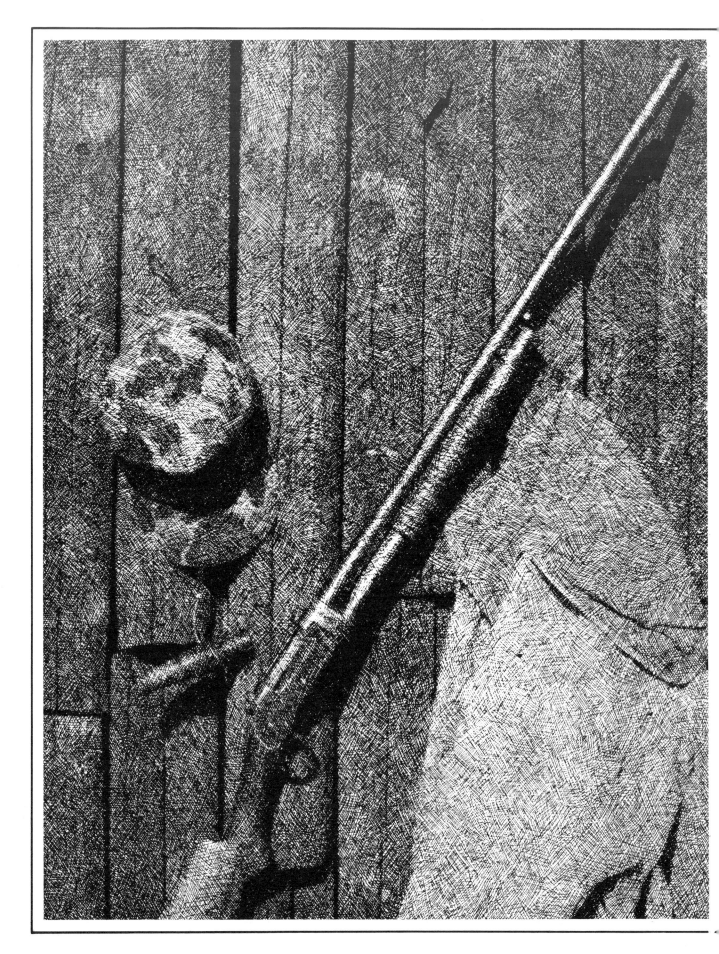

1
The Long Tom Tradition

From the time when punt guns and 8 gauges were everyday waterfowling pieces, duck and goose hunting have traditionally been equated with long, ponderous, full-choked shotguns that throw heavy charges of big pellets. Barrels of 30–34 inches reigned supreme; anything shorter and lighter was deemed racy, if not radical. Early pumpgun makers included 32-inch barrels as a natural part of the business, and there was a certain fascination for such catchy trade names as Long Range Wonder, Super Ranger, and Long Tom. These enticingly labeled guns were normally single-shots with pronounced barrels of 36– 40 inches, and old-timers who didn't bother about such things as actual patterning and comparative ballistics thought such chimneylike barrels turned the smoothbore into a veritable rifle.

Americans and Canadians weren't the only ones afflicted with such an obsession, either. In fact, they probably caught it from the British and Europeans who demonstrated almost blind loyalty to lengthy tubes. When noted British gunmaker Robert Churchill introduced his famous 25-inch-barreled XXV double in the early 1920s, for instance, he was severely chastised in print for years by contemporary shooting editors. How dare Churchill question the 30-inch barrel? How dare he even think of saying the 25-inch barrels were the equal of 30-inchers afield? And, of course, long barrels were characteristic on that early classic among specialized waterfowling doubles, Greener's Far-Killer Duck Gun. And, since stateside sportsmen often looked to England and the Continent for conceptual leadership, the long barrels were accepted without question and became traditional.

This penchant for long, heavy shotguns with gaping muzzles can be understood if one considers the evolution of shotshell performance and the popular tenets of wingshooting theory.

The use of long barrels actually dates back to the black powder era, which helps explain the reliance on sheer length: black powder burns slower than modern smokeless powder; consequently, it needs more confined combustion area in order to generate its full thrust. Westley Richards, another famous British gunmaker, came up with a mathematical axiom when he advocated that, for optimum burning efficiency with black powder, a shotgun's barrel should be forty times its inner diameter. That figures out to 29.16 inches for the conventional 12- gauge, and 31.0 inches for the 10-gauge. The Westley Richards dictum thereby not only justified considerable barrel lenght, but also gave encouragement to the hunters who thought that more barrel length would give substantially more velocity. When this type of thinking ran rampant, barrels of 32 – 40 inches appeared. For whatever reasons, this same kind of thinking has continued even though modern smokeless powders develop adequate energy and velocity within just 18–20 inches of confinement.

If velocity considerations no longer dictate barrel length—if Westley Richards' dictum has fallen before modern technology — why have long, heavy, big-bore shotguns remained symbolic of waterfowling? Mainly, it seems, because the sporting press and hand-me-down advice have drummed certain wing-gunning concepts into our minds. The long barrel, we have been told, is needed as an extended sighting radius for better accuracy on distant targets, and its "hang" (muzzle-heavy quality) provides forward momentum for a smooth swing and positive follow-through. The gun's overall weight, it has also been pointed out endlessly, helps absorb some of the brutal recoil of heavy loads. Thus, once a hunter gets such a long, heavy gun mounted and moving, its mass, theoretically, can be an asset — no question about it.

NEW GUNS TRUE TO TRADITION

For hunters who can handle a lot of gun and load, there are many on the market. One

Harrington & Richardson markets an inexpensive single-shot 10-gauge Magnum with a yard-long barrel.

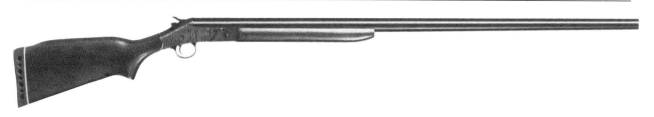

Marlin's Model 5510 is a 34-inch-barreled bolt-action in 10-gauge Magnum.

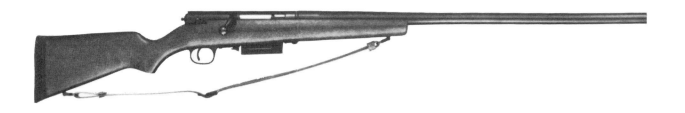

For those who can handle it, Ithaca's Mag-10 is the epitome of traditional waterfowl guns — long, heavy, and made to throw tremendous charges of large shot.

need not shop very long before finding special waterfowl models designed and built according to historical concepts.

Harrington & Richardson, for example, has kept the old Long Tom tradition alive with its 36-inch-barreled 10-gauge Magnum cataloged simply as the Model 176. Specially constructed for steel shot, but equally adept at patterning lead, the Model 176 has an extended forend to help the hunter elevate its 10-pound heft.

The H&R Model 088 can be had in a similar style in 12-gauge Magnum with a 36-inch barrel for somewhat less handling weight and recoil. At one point in the recent past, H&R made a 32-inch-barreled 20-gauge Magnum in the Model 088 configuration, but it didn't catch the public's fancy and has been discontinued. Perhaps one day it will be a collector's item like the Super Range and Long Range Wonder of yesteryear.

The Savage-Stevens organization has also breathed life into the extra-length barrel with a pair of single-shots — the Savage Model 94 and the Stevens Model 9478 — with 36-inch 12-gauge Magnum tubes. The main difference between them is that the Savage M94 has a tang-top opening lever, while the Stevens M9478 is opened by means of a bottom-mounted lever located just ahead of the trigger guard. The Stevens M9478 can also be had in the massive 10-gauge Magnum version with a yard-long barrel to match the H&R M176.

Nor has Marlin forsaken traditionalists. This company's two models of long-barreled bolt-actions have become common sights along the perimeters of waterfowl refuges where hunters snipe at fast-winging birds that have learned to stay high when crossing the boundary lines. Marlin's super-long turnbolts combine all the theoretically sound traditional features into the form of affordable repeaters which, although they lack the rapidity of a pump or autoloader, can be operated for at least two shots on passing geese. The giant member of this Marlin duo is the Model 5510 Supergoose, a 10-gauge Magnum with a 34-inch barrel and an overall weight of 10½ pounds. The lesser member is the Model 55 Goose Gun sporting a 36-inch full-choke barrel and scaling 8 pounds. Both now come with mounted swivels and a carrying strap for easier car-to-blind transit.

An interesting accessory on the Marlin long-barreled bolt guns is a high-sitting appurtenance found just ahead of the front receiver ring. It is advertised as a rear sight and looks like a rear sight, but, in reality, it serves another purpose: the sightlike device forces a hunter to elevate the muzzle slightly to correct the potential low-shooting tendencies of long, limber, vibration-prone barrels. For when a shotgun is fired, its barrel, no matter how long, vibrates under the impact of chamber pressure, and the initial movement is a downward dip of the muzzle despite the apparent upward recoil jump (just as a flyrod's tip ducks downward at the start of a backcast). This dip can have a bearing on the point of impact at long range, because the pattern will fly low if the shot charge emerges when the muzzle is still in its downward attitude, which is often the case with long, supple barrels that don't recover with the same speed as short, springy ones. Thus, the appurtenance is not a true sight, and hunters make mistakes if they use it for aiming. The feature's job is countering the low-shooting tendencies of lengthy barrels, and it should be viewed only as a reference point when swinging on game. Shotguns, after all, are dynamic arms meant to be pointed and swung, not aimed and held tightly. Aiming carefully with a shotgun only slows the swing and encourages missing well behind a moving mark. Indeed, whether the target is in close or at the extreme limits of scattergun effectiveness, the proper technique remains a reliance on hand-to-eye coordination with the shooter's eye placed squarely atop the comb as the de facto rear sight.

Other manufacturers are also in the game with their own specialized waterfowling models. Winchester offers long barrels on its robust over-under, the Model 101 Waterfowl-Winchoke. A 3-inch 12-gauge Magnum, it has 32-inch barrels machined to accept steel loads and various Winchoke tubes. Four tubes are supplied to cover intermediate and long-range hunting: modified, improved modified, full, and extra-full. The gun has a raised ventilated rib that guides one's eye quickly to the front bead, and its 8¼-pound empty weight is distributed in the weight-forward manner, which injects smoothness and momentum into the swing. The overall weight, plus a comb line that is higher than that of many other field-grade doubles (2¼-inch drop at heel) for a straight-line effect, helps tame recoil considerably and makes possible a rapid recovery for quick second shots. Unlike the other Model 101s which generally have silvery, brushed-metal receivers, the Waterfowl-Winchoke has a blued receiver to eliminate glint. Tasteful, lifelike waterfowl scenes are hand-etched into the receiver — a nice touch.

Although side-by-side waterfowl guns are hardly in vogue these days, Winchester did produce a limited edition of five hundred Model 23 Heavy Duck guns. Given a fancy walnut stock and a generous beavertail forearm, this model scales 8½ pounds, thanks

Browning's venerable A-5 Magnum sports a 32-inch barrel.

also to the heavy-walled, 30-inch tubes built for magnum loads. Choked full and full, the barrels give a weight-forward hang and a balance point well ahead of the knuckle joint. In other words, it is totally unlike the quick-handling upland doubles which have between-the-hands weight distribution, and it will be a bit slower swinging into action. But once it starts, it keeps on moving to overcome the hunter's hitches. Like the Model 101 Waterfowl-Winchoke, the Model 23 Heavy Duck gun has a blued receiver. Undoubtedly the classiest side-by-side duck gun made in recent years, the Model 23 not only has traditional waterfowling characteristics, but will probably become a collector's item. Both the Model 101 and Model 23 make pleasant viewing in any blind when the flights slow down, and the hunter who thinks in terms of fine, specialized shotguns and overall aesthetics should enjoy either or both.

Browning does not label its 30-inch barreled Citori over-under or B-SS horizontal double as specialized waterfowling guns, but both fill the bill. Traditional values are definitely upheld in Browning's 32-inch-barreled Automatic-5 Magnum, which weighs about 9 pounds. Now made in Japan, the A-5 12-gauge Magnum hasn't lost anything in functional reliability, but some of the Belgian-made A-5 Magnums had oily-slick actions resulting from hand finishing and fitting of parts that is unknown in today's repeaters.

Browning caters to waterfowlers in its pumpgun offerings, too. The steel-receivered, bottom-ejecting BPS pump can be had with a 32-inch full-choked barrel that is reminiscent of the days when long-barreled Model 97 Winchesters swept the autumn skies. The BPS is chambered for 3-inch shells, and the 32-inch barrel can also be had with the increasingly popular Invector screw-in choke feature. At 8 pounds empty, it is manageable with most magnum loads.

From U.S. Repeating Arms comes perhaps the least expensive waterfowling specialty, the Model 1300 XTR Waterfowl pump with a 30-inch, Winchoke-equipped barrel chambered for the 3-inch 12-gauge Magnum. The gun has a nice long beavertail forend and ventilated rib, along with a full-sized rubber recoil pad. It is somewhat of a lighter gun than the other traditional models, because its receiver is made of high-strength aluminum alloy rather than steel. However, the breech block's front lugs nest directly into the barrel's steel extension, and there is no metallic weakness. Empty, the Model 1300 XTR Waterfowl weighs about 7½ pounds as compared to 8–11 pounds for a lot of other 12- and 10-gauge guns.

Smith & Wesson also offered a waterfowl pumpgun, introducing it in 1982 as the Model 3000 Waterfowler. It had a 30-inch barrel, Parkerized metal, black oxidized bolt, and a dull oil finish. A padded, camouflaged sling and installed swivels were included, as was a rubber recoil pad. The Model 3000 was a

Shown at right:

Left / As a traditional long-barreled pump, the Browning bottom-ejecting BPS can be had with a 30- or 32-inch full-choke barrel.

Center / Remington's 3-inch 12-gauge Magnum 1100 is made with a 32-inch barrel on the DU commemorative designated the Atlantic.

Right / U.S. Repeating Arms has introduced a traditional-style pump, calling it the Model 1300 Magnum Waterfowl with Winchoke. The gun has a non-glare matte finish on its metal, and a low-luster finish on stock and forend.

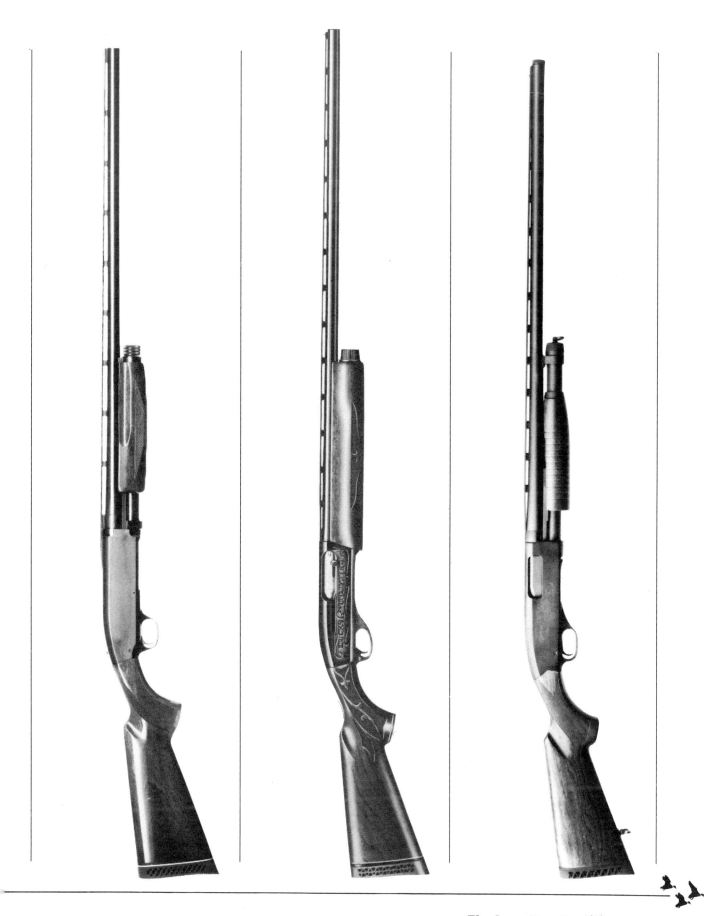

very modern pump in every sense of the word. Those shotguns are no longer in the Smith & Wesson line; the guns are now being distributed by Mossberg.

For a number of seasons, Remington has made various Ducks Unlimited commemorative models, and some of these have been given 32-inch full-choke barrels. The 1983 DU commemorative, for instance, was a 12-gauge Model 870 Magnum called the Mississippi. It carried distinctive engraving on the receiver to celebrate the specific flyway and sported a special DU serial number. A year earlier the Remington DU commemorative had been a Model 1100 12-gauge Magnum, the Atlantic, which also had a 32-inch barrel. These guns can still be found, but you may have to hunt for them among collectors and used gun shops as they were made in limited quantities.

Ithaca has jumped into the duck and goose gun business with a specially finished version of the Model 51 Magnum Autoloader in 12 gauge. To guard against bird-scaring reflections, all exposed metal components, including the 30-inch full-choked barrel, have a matte finish; the bolt has a black oxidized surface; and the stock and forend, bearing impressed checkering, have flat oil finishes. The gun comes with sling swivels in place, and the gun has been strengthened by the inclusion of stainless steel links. The trigger is as light and smooth as any yet found on contem-porary autoloaders, and each rib is capped at the muzzle by the glowing Raybar bead that stands out in rain, snow, gloom, or sun. Although Ithaca advertises the Model 51 as a featherweight gun, the Waterfowl grade tugs most scales to a full 8½ pounds and absorbs recoil nicely for minimal disturbance.

One cannot mention Ithaca without dwelling on the Mag-10. This creative step of teaming the monstrous 10-gauge Magnum shotshell with a softer-recoiling, gas-operated action is the pièce de résistance for modern waterfowlers, blending traditional length, weight, and load concepts with advanced technology. Everything is there: heavy shot loads, gun weight to offset recoil and to help build momentum for a positive follow-through, barrel length (32 inches if you want it) for accurate pointing and a muzzle-heavy hang, three rapid shots for sustained fire, and, above all, reduced recoil.

Several grades of the Mag-10 are available, and the gun can be had in either plain Jane or dolled-up versions. The standard, plain-barreled model is Parkerized and given un-checkered, straight-grained walnut blandly finished in oil. Thereafter, the styles improve as the Mag-10 goes from the Deluxe through the Supreme and Presentation grades with progressively fancier American black walnut stocks and forends. Obviously, the Mag-10's overall weight will increase variously as the added density of full-fancy walnut is com-

Ithaca MAG—10 Deluxe Vent

bined with the 32-inch ventilated rib barrel and basic 11-pound heft. For the hunter who can handle that much gun, then, Ithaca's Mag-10 epitomizes the tradition and theory of combining massive guns, long barrels, and wide bores with lots of big pellets.

But within that last sentence lies food for thought: what about the hunter who can't handle that much gun effectively? It's an important point, because individuals have markedly different physical and athletic abilities; and, if the truth were faced, it would be obvious that many of today's waterfowlers honestly don't have the strength and/or technique to handle such traditional pieces properly. True, hunters can lug them to the blinds. True, hunters can hoist them to their shoulders. And, true, hunters can push such long, heavy guns after the birds and fire off some salvos. Equally true, however, is the fact that they do plenteous missing — as is readily apparent to anyone who observes the fusillades that erupt along refuge boundaries whenever waterfowl pass over — since lugging, struggling, and pushing aren't exactly finesse points in expert wingshooting technique. Such labored gun handling, in fact represents nothing more than a primitive, clumsy, totally inexpert form of shotgunning akin to no technique at all. But, for the hunter who can honestly handle the long, heavy guns apropos to waterfowling traditions, there is nothing better. The current market has a broad selection of models designed and built specially for him. But as we introduce the next chapter, we do so with a constructive, albeit iconoclastic sort of question: must the modern waterfowler who feels slow, labored, and uncomfortable with Long Tom-type guns continue to be a slave to tradition?

2
Lighter Guns and Shorter Barrels

A wise old prophet once observed that "time changes all things," and the logic of his observation is certainly applicable to our topic. Time certainly has had an impact on duck and goose guns and loads. Technology, too, has played a major role in changing equipment and performance. And we have reached a period in history when the impetus of tradition must be questioned. Is the Long Tom attitude still the only viable approach to duck and goose gun selection?

Dedicated old-timers and other traditionalists may shudder at this, but advanced technology, along with a critical assessment of wingshooting technique, permit a serious, scientific reconsideration of the waterfowl gun's physical form and handling qualities. Bluntly stated, we have reached a time when the old Long Tom can be replaced without sacrificing effective ballistic output.

Why would anyone want less than a 30-inch barrel for waterfowling? Because lighter, somewhat shorter guns respond better in the hands of those who aren't built like NFL linebackers, that's why. Indeed, if a shotgun's bulky proportions impede the application of sound handling and swinging technique, that gun is counterproductive regardless of how much shot it spews. Missing a bird is not usually due to a weak shot pattern and/or velocity. More birds are missed by horrible shooting technique than by puny patterns or slow pellets. If a hunter can't score consistently with a 30-inch-barreled Magnum 12, he certainly won't be able to handle a 10-gauge Magnum any better. In all probability, his performance will worsen because his swing will deteriorate to a mere drag, and he'll shoot farther behind the birds than he did with the 12-gauge.

LIGHTER GUNS

Before a hunter can reap the advantages of a faster-handling shotgun, however, he must admit to himself that one of the ponderous long-range cannons is too much gun for him. He can do that by taking an honest look at his gun handling and scoring. When gun mounting is a chore requiring extensive arm and shoulder effort; when the swing is nothing more than a labored dragging of the muzzle without speed or spirit; and when more than four or five empties pile up on the floor of the blind for every bird taken cleanly — it's time to lighten up. He's got too much gun for his size, strength, and technique.

One problem is getting hunters to admit (even to themselves) that they can't handle a 10-gauge Magnum. Big guns are ego trips. Handgunners like to use .45s and .44 Magnums. Rifle buffs frequently gravitate to the husky belted magnums. And, if the truth were out, we'd see that very few shooters of either persuasion are any good with those heavy, hard-kicking pieces. So, too, is the typical duck or goose hunter overgunned with much of the traditional-type ordnance he often buys more for the sake of machismo than common sense. Therefore, whereas some shooters are drawn toward larger gauges, longer barrels, and heavier guns, the reverse approach would undoubtedly be more productive for typical hunters.

A shotgun, for use at whatever ranges, should match a particular hunter's physical

---

The lightweight over-under being carried here by the author may very well be the duck gun of the future, as the trend is away from those heavy, sluggish, long-barreled guns of yesteryear and toward shorter, lighter magnum-grade pieces that are easier to swing.

and athletic abilities for easy mounting, accurate pointing, brisk and controlled swings, and coordinated timing. For some people, this means only a 7½-pound gun — anything heavier placing a strain on muscles and causing a breakdown in technique and timing. Others can handle a full 8½ pounds of gun before feeling encumbered, and a few can actually take the 11-pound 10-gauge Magnum through its paces without sacrificing smoothness, timing, or overall technique. But those who can honestly and effectively handle a gun weighing more than 8½–9 pounds are few and far between.

Lighter shotguns have a more delightful dynamic quality about them. They swing into action enthusiastically, sprint through the swing to set up the necessary forward allowance, and are entirely controllable for "grooved" timing and accurate pointing.

Back in the early 1970s, my partners and I used either skeet guns or doubles bored IC&M on the prairie potholes of southern Manitoba, while the local hunters used 30-inch-barreled pumpguns. We had an excellent bird-to-shell ratio, while the Canadians racked up poor averages. Most of the potholes weren't any larger than a softball diamond or skeet field, and our short, fast-handling guns got on the teal and mallards with ease, while the Canadians had all sorts of trouble unlimbering those longer guns on close, quick targets.

This same improved handling quality also applies to long-range wingshooting; if a hunter's technique is sound, a lighter, shorter gun will score as well as a long, ponderous one. The difficulty is getting hunters to accept the fact that they are not great shots and to start blaming themselves for missing, not their guns and loads.

The British have long demonstrated that high birds can be taken with trim, delightfully balanced doubles that weigh only 6½ pounds or a tad less. Known as game guns, such British doubles will balance nicely between the shooter's hands with the remainder of their weight divided evenly fore and aft for responsive pivoting; they do not have the muzzle-heavy sag that dampens initial movement and swing speed as do repeating guns with long barrels and substantial overall weight. And the millions of high pheasants that British sportsmen have stroked from the sky with those relatively light game guns at-

Although this Merkel over-under weighs only 6¾ pounds, it does an excellent job for the writer on high passing birds because it swings with more spirit and speed than does a long, heavy-barreled gun of the traditional sort.

test to the correctness of the concept. Moreover, the British regularly shoot loads of just 1 or 1$\frac{1}{16}$ ounces of shot, proving again that technique counts more than sheer gun/load potency.

My own experience with lighter guns for long-range pass shooting has caused me to cock a skeptical eyebrow at the conventional Long Tom concept. On my rack is a 12-gauge Merkel over-under with handling qualities almost like a British game gun. It scales just 6¾ pounds, and it differs from the true game gun only in that its 28⅝-inch barrels have slightly thicker walls. Sensitive shotgunners will detect slightly more forward weight in the Merkel than in a British classic, but just slightly more. Otherwise the Merkel flows almost effortlessly toward a moving mark, placing no strain whatsoever on the shooter's muscles, and I have used it often with scatter loads for close-breaking upland game; the scatter loads being necessary because the lean, tapered barrels pattern full and extra-full with normal loads. But in addition to the upland handling qualities of that Merkel, it is also a pet of mine for pass shooting. I have developed a 1$\frac{3}{16}$-ounce reload for it, which, with buffered, copper-plated No. 2s, patterns 88–90 percent from both barrels for extremely stiff center densities; and with that combination of a lively gun and effective reloads, I have done far better on geese than tradition-bound hunters, lugging 9–11-pound guns, would care to believe.

It is quite possible that hunters who can't hit with a standard-weight 12 would do far better if they dropped back to a lighter, shorter-barreled 12 or a 3-inch 20-gauge instead of jumping helter-skelter to a heavier Magnum 12 or a massive 10-gauge Magnum. The larger

The Remington Model 870 S.P. Magnum illustrates the current trend. It is Parkerized and given a flat finish to eliminate bird-scaring glints. This traditional style has a 30-inch barrel, but the gun is available with a faster-swinging 26-inch barrel, also full-choked.

The Ithaca Model 51-A Turkey Gun has a trim, 26-inch full-choke barrel.

A Canada goose taken with Ithaca's Turkey Gun.

guns put added demands on technique, and a hunter who can't handle a standard 12 certainly won't be able to master more gun. With the right ammunition giving good patterns, a lightweight 12 or a 3-inch 20 can turn in stellar performances merely because the hunter can handle it. And since ranges are frequently overestimated anyway, the standard-chambered 12 and 3-inch 20 can generally stop all birds that come within the range of a typical hunter's ability.

This author had an enlightening experience with Ruger's Red Label over-under. When that gun first came out, it was only made in 20 gauge with 26-inch barrels. I got an early one bored IC&M, the kind most hunters would automatically relegate to uplanding. But I wanted to give the gun a thorough wringing out before writing about

it, so I developed reloads which, with copper-plated shot, would provide modified pattern percentages through the improved cylinder choke and full-choke patterns through the modified barrel. The 7-pound Ruger then went duck and goose hunting, and it was a delight in pass shooting. My bird-to-shell ratio was as good as, or better than, my prior best. The gun moved briskly, yet hit with authority. Even when hip-deep in weed-cluttered water with both feet sucked tight by muck, I could spin the little gun into action almost effortlessly for shots on either side. The same physical flow isn't possible with a hulking 10 gauge or long-barreled Magnum 12.

Twenty-six-inch barrels may be a bit stubby for serious pass shooting with the 3-inch 20, of course. Those of 28 inches are suggested for their extra weight up front. But my results with the 26-inchers prove what a dynamic gun can do if the loads and the hunter's technique are right.

THE EMERGING TREND

Not all waterfowlers will want to try the 3-inch 20, nor will many of them opt for a truly featherweight 12-gauge. How can greater handling ease be bred into magnum-grade 12s and the monster 10-gauge Magnum? It's done by shrugging off traditions and ancient ballistics beliefs and selecting barrels of just 26–28 inches for 10- and 12-gauge guns of standard and magnum weights. That may sound radical, but abbreviated barrels are becoming very common for magnum shotguns, and the trend is gaining momentum.

A shorter barrel not only reduces overall weight and muzzle-heavy sag, but also lets the hunter accelerate his swing for a faster arc. Contrary to some popular notions, a shorter gun doesn't move through a shorter arc than a longer gun; the geometry remains the same. The advantage is in speed, which makes all the difference in the world when one is trying to set up those forward allowances needed on fast, far-out birds.

Perhaps the first step in this direction was taken several years ago when Remington made a limited run of 26-inch full-choke barrels for both the 870 pump and 1100 auto. The idea was to facilitate gun handling in cramped waterfowl and turkey blinds without sacrificing pattern density. Although the barrels sold, there was no loud clamor for more. Historically speaking, the time was not right.

Today, though, the emerging trend is toward shorter barrels on all repeating guns, standard and magnum alike. Remington and Ithaca are foremost in the field of trimming

Ithaca has improved the handling qualities of the massive Mag-10 by giving it a 26-inch full-choke barrel, which moves better than the original 32-inch tube.

full-choked barrels, and hunters have begun to sit up in their duck skiffs and take notice. What really got their attention is Remington's 21-inch-barreled Special Field variant of their Models 870 and 1100. This is such a radical departure from the norm that the public simply had to notice it, and, once John and Jane Q. Public handled the guns, they liked them.

Other gunmakers were quick to follow Remington's lead with barrels of 21–24 inches. However, the emphasis has always been on upland hunting rather than waterfowl models.

Except at Ithaca, that is. Here, the formerly heavy, long-barreled, magnum-chambered guns have been bobbed for easier handling. The Model 51 Magnum, for example, has been given a 26-inch full-choke barrel and labeled the Turkey Gun. In all respects it is otherwise the very same gun as the 30-inch-barreled Model 51 Magnum Waterfowler. As its name implies, the Ithaca Turkey Gun is intended for convenience in the turkey woods; however, that doesn't detract from the gun's potential on waterfowl. Forget the name and the Turkey Gun also becomes a somewhat faster-handling, quicker-swinging gun than its companion Waterfowl model. This writer has used both and will lay odds that an average duck hunter will score better with the 26-inch Turkey Gun because it doesn't weigh down and overpower his technique. The styling is, in fact, a good compromise between the heft of a long-range gun for smooth, steady swinging and the brevity of an intermediate- or close-range gun for snappier movement. Taking a Turkey Gun into a duck blind or goose pit may not sound exactly right, but guns should be picked for their effectiveness in the individual hunter's hands, not their trade name.

In a move that may surprise many, Ithaca has also begun to make available 26-inch full-choke barrels for the great Mag-10. It is

definitely a stride in the right direction. By taking six inches off the Mag-10's normal waterfowling barrel, Ithaca has made the basically huge gun somewhat more manageable and a bit faster pointing and swinging. Indeed, one reason why hunters pound so many two- and three-shot salutes at passing birds without disturbing a feather is failure to generate ample swing speed with long-tubed 10s. Thus, although the Mag-10 with a 26-inch barrel is still not a lightweight by any means (it weighs 10¾ pounds empty), it does handle better than the same gun with a 32-inch barrel. As a rule, this writer can live without a 10-gauge duck gun, but the shorter barrel length does move acceptably fast and speaks with authority when the mallards hang high.

The abbreviated Mag-10 and a pair of greenheads that couldn't outfly it.

Hunters who use intermediate-weight shotguns — the Remington 870, Winchester 1300 or 1500, Mossberg or Stevens pumps, Savage/Fox autoloader, or Weatherby Eighty-Two auto or Ninety-Two pump — might think in terms of 28-inch barrels rather than longer ones. On over-unders, most of which are now chambered for 3-inch shells, 28-inch barrels are suggested instead of 30-inchers as the merest concession to handling ease. A gun like that splits differences nicely and doesn't inject any serious disadvantages for either long- or close-range gunning.

For pumpgunners, an outstanding magnum-grade candidate in 12 or 20 gauge is Ithaca's Model 37 field-grade Magnum with ventilated rib, 28-inch barrel, and screw-in chokes for versatility. The 12-gauge weighs 7¼ pounds, and, with a full-sized recoil pad in place, is tolerable with all magnums except the newest 2-ounce 12-gauge load from Federal. Another good choice is Remington's

The point limit taken with one of the author's favorite waterfowl guns, the Remington Model 1100 12-gauge Magnum with a 28-inch modified barrel. The difference between a 30- and a 28-inch barrel is frequently quite noticeable to serious shotgunners, and the shorter version swings quicker to catch and pass speeding targets.

economy copy of the Model 870, the Sportsman 12, which has excellent handling qualities with the 28-inch barrel in place.

When shorter, tightly choked barrels aren't available for a certain type of shotgun, the new screw-in choke tube installations solve the problem. Several custom gunsmithing firms offer the service and will either shorten a repeater's barrel to the desired length, or thread the muzzle of a side-by-side or over-under to receive hidden tubes that throw dense clusters. Walker Arms Company, Rt. 2, P.O. Box 73, Selma, Alabama 36701, can counterbore and tap any type of shotgun barrel to accept their own brand of full-thread choke tubes. On my rack is a Remington 12-gauge M1100 barrel that started life as a 28-inch modified but was cut to 26 inches by Walker and threaded for internal choke tubes. The gun handles like a skeet grade, but the full- and Xtra-full choke tubes make it shoot like a Long Tom. Incidentally, Walker's No. 2 skeet tube has produced the most evenly distributed patterns with steel shot I've seen to date. In a nutshell you don't have to be stuck with a long, unwieldy barrel on a favorite gun. Specialty gunsmiths can cut and rechoke barrels, thus making the gun faster to swing and tremendously versatile.

The point needs no further elaboration. Shorter barrels with modified or full choke are coming into vogue, and they can help the hunter whose technique and physical prowess aren't up to getting the most from robust, obese guns that handle like tall smokestacks.

PERFORMANCE FACTS

But although most hunters would admit that shorter, lighter shotguns do handle better than the Long Tom types, they still have qualms about downrange performance. Will short barrels develop enough velocity to "hit hard" at long range? Will they pattern as tightly as 30–36-inchers? And can they be pointed accurately for hits at 60 to 75 yards?

To lay a groundwork of scientific facts rather than proceed via guesstimates, some patterning, chronographing, and accuracy work was done with a trio of the newest short-barreled models: a Remington 12-gauge Special Field, an Ithaca Model 51 Turkey Gun, and an Ithaca Mag-10 with 26-inch FC barrel.

Patterning came first. Shooting at 40 yards, the Mag-10's full-choke 26-inch barrel averaged 78 percent with 2-ounce loads of copper-plated BBs, and some individual patterns got to 82–83 percent. With 2-ounce reloads of high-antimony, magnum-grade No. 2s, patterns averaged 73 percent. Thus, with both loads tested, the shorter-barreled Mag-10 did reach full-choke percentages, and it could be viewed as flirting with extra-full with copper-plated BBs.

The Ithaca Turkey Gun shot between 70 and 75 percent with buffered loads of copper-plated 4s and 2s of Winchester and Remington manufacture. That, again, is honest full-choke work.

My personal 21-inch Special Field barrel had an improved cylinder choke, but a friend patterned his full-choked specimen at 75 percent with No. 7½ trap loads, and 68 percent with Remington 1½-ounce Nitro Mags throwing 4s. That might not be rifle-tight, but it's substantial and better than a lot of 30-inch full chokes shoot with deformation-prone Duck & Pheasant loads. More about these later.

With quality loads of hard or plated shot, then, the shorter barrels definitely got to the full-choke level, and they probably can be made to perform even better when trial-and-error load testing is carried further with buffered handloads.

VELOCITIES

Unlike the days of black powder, barrels no longer have to be forty times as long as

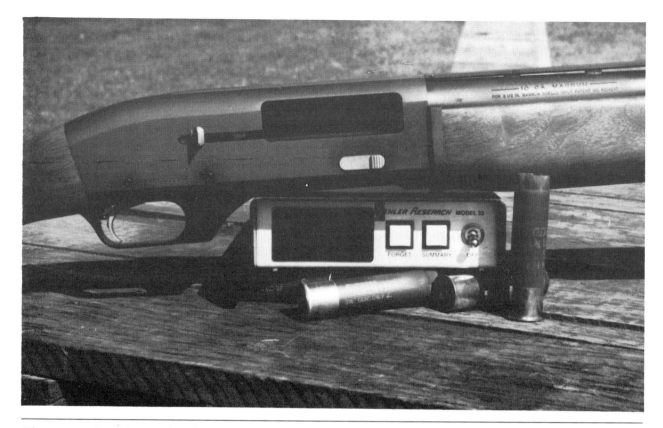

Chronograph tests run by the author prove that there is no significant velocity loss in the 26-inch Mag-10 barrel. Modern powders deliver adequate speeds for all practical waterfowling.

their inside diameter for effective burning. Smokeless powder develops most of its thrust in just 18 to 20 inches. For whatever reasons, however, short barrels don't seem powerful enough to the average hunter who is used to believing that anything less than 30 inches sacrifices important velocity. However, when chronograph results done for this book are compared to retained velocity/energy tables, it will be proof positive that barrels of just 21–26 inches do indeed supply adequate confinement for effective waterfowling velocities.

Chronographing was done with an Oehler Model 33 Chronotach and Skyscreens placed three feet apart. The velocities reported herein are not muzzle velocities, but are instead readings recorded five feet from the gun's muzzle. The use of a baffle eliminated the chance of muzzle blast and shock waves upsetting the operation.

The Mag-10 came first. Its 26-inch barrel averaged 1,325 f.p.s. with Federal's 1⅝-ounce load of steel 2s, which compared favorably with the company's published average of 1,350 f.p.s. from a 32-inch lab barrel. A Remington 2-ounce load of No. 2s clocked 1,185 f.p.s., whereas the same factory load is listed at 1,250 f.p.s. This drop in velocity is certainly not a disaster. It equals the speed of a 3-inch 20's 1¼-ounce load from 28-inch tubes. And, if one checks it against retained energy/velocity charts, he finds that 2s launched at about 1,185 f.p.s. still have at least 5 foot-pounds of energy at 60 yards. Switch to BBs, and the energy factor rises to double the amount needed for positive penetration on 60-yard geese. Therefore, with the copper-plated BB load, which patterned so nicely, this particular Mag-10's 26-inch barrel could do a clean job to 75 yards, ballistically speaking. These stout muzzle velocities are no doubt attributed to the 10's efficient expansion ratio; powder gases find a big, broad wad base upon which to shove, and they transfer their chemical energy into kinetic energy very rapidly.

The Ithaca 26-inch-barreled Turkey Gun also gave a good account of itself. Remington 1¼-ounce, 3-inch loads of steel 2s did 1,300 f.p.s. Federal's 2-ounce load of copper-plated 2s churned up a spritely 1,204 f.p.s., and 1½-ounce Remington Nitro Mags averaged 1,274 f.p.s. with hard 2s. The following handload, which Hercules lists at a nominal 1,300 f.p.s., was also tested:

Federal 3″ plastic case
Federal 209 primer
39.0 gr. Blue Dot powder
Winchester WAA12F114 wad
1⅝ oz. No. 2 hard shot
Pressure: 9,900 p.s.i.

It averaged 1,283 f.p.s. from the 26-inch Ithaca barrel while, in a tangent test, could do no better than 1,319 f.p.s. in the imposing 32-inch barrel of a Browning A-5 Magnum. Despite giving up six inches of barrel length to the A-5, the Ithaca Turkey Gun lost but 36 f.p.s. on the average, or about 6 f.p.s. for each inch of barrel. With velocities already at 1,200 f.p.s. or higher for these loads of coarse shot, the added *bazatz* contributed by the longer barrel is insignificant. A typical hunter would be wiser to think in terms of gun handling qualities rather than a few more feet-per-second velocity from his load.

It is possible that tradition-bound waterfowlers view a 21-inch barrel as a joke; it doesn't project an image of power. When chronographed with Remington 1½-ounce Nitro Mags, however, the 12-gauge Special

Field averaged 1,210 f.p.s., which is about 25 f.p.s. faster than the 3-inch 20 launches its 1¼-ouncer from a 28-inch barrel! Number 4s doing 1,210 f.p.s. at the muzzle retain 3.05 foot-pounds of energy at 60 yards when they retain their spherical form for optimum aerodynamics. Thus, copper-plated 2s or 4s from a 21-inch barrel can give clean-killing penetration at 55–60 yards.

This review of chronoraphing results is not intended to be a sales pitch for 21-inch-barreled duck and goose guns. I might like something longer myself, if for no other reason than moving the blast from magnum loads farther away from my tender ears. But the readings do justify 26-inch 10- and 12-gauge barrels for waterfowl at ranges out to 65–75 yards with the appropriate patterns and loads, which is generally 20 to 30 yards beyond the skill of most hunters. The guns are easier to handle on close- or intermediate-range shots while still being effective at long range.

EXPLODING THE SIGHT RADIUS MYTH

Although chronographing can dispell mistaken beliefs about barrel lengths and their effect on velocity, many hunters will still be perplexed by sighting changes. There is an aged notion, still popular, that long barrels extend the sighting radius for maximum long-range accuracy, and sportsmen do get hung up on the idea.

The fact is, however, that much about the shotgun's sighting radius is overrated and predicated, to a large degree, on optical illusion. In expert shotgunning, for instance, the shooter's head is supposed to be down firmly on the comb so that his eye can serve as the rear sight for that all-important eye-to-muzzle-to-target alignment; and, if one's head is indeed down properly he can't see the top of the long barrel or its rib. The only visual contact should be the very top of the crown of the muzzle or the front bead, and even then those features should be seen only as fuzzy reference points as the eyes remain focused sharply on the target for optimum hand-to-eye coordination. Hunters who aim with the rib, barrel top, and/or use the matted receiver top as a rear sight, are doing it wrong! It's no wonder that they miss; they're concentrating on the gun, not the bird.

Thus, the logical question is: if one doesn't look directly at the barrel, rib, bead, or receiver top, how can their length or size be serious elements in shotgun pointing? The answer is, of course, that they aren't as vital as traditional opinions have made them out to be. The simple act of getting one's head

down tightly on the comb and keeping it there for good alignment throughout the swing is vastly more important than sheer barrel length. A good shot will score more often and more consistently at 50 yards with a 21-inch barrel than a poor shot will with a 30-incher.

Shooters who insist on having the optical image of barrel length can create that effect by replacing the large front bead on their gun with a smaller bead. Trap shooters have done this to keep the bead's size relative to the outgoing trap clays that obviously appear to get smaller as they fly away from the trap house. A large bead on a trap gun can actually blot out clay targets at handicap distances, and going to a smaller bead brings things

Ithaca's Model 37 Field Grade Magnum is basically a lightweight pump with good handling qualities for those who don't like the heftier magnum-grade pumps. Its 28-inch barrel comes with three choke tubes.

Remington's 3-inch 20-gauge Lightweight Magnum is an easy-swinging duck gun that may be just the ticket for hunters who have difficulty handling heavier shotguns.

back into perspective. The same can be done on any short-barreled waterfowl gun to provide the optical illusion of greater barrel length.

The age of black powder is far behind us, and waterfowlers no longer need to be bound by the Long Tom approach when selecting their shotguns. Modern powders, even the progressive types, burn faster and negate the need for long-barreled heavyweights. Far more important than traditional values is the matter of picking a gun that you, as an individual, can handle and swing with sound technique and speed. If that happens to be a 26-inch-barreled Ithaca Turkey Gun or Remington Model 870 or Model 1100 S.P., or even a 28-inch-barreled 20-gauge Magnum instead of a 32-inch-tubed 10-bore, so be it. The necessary ballistics will be there if ammunition is intelligently selected for the game and the range. Today's enlightened shooters are definitely looking toward shorter and livelier repeaters and doubles despite the fact that traditions die hard and still capture the imagination in some respects. There is always an overlapping period when changes occur, and we may well be living in such a transitional era.

FLAT FINISHES

Another obvious change taking place in waterfowl guns is that of finish. Whereas guns have long been expected to have brightly blued barrels and receivers, and glossy stocks and forends, production models are now coming out with flat finishes to reduce potential reflections that scare game. This involves a matte or Parkerized finish on the metal and a dull oil finish on the wood. Ithaca has gone one step further, announcing recently a highly rust-resistant camouflage finish for the metallic parts of the Model 37 pump, Model 51 auto, and Mag-10. These Ithacas are listed under the Camo-Seal banner, and have screw in choke tubes, recoil pads, and lacquered wood with a dull tone. The guns, as of this writing, have no checkering. It would not be surprising if other manufacturers followed suit, extending the camouflage decor even to the wood.

There can be little doubt that such flat and camouflaged finishes will blend nicely into waterfowling. It may take a bit of time, however, for sportsmen to get used to these drab gun exteriors after decades of admiring deep luster bluing on barrels, case coloring on receivers, and glossy finishes or hand-rubbed satin oil on stocks and forends. But as in the case of shorter barrels, the time is ripe for a change in the finish of waterfowl shotguns.

A pair of short-barreled autos in the modern mode: Ithaca's Mag-10 (top), and Model 51A Magnum Turkey Gun (bottom).

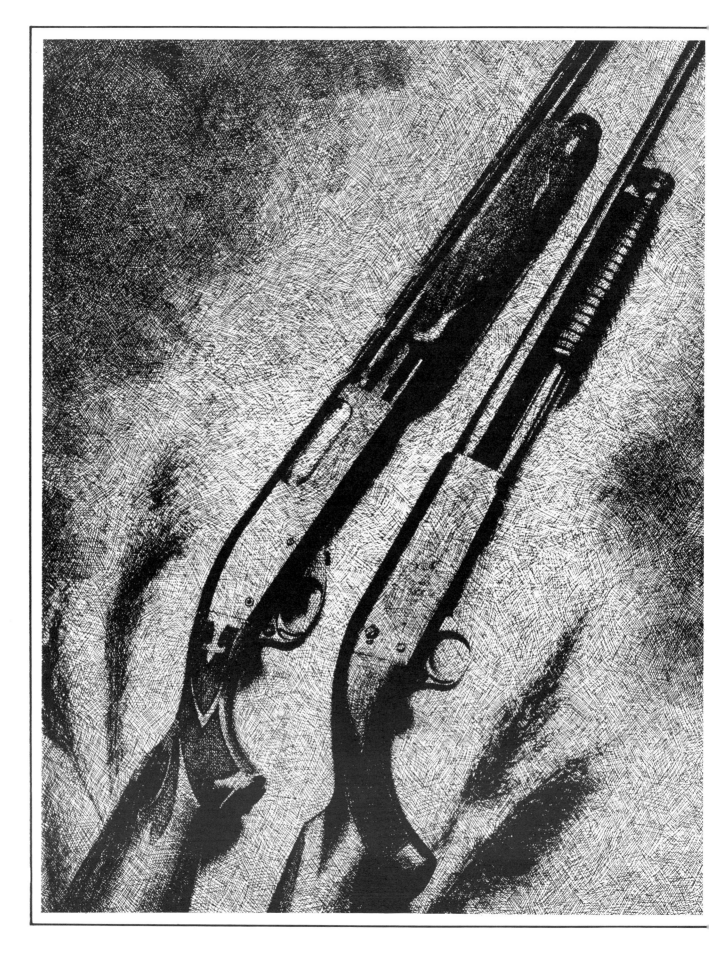

3
Pumpguns and Their Use

In North America, pumpguns are firmly entrenched in the world of waterfowling. According to some of the earlier hunting and shotgun authorities, however, it wasn't supposed to happen that way. They looked upon the pumpgun as an intermediate step on the way to autoloading arms. When Charles Askins published his 1928 tome, *The American Shotgun,* he reflected this opinion by writing, "I believe an auto-loading mechanism is the ultimate fate of all pump repeaters. Within another decade I expect to see every gun builder, who now places a pumpgun on the market, extolling the virtues of his own particular automatic." Moreover, anyone conversant in British and European sporting arms lore knows that these camps never accepted the pumpgun concept. When W.W. Greener discussed repeating shotguns in his massive volume, *The Gun And Its Development,* he had lively verbal sport indeed with the failures and frustrations of Dr. W. F. Carver, the great American shotgunner, who had nothing but jams and malfunctions when he tried publically to demonstrate the rapidity of trombone-actioned guns. Greener believed then, as do most British and Europeans still, that doubles with automatic ejectors provide adequate firepower for sporting use, and that the mechanisms and changing point of balance, plus the hand movement between shots, detract from the purities of wingshooting theory. The additional moving parts and lengthy receiver also cause chagrin among those devoted to the simplicity of a double.

But despite predictions from early gun writers, and despite functional problems, the pumpgun is still alive and kicking (if you'll pardon the pun). Instead of becoming less desirable, pumpguns have become bread-and-butter items with many gun manufacturers. And rather than being supplanted by autoloaders and doubles, the pump remains the most popular waterfowling design.

What is it that keeps the pumpgun viable after nearly a hundred years? Apparently the pumpgun, as it has evolved, offers the most firepower at the lowest price. The improvements worked into pumpguns have made them relatively trouble-free and fast-stroking. The self-lubricating, non-swelling qualities of plastic shotshells have also helped the pumpgun remain popular, as they feed slickety-click through the cycle. Money is also a factor. When a waterfowler thinks in terms of how his gun will probably be treated by harsh weather and indifferent handling, he tends to opt for a $150 pumpgun rather than

a $1,000 over-under. Too, a lot of enthusiastic duck hunters are people of average or low income, and they simply can't afford an expensive sporting arm.

But there is an aspect of the pumpgun's heritage that must be viewed critically. This is the oft-heard brag that "I can shoot as fast with my pumpgun as you can with your expensive autoloader." On a purely theoretical basis, a pumpgun may be able to outrace an autoloader, because one must wait for a gas- or recoil-operated autoloader to shuffle through its sequence mechanically, while a pumpgunner can shuck his gun without waiting for gas or recoil energies to build. That possibility, however, is only a matter of potential; it is hardly a universal accomplishment common to all pumpgun shooters. Indeed, most pumpgunners observed afield are

A pumpgun may not be the connoisseur's idea of a truly fine design, but it can take the rigors of waterfowling and keep on shooting.

significantly slower than hunters using semiautomatics, and their second shot is definitely behind that of sportsmen handling over-unders or single-triggered side-by-sides. Bluntly stated, most hunters have not practiced enough — nor have they taken into account the mechanical aspects of the slide action — to equal the speed and ease of autoloaders. Here's what the average pumpgunner does wrong:

Instead of starting to pump immediately after pulling the trigger, he (1) absorbs recoil, (2) makes a follow-through of sorts, and (3) watches to see if he hit the target before initiating any part of the pumping move. Only after viewing the results of the first shot does a typical hunter turn his attention to pumping — by which time an autoloader would have a fresh shell already chambered. True,

while pumpguns have the potential to equal an autoloader's reloading speed, very few are used at peak operational efficiency because of their owners' lack of expertise.

WHEN AND HOW TO PUMP

The secret to making a pumpgun work as fast as an autoloader lies in two things: (1) hand speed, and (2) timing the start of the stroke. The need for hand speed is self-explanatory. The hand can be quicker than the eye only if one's muscles carry out the correct mental command with grace and dispatch. How fast is fast? When a truly expert pumpgunner puts a trombone gun through its paces fast enough to challenge an autoloader, the sights and sounds of pumping are virtually nonexistent. They are covered

Rapid firepower with a pumpgun requires proper handling. Here, an empty pops out of a Remington Model 31, probably the slickest slide-action ever produced.

by recoil and muzzle blast. About all that can be heard, if anything, is the final closing metallic snap. When any sounds of the rearward stroke are audible, there is no chance of the pumpgun equaling the autoloader.

But hand speed alone isn't enough. The key lies in timing the pumping hand's rearward move with recoil energy. In modern pumpguns the action is released when the trigger falls, and if a hunter takes advantage of this mechanical fact he'll get a surprising assist from recoil energy as it acts against the breech bolt; the slide will come back almost effortlessly if the hand's impetus comes on hammer fall. This assist from recoil can be seen in a simple test. Put a high-velocity or slug load into a pumpgun, place the gun's forend on a sandbag or similar rest, and pull the trigger while letting the forend float freely on the sandbag the way a benchrested rifle would be treated. Apply little or no shoulder pressure to the pumpgun's butt. In other words, let the gun kick. On firing, the gun will practically open itself with no help whatsoever from the shooter. Accordingly, any pumpgunner who wants to be truly fast must practice timing his stroke with trigger yield so that the gun's action gets an assist from recoil. (The exceptions to this were the Winchester Model 97, Model 12, and Model 42 pumpguns. They unlocked only after a short forward jab of the pump handle was caused by recoil.)

Another major flaw in many pumpgunners' techniques is stopping at the end of the opening stroke. The fastest closing strokes are made when the pumping hand utilizes rebound energy immediately to initiate the closing move. Moreover, the faster a pumpgun is closed, the less chance there is for malfunctions. This is true because, in a slowly worked gun, the shotshell has more time to feel the effects of gravity and/or mechanical wiggle-wobble, and those factors can produce shotshell misalignments which hinder smooth chambering. Pumping speed can be especially important with the longer 3-inch magnum loads, as their potential for wobble and/or tilting seems greater than that of the shorter rounds. The point is that the faster a pumpgun is shucked, the less troublesome it becomes.

Crisp, accurately timed pumping comes only with practice. There's nothing instinctive about it; the move must be learned. The best practice comes on the skeet field in doubles shooting. Those who don't have a skeet field handy can work on timing by throwing up a clay pigeon, breaking it, and then pumping in a second load to hit the largest remaining chip before it reaches the ground.

THE CLASSIC PUMPGUNS

The trim elegance of a side-by-side double may be the British sportsman's idea of a classic shotgun, but generations of American and Canadian hunters have been

Shown at right:

Left / Ithaca's Model 37 Deluxe Magnum with ventilated rib.

Center / Marlin's Model 120 pump can be had with various barrel lengths and is a sound, sturdy pumpgun.

Right / A Duck Unlimited commemorative celebrating the Mississippi flyway: the Remington Model 870 Magnum known as the River with duck medallion and minor scroll.

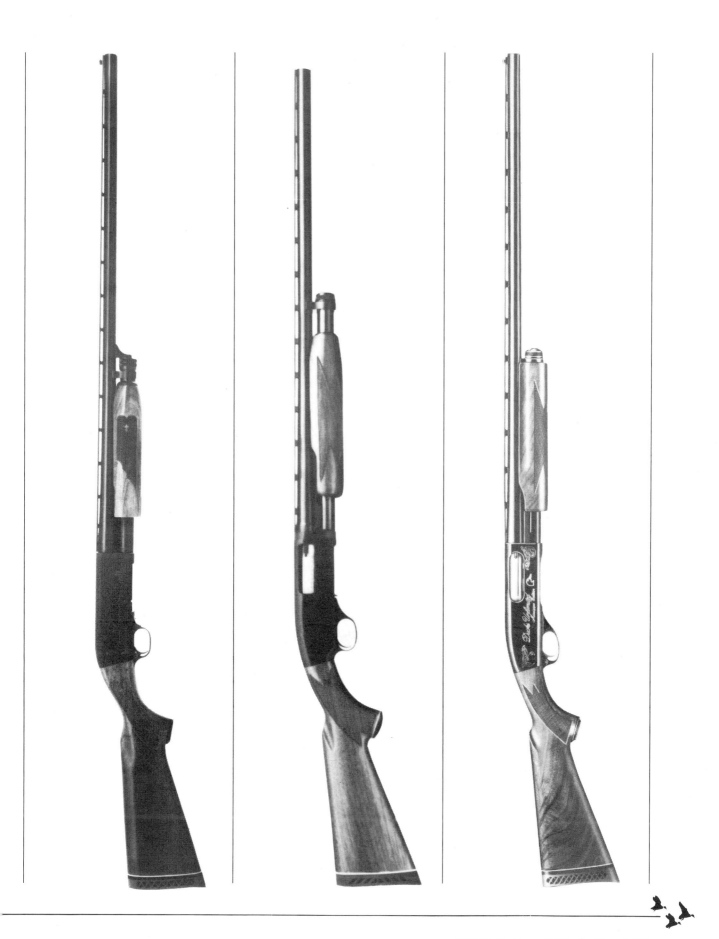

heavily influenced by their grandfathers' long-barreled pumps. The pumpgun legacy dates back to the late 1800s when slide-actions were first introduced to American shooters.

The first successful pumpguns were created by John M. Browning, who was a leading designer of repeating arms of all sorts. His first commercial pump was the Winchester Model 93, which the company updated into the famous Model 97 hammer gun. Its six-shot capacity and 30–32-inch barrels gave meat and market hunters the firepower they wanted.

But Browning wasn't satisfied with those early hammer guns. They didn't have the streamlined profile he envisioned, and he strove for a hammerless system that could also be taken down for cleaning, storage, and transportation. He reached this goal in the Stevens Model 520, which was introduced in 1904 as the world's first hammerless repeater. Stevens carried the basic design into the post-WWII years, switching from machined parts to punch-press parts in the 1960s.

Competition for sales thereupon forced other gunmakers to streamline their pumps.

Winchester's in-house designer, Thomas Crossly Johnson, developed the Model 12, and Winchester advertising dubbed it "The Perfect Repeaters." A lot of hunters must have believed the Winchester copywriter, as over two million Model 12s were sold between 1912 and 1980. One researcher has estimated that if all the Model 12s ever made were laid end to end, they would stretch for about 1,200 miles.

During these same years, Remington was going through a succession of bottom-ejecting pumpguns like the Models 10, 17, and 29. The public didn't exactly flock to these guns, and in 1931 Remington unveiled a new pump that went on to become the slickest slide-action of all time. This was the Model 31, known affectionately as "the gun with the ball bearing action." Made in 12, 16, and 20 gauge, and in all sorts of grades and styles, the Model 31 had a short, smooth stroke unequaled by any other pump of the period, Winchester's famed Model 12 included. Bob Nichols was the shotgunner's guru of that period, and in his book, *The Shotgunner,* he wrote, "The willowy, 'ball-bearing' quality of the smooth, fast action of the Model 31 Remington pump-

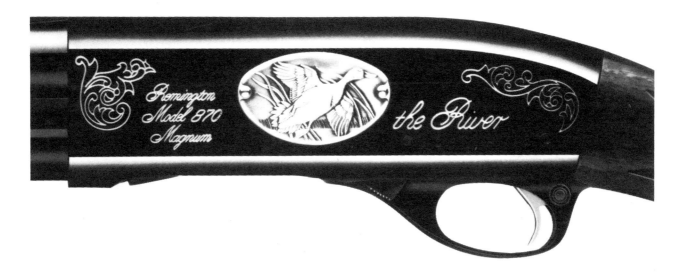

Attractive detail of the Remington commemorative 870 Magnum pump-action.

gun is just a bit superior, we feel, to any other American pumpgun..." Today, however, collectors and hunters who want an old-timer flock to the Winchester Model 12 while almost totally ignoring the Remington M31. For a savvy shotgunner, of course, that's just fine; it means the collector's price of Model 31s will be lower than those of Model 12s in identical condition because of a lesser demand, and he'll be able to get one of yesteryear's truly great pumpguns for hundreds of dollars below the price of a Model 12. In terms of quality and stroking speed, the Remington Model 31 is an all-time classic repeater.

No review of pumpgun history would be complete without mention of Ithaca, which became involved in pumpgun production in the 1930s when Remington, concentrating on the then-new Model 31, dropped a neat little 20-gauge cataloged as the Model 17. John M. Browning had designed the bottom-ejecting, slab-sided Model 17, and Remington had only made it in the trim 20-gauge model. Lou Smith, then president of Ithaca, managed to obtain rights to the Browning-designed M17, and it was his company's initial venture into repeating shotguns. The former Remington M17 was modified for 12- and 16-gauge shells as well, and Ithaca began to market it in 1937, calling it the Model 37 in honor of the year of introduction. The Ithaca M37's closed sides and bottom loading/ejecting features have endeared it to waterfowlers who like the way rain and snow are kept out of the mechanism. Of all those early pumpgun designs, only the Model 17/37 is still with us, albeit in further modified form. More about that shortly.

THE CURRENT SCENE

The year 1950 marked the end of an era insofar as repeating shotguns are concerned. In that year Remington dropped the Model 31 and its machined, carefully fitted parts in favor of the Model 870 and its stamped parts,

plus, apparently, less precise factory fitting. Post-war inflation was behind the change. With labor costs going up and people unwilling to pay higher prices for precision-quality items, there was no alternative; Remington had to cut production costs to keep its guns competitively priced. There was some dissatisfaction among hunters, of course. "They don't make 'em the way they used to," was a common remark. And since Winchester continued to make the Model 12 for another ten years or so, there was still a remnant of the old days to serve as a measuring stick. What hunters didn't realize, however, was that Remington's move to the 870 was a brilliant business step. The gun companies simply couldn't keep making guns with hand-fitted machined parts and turn enough profit to stay healthy. Within the firearms industry it has been widely (although unofficially) maintained that, at least during the latter part of its existence, the Winchester Model 12 lost money for the company despite the volume sales; the machine and assembly times were too extensive and costly.

Economic factors finally caught up with Winchester and the other firearms manufacturers in the 1960s. In 1961, some castings were being used instead of machined parts in the Model 12, and by 1964 the original series was dropped. It was followed by the Y-series of the Model 12, which employed more castings, and sported a much higher price tag. If the great old Remington 31 and Model 12 guns were still made today with their original machined parts and judicious hand fitting, they would probably cost a cool $1,000 or more, retail.

By the end of the 1960s, affordable pumpguns were all made of castings and stamped parts. The same holds true today, and the hunter who wishes machined parts must shop the gun shows and used gun racks. And he must also be willing to pay several hundred dollars more than he would for a current, off-the-rack shucker.

Winchester's answer to the Remington 870 was the Model 1200, which eventually was revamped and called the Model 1300 XTR. Both guns have high-strength aluminum receivers, cast and stamped parts, and mass-production assembly.

Making a profit on domestically produced sporting guns became such a headache for Winchester that the parent corporation, Olin, sold the historic New Haven, Connecticut, plant to a new group of investors known as U.S. Repeating Arms. Part of the deal included the use of the Winchester trade name; hence, all Winchester brand guns being produced in the United States are being made by U.S. Repeating Arms. The original Winchester group now markets only doubles made in Japan.

One of the pumps made in New Haven is a flat-finished Model 1300 XTR Waterfowl gun specially outfitted for long-range shooting. Made in 12 gauge only, it carries a 3-inch-chambered, 30-inch barrel that is topped by a ventilated rib and terminated by the versatile Winchoke feature. Three choke tubes are supplied for this specialized rig: improved modified, full, and extra full. The gun scales 7½ pounds empty, which puts it in the intermediate weight category.

Budget-minded hunters or those looking for a gun they won't mind exposing to the elements can inspect U.S. Repeating Arms' Ranger series of pumps. Ranger pumpguns are the Model 1300 with fewer frills. Like the Remington Sportsman 12, they have stained hardwood stocks and forearms instead of genuine walnut, and the final appearance isn't as attractive as the higher-priced guns. But the Ranger line is indeed serviceable, its on-

ly shortcoming (in this writer's opinion) is an abbreviated forend that causes a hunter to reach too far, a weakness when pumping during high-angle fire.

Today, all pumpgun manufacturers make considerable use of stampings and castings, and further inflation has forced them to take additional shortcuts in order to keep the retail prices within an average hunter's budget. One of the lowest priced pumpguns at this writing is Mossberg's Model 500, which can be had for less than $200. It features interchangeable barrels that are offered for amazingly low prices and has a top-tang sliding safety like double-barreled guns. The gun has a relatively long stroke that takes some time to smooth out, but it does have good stock dimensions for lining up on passing birds.

As of 1984, Remington also began offering an economy-grade pump, the Sportsman 12. This is a lower-priced version of the Model 870 with less attention to finish. The stock and forend of the Sportsman 12 are stained hardwood, not walnut, and the receiver top doesn't have a matted groove. But the gun's fit and feel are identical to the more expensive 870s, and a hunter can't tell the difference when the gun is at his shoulder. Of all the low-priced pumps, the Sportsman 12 is tops. The presence of a 3-inch chamber makes it quite versatile and competitive, and an outstanding feature of the Sportsman 12 is the same excellent trigger as that of the parent 870. Unfortunately, many other low-priced pumpguns have stiff, hard trigger pulls that upset one's timing.

Ithaca's line of Model 37s should interest waterfowlers who like lighter, easily handled guns. The 12-gauge 3-inch Magnum model with a 30-inch barrel weighs only 7¼ pounds,

Left / U.S. Repeating Arms' Model 1300 XTR with a 30-inch, Winchoke-equipped barrel.

Center / Remington's ever-popular Model 870 can be had in a left-hand version in 12 and 20 gauge.

Right / An economy model of the Remington 870 with a flat finish on the wood is the Sportsman 12.

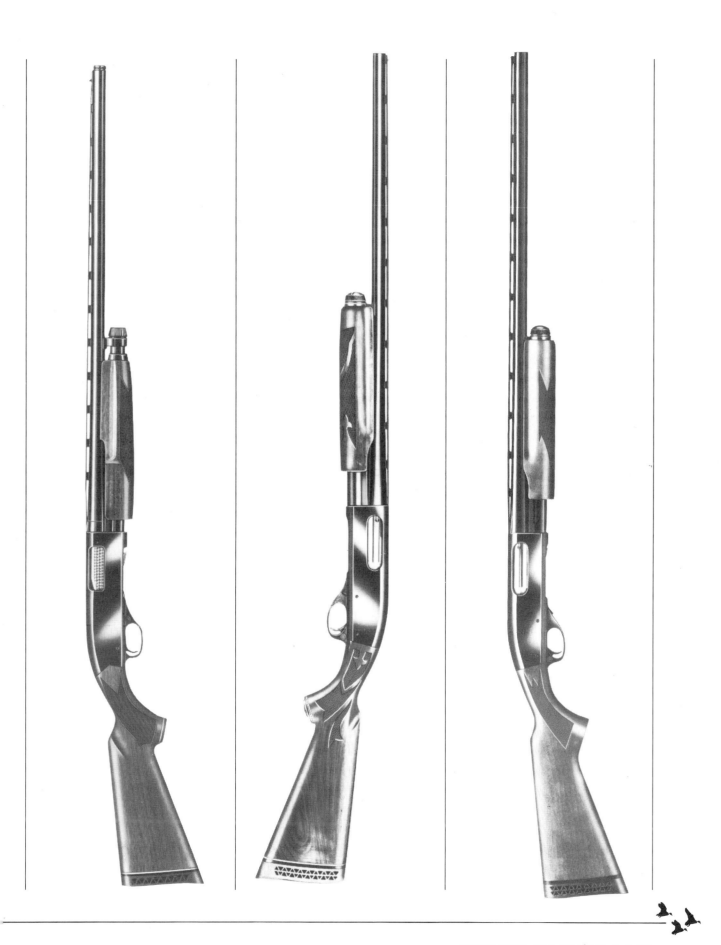

An old Winchester Model 12 downed this Canada goose.

and it may be just the ticket for hunters who can't get the heftier shotguns moving as briskly as they need to for effective long-range work. This author has had the opportunity to pattern a pair of Ithaca Model 37 Magnums, and they turned in superb performances.

An economy offering also awaits. This is Ithaca's Model 37 Featherlight Field Grade with hardwood accouterments instead of walnut, plus the screw-in choke tube feature. The gun also has the famous old "ring-tail" forearm of the original M37s.

The concept of bottom ejection is also employed by Browning on its husky BPS pumpgun. Unlike the lively Model 37, however, the BPS offers hunters the opposite weight extreme; it's a robust slide-action, having a solid steel receiver rather than an alloy frame, and it's stock and forend are equally generous. Browning barrels are heavily walled, all of which brings the gun to a full 8 pounds or slightly more with magnum loads aboard. The weight and bulk aren,t all bad, of course. They play into the hands of hunters who want a heavy gun for recoil reduction and swing momentum plus a positive follow-through. The recoil pad on each BPS is quite broad for widespread distribution of recoil. Chambered for the 3-inch shell, the BPS and its $9/_{32}$-inch rib are nicely suited to the waterfowler who can handle a lot of gun.

At one time, Smith & Wesson offered a Model 3000 pumpgun series which included a specialized pump known as the Waterfowler. It had two barrel types: one a 30-inch full-choke barrel; the other a 28-incher threaded for the Multi-Choke tubes. Both guns were Parkerized, chambered for 3-inch shells, and had removable flush-fitted swivels complete with camouflaged sling. Full-sized recoil pads and ventilated ribs completed these intermediate-weight guns. These Waterfowlers have good pointing qualities, and their actions become slick in a hurry. Currently, that same gun is marketed by Mossberg.

The shortest stroke on any pumpgun today is on Weatherby's Model Ninety-Two. As with all Weatherby guns, the Ninety-Two has distinctive lines. The receiver is semi-humpbacked, the pistol grip is carried out and capped, and the forend is squared at the front. Weatherby wood is generally a grade or two ahead of the field, and that on the Ninety-Two is an advanced grade of Claro walnut attractively finished. The gun can be had with either screw-in tubes or solid chokes. One advantage on the Ninety-Two is its long beavertail forend which extends back to the receiver and permits a shorter grip for easier pumping on high-angle shots. Although the Weatherby Ninety-Two isn't precisely labeled a waterfowling pump, it certainly does fill the bill. And its full, rounded comb, along with the wide recoil pad, help dampen recoil.

The pumpgun may not be universally admired throughout the world, but American and Canadian duck hunters couldn't care less. It will probably be a part of our waterfowling scene as long as men are free to hunt.

Wherever waterfowlers shop, there will always be an interest in pumpguns.

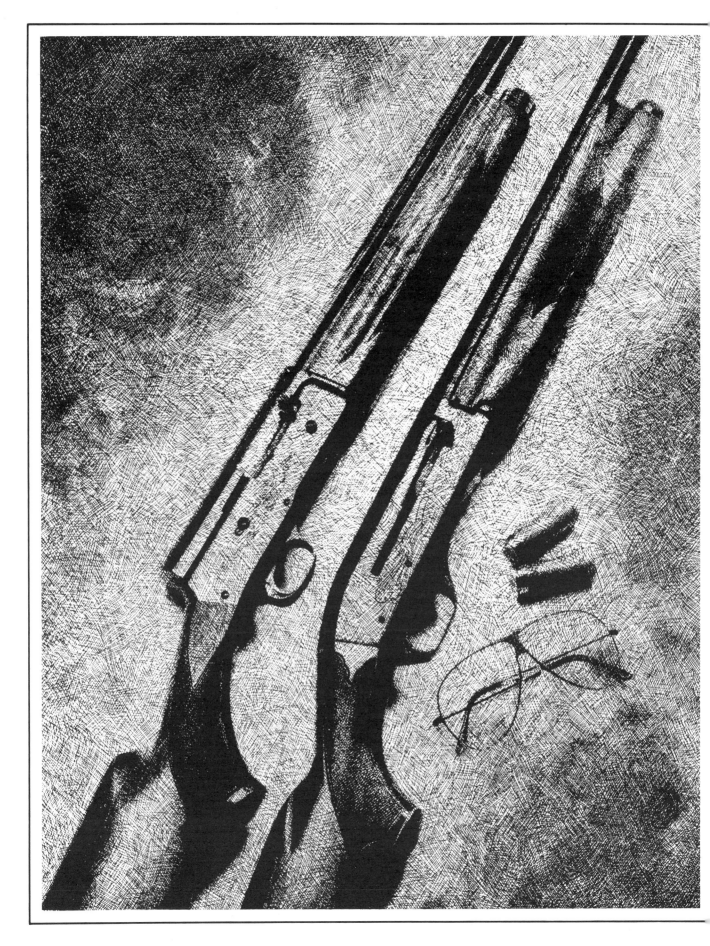

4
Autoloaders

When autoloading shotguns first came on the market in the early 1900s, the sporting press editorialized against them and conservationists argued that they should be declared illegal for hunting. Flock after flock of waterfowl would be decimated by hunters with all that firepower, it was feared, and eventually a federal law was passed making it illegal to have more than three shells in any repeating gun used for waterfowling. Today, the autoloading shotgun is perfectly acceptable in most sporting circles on our side of the Atlantic. We can all be thankful for that, because modern self-shuckers take the sting out of hard-recoiling loads.

There is no legitimate reason for stigmatizing any shotgun design as unethical or unsporting. The guns are inanimate; they don't point and fire themselves. Issues of ethics and sportsmanship must be applied to those who use them, and if anyone wishes to violate game laws, he can do so with a single-shot, pumpgun, or double-barrel as well as with an autoloader. Indeed, any criticism of the autoloader's rate of fire is laughable when it comes from pump-gunners who almost invariably claim they can pump as rapidly as any autoloader can operate. What's the difference between rapid fire from a pump and the same from an auto or a single-triggered double? Stroking a trombone action doesn't enhance the ethics of a hunter.

In any case, the public's attitude toward autoloading shotguns has changed. The person who uses one nowadays is no longer equated with meat hunting, thanks in part to design improvements that have taken the machinelike qualities out of autoloaders and given them clean, sporty lines and eye appeal.

The first successful autoloading shotgun was invented by John M. Browning and patented in 1900. Gun tinkerers had known all along that the energy of a shotshell could be harnessed and made to operate the eject/reload cycle, but their technology was wanting. The major problem was getting one mechanism to function with all the types of ammunition then available; light loads wouldn't impel the same mechanism as heavy loads, and the gun had to handle every load if it were to be a commercial success. Browning beat everyone else to the breakthrough by devising an adjustable shock absorber (friction ring) assembly that fits on the magazine tube just ahead of the recoil spring. By manipulating these rings, the hunter could make one gun function with light or heavy loads.

That gun, of course, was the famous "humpback" Browning Auto-5, and it dominated the market for generations. The A-5 is still with us, now being made in Japan instead of Belgium. It has recently been updated by Browning with the inclusion of the screw-in Invector choke tubes. There can be little doubt that the Belgian-assembled Browning A-5s were some of the most carefully fitted production-grade shotguns of all time, their actions rolling like oily glass.

The first commercially successful autoloading shotgun was John M. Browning's Automatic-5, the so-called "humpback," shown here in the hand of its creator.

The current Japanese-made Browning A-5, now available with the screw-in Invector choke system.

The Browning A-5 was based on the so-called long-recoil system in which the breech bolt and barrel remained locked while they were driven backward by recoil energy. As this tandem neared its rearward extent, a series of latches released the barrel to jump forward while the next load was released from the magazine and elevated by the carrier. The energy of the spring-urged shell popping out of the tubular magazine tripped another latch that released the breech bolt to pick up the fresh round and slam back into place. Eventually, this same long-recoil system was used on guns like the Remington Model 11, Savage Model 750, and Winchester Models 11 and 40.

The humpbacked configuration of Browning's A-5 was necessitated by breech block travel, and, in many eyes, was hardly streamlined or appealing. Overall, the guns had a slab-sided appearance as compared to the trim doubles and low-profiled Model 97 and Model 12 pumpguns. The flat, upright, high receiver thus became a controversial point among wingshooters. Many felt it blocked out too much of the field for good visual contact with the target, and they rejected the design. However, others took a reverse view of the same feature and claimed that the bold, blank obstruction helped them point quickly because the muzzle/bead area stood out in such contrast. This controversy has never been resolved except on personal bases, and it will probably remain that way.

The high, flat-backed receiver of Browning's A-5 is controversial; some hunters saying it is a hindrance to good shooting, and others praising it as a subconscious visual reference point or a feature that makes the rib and bead stand out sharply in contrast.

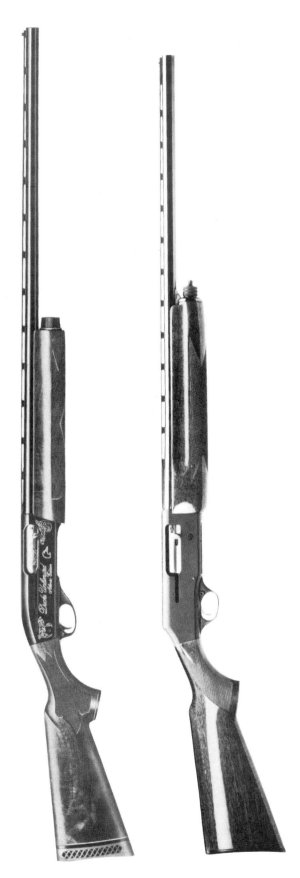

Meanwhile, the humpbacked A-5 is still ringing up sales and knocking down ducks.

To jibe with the then-new federal three-shot limit for repeaters, Remington made a three-shot version of their Model 11, calling it the Sportsman. It had a slightly bulkier forearm than the standard five-shot Model 11 and the Browning A-5, and it gained a following among early skeet shooters as well as waterfowlers. Through the middle 1930s, from about 1932 to 1939, Remington offered an overbored barrel for the Model 11 12-gauge autos to improve the patterning and to lessen the recoil with heavy, high-velocity duck loads.

GAS-OPERATED AUTOLOADERS

Shotguns built on the long-recoil system were known as "clankers," and more than a few sportsmen disliked the shuffling-barrel sensation. World War II brought about the technology that switched the sporting arms industry from the use of recoil energy in autoloading shotguns to the utilization of gas energy. Some very popular guns evolved, none more popular than Remington's Model 1100. Over three million have been made. Part of its allure is a soft-shooting quality, but another important aspect is a stock design that fits practically everyone.

The major problem with gas-operated autoloaders is the same one encountered by Browning and the other early experimenters:

The most famous and most widely used American-made autoloader is Remington's Model 1100, of which over three million have been sold. This is the 12-gauge Magnum, a soft-recoiling gun with a stock design that fits just about everybody. It is the Ducks Unlimited Chesapeake commemorative.

Browning's current B-80 has a semi-humpback configuration, but mechanically it's akin to the Beretta Model 302.

how can one mechanism be made to function perfectly with everything from light to magnum loads? This has been a stumbling point, because light loads use faster-burning powders than do heavy or magnum loads, and the gas pressures will differ significantly when they reach the bleeder valves. Magnum loads with their great gobs of slow-burning powder will have higher gas pressures down the bore than will lighter field or target loads; consequently, the bleeder valves must vary according to the gas pressure for proper operation.

Some strides have been made in improving the situation. Remington's M1100 Magnum will function with light loads *if* a standard (non-magnum) barrel is installed so that the bleeder valves are appropriately sized. Moreover, the standard-chambered M1100 will function with everything from light target loads through short magnums without any adjustment.

Beretta's Model 302 Autoloader has the same versatility as the Model 1100 Remington; any Beretta M302 receiver can take magnum-chambered barrels and function perfectly with 3-inch shells. Browning's Italian-made B-80 is essentially the Beretta M302 with a different profile (semi-humpbacked), and it also can be used with standard or magnum barrels interchangeably.

One of the more significant steps taken to increase the versatility of gas-operated shotguns is on the Japanese-made Super 12 as formerly imported by Smith & Wesson. This gun was given a metering system that controls gas flow to the operating mechanism,

With light loads the M1000 system closes the forward valves and utilizes all necessary gas for operation.

The self-metering gas unit of the M1000 Super 12 permits a forward escape of powder gases when loads have a high gas pressure at the bleeder valve.

SMITH & WESSON MODEL 1000
SUPER 12

LIGHT LOAD OPERATION

- ▨ GAS FLOW
- ▨ VALVE
- ▢ GAS PISTON
- ▰ MAGAZINE CAP

SMITH & WESSON MODEL 1000
SUPER 12

MAGNUM LOAD OPERATION

- ▨ GAS FLOW
- ▨ VALVE
- ▢ GAS PISTON
- ▰ MAGAZINE CAP

which cycles faster with light loads and slower with magnums. The stress on the gun is said to be less than with other autoloaders that do not regulate the gas flow on a variable basis. Although the Super 12 looks like the old S&W Model 1000 autoloader, it is an entirely different gun and barrels do not interchange. The screw-in Multi-Choke feature can be had on Super 12 barrels of 26, 28, or 30 inches.

For complete details, check out the Mossberg catalog, as this firm now handles these long guns.

The Ithaca Model 51 has recently been upgraded and deserves some attention. It has a redesigned trigger group, an action slide with a shot-peened finish, a link made of stainless steel, and a bolt buffer fashioned of a nylon-based material for longevity. A basic three-shot, the revamped gun is known as the Model 51-A, and its maker emphasizes its overall simplicity. Each 51-A has about one third fewer parts than comparable guns, and the gas system is soft-shooting although it has just one moving part. Field stripping is easy; no tools are needed, and the job takes but half a minute. When the Model 51 was first produced, it had a rather odd lift-type move on the trigger, but that has been changed for a crisp straightline pull that is among the very best on modern autoloaders.

THE BENELLI DARES TO BE DIFFERENT

Not all hunters and gun designers are convinced that gas-urged operation is the ultimate for autoloading shotguns. One drawback is the accumulation of gunk that can foul up the system. The Italian firm of

---

The former Smith & Wesson Model 1000 Super 12 has an advanced gas system that lets hunters use anything from light 1-ounce loads to 3-inch Magnums without any adjustment. The system is self-metering.

The Benelli autoloader is a trim, light-recoiling gun with a unique operating system. It is reputed to be the fastest-firing autoloader among sporting shotguns, a feature that helped the author double on these early-season ducks.

Benelli has an interesting alternative that utilizes recoil energy plus residual gas energy to produce a soft-kicking, ultra-fast-firing autoloader.

Distributed stateside by Heckler & Koch, the Benelli is a trim gun that handles and points much like a fine over-under. I had the pleasure of using one for a waterfowl season, and, even without a recoil pad of any sort, the gun was gentle, fast-shucking, and quick into follow-up shots. It has the reputation of being the fastest-cycling autoloader in the scattergun field, and trick shooters who match

slicked-up pumpguns against autos no longer take on the Benelli.

Although the Benelli uses recoil energy, it doesn't have a shuffling barrel like the Browning A-5. Nor is the breech bolt driven back by sheer recoil energy. The barrel is rigid, and the overall operation is more complicated; however, it seems to work flawlessly without any field problems.

The designers at Benelli say the gun was made to recoil *around* a fixed breech bolt which, for a split second, holds its own against recoil energy as the rest of the gun moves backward. That sounds confusing, of course, so here is how it happens in detail:

The breech bolt assembly is the vital nucleus of a Benelli autoloader. It is made of three components: (1) the bolt head, which locks in place behind the shotshell when the gun is cocked and closed; (2) the breech bolt body, or block, which is a longer part than the bolt head and which floats freely behind the head; and (3) a sizeable coil spring, which is placed between the body and the bolt head. The interaction of this bolt head/spring/bolt body assembly produces the soft, fast operation.

When a Benelli autoloader is fired, the locked bolt head remains in place momentarily, firmly locked to the rigid barrel. Meanwhile, recoil sends *most* of the other parts backward. I say "most" because the lengthy breech body, floating free and separated from the bolt head by the coil spring, tends to maintain its position due to inertia. If one can picture in his mind's eye the body bolt holding its prior position during recoil, he can see the gun kicking back and around the breech bolt assembly. What happens mechanically in that split instant is that the bolt's body moves forward relative to the spring and bolt head, thus compressing the strong coil spring trapped there.

Now the power of the compressed spring takes over. Its energy overcomes the inertia of the breech bolt body, shoving it backward smartly to cam a locking bar out of the way and to release the bolt head. Once the bolt head is unlocked, residual gas chamber pressures force it open to initiate the extract/reject/reload sequence. Thus, without the rearward thrust of the raw recoil, the coil spring wouldn't be compressed and the opening routine wouldn't be initiated.

While all this happens incredibly fast, Benelli technicians say that the bolt remains closed until after the ejecta has left the muz-

An internal look at the Benelli system, illustrating the massive coil spring between the bolt head and bolt body.

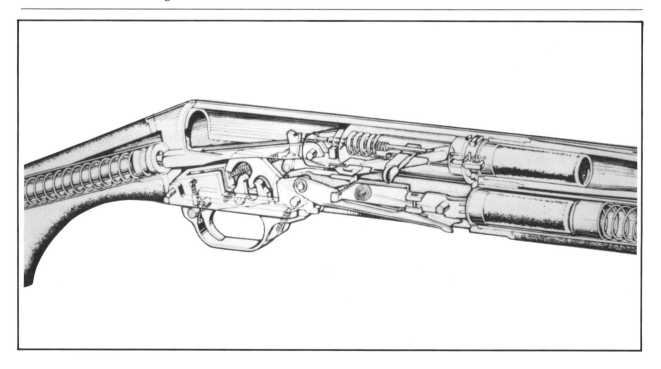

zle. I've chronographed loads from the gun and, indeed, have found them to be the equivalent of other guns with the same barrel lengths.

Remington's newest styling of the Model 1100 12-gauge Magnum has given hunters the best of two worlds. Called the Special Purpose Magnum (S.P.), it can be had with either 26- or 30-inch full-choke barrels. The guns are given dull finishes, Parkerized metal and flat oil wood. They come with swivels and a camouflaged sling, and, to reduce bore maintenance woes, they have chrome-lined bores. By interchanging barrels, one can employ the Long Tom tradition or the faster-swinging concept and still get soft shooting, tight patterning, and excellent pointing.

The world of autoloaders is wide open to the waterfowler. Mechanical types abound: long-recoil, gas-operated, Benelli principle. Winchester once used an inertia-block system in the Models 50/59, which were some of the lightest-kicking guns ever made outside of the gas-impelled models. Val Browning designed a short-recoil system, using it on the ill-fated Double Auto. And the modern gas pistons are becoming ultra-simple, as is the case of Ithaca's Model 51-A. Study the catalogs seriously before buying; handle every model you can get your hands on to see which feels best. Check all the features. The companies are competing for sales by making their guns more specialized for certain types of hunting, and the autoloaders have much more to offer than just three fast shots.

Beretta's Model 301/302 line of Italian-made autoloaders has an efficient gas-operated system and a flat rib. It accounted for this pair of greenheads from Manitoba's pothole country.

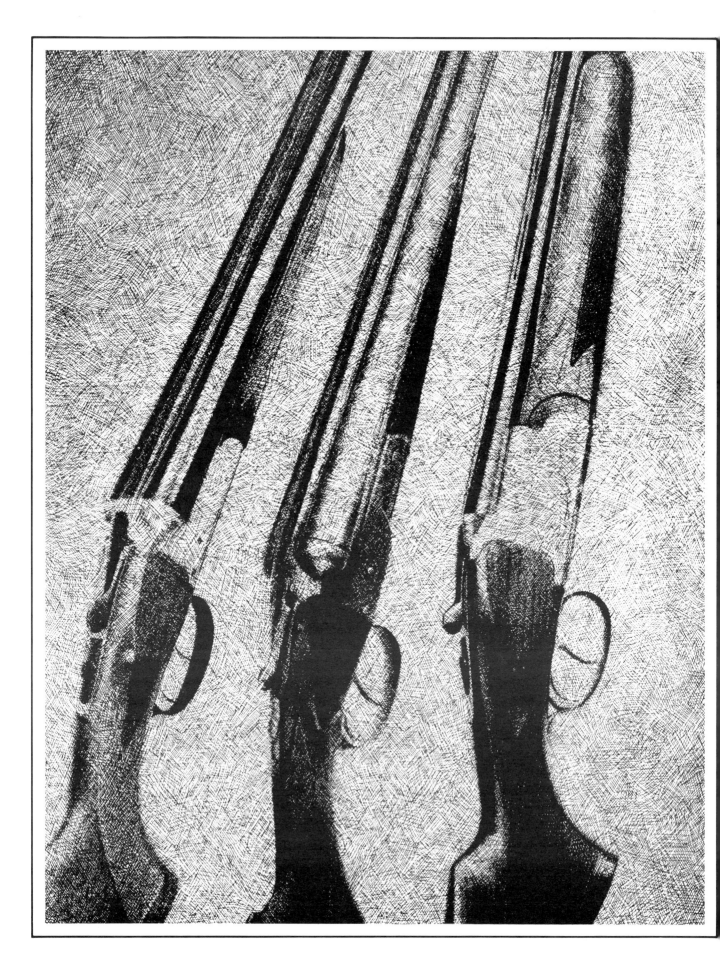

5
Double-barreled Guns

The double's clean lines and appealing aesthetics, simple and compact mechanics, and lively dynamics have made it the most prestigious of shotguns. Indeed, Grandfather may boast that his rusty pumpgun has "bagged more ducks than you'll ever see," but modern sportsmen who appreciate the finer things have been leaning toward doubles. The only question has been: which one has the most to offer a waterfowler, the side-by-side or the over-under? This chapter will spell out the strengths and weaknesses of each type as they pertain to duck and goose hunting.

THE SIDE-BY-SIDE

During some of the best years of American waterfowling, which included the market hunting era, the side-by-side double was widely and effectively employed by the best shots. Surprisingly, then, it is always thought-provoking to hear a modern hunter say, "I just can't hit with the side-by-side; it doesn't point right. Every time I bring one to my shoulder, it seems as if I am looking down a highway." That negative reaction to the horizontal double's breadth, of course, does more than hint that such a pointing plane cannot be used accurately, especially at long range.

However, that negative assessment of the side-by-side always raises the moot follow-up inquiry of why an earlier generation of wingshots could drop millions of passenger pigeons and made serious inroads into duck and goose populations with side-by-sides, while a later generation finds something inherently wrong with the gun's pointability. Is it the gun — or is it the technique of the shooter? For the fact is that, properly mounted and cheeked, a side-by-side can be pointed as rapidly and as accurately as any single-barreled gun. The key is getting your cheek down firmly on the comb and ignoring the barrels to look right down and over the raised

The side-by-side does very well on high-angle shots when the shooter uses good technique and keeps his head down firmly on the comb.

rib between the tubes. As explained in a later chapter on shotgunning fundamentals, the shooter's eyes must focus sharply on the target and remain there, while pointing and swinging are done by hand-to-eye coordination. If the barrels are seen at all, they should be fuzzy. Some hunters probably feel uncomfortable with a side-by-side because they're making two mistakes: (1) the gun isn't being mounted and/or cheeked correctly (the hunter has his head too high and sees the upper barrel surfaces foreshortened, which he shouldn't); and (2) the hunter is probably concentrating on the gun instead of focusing on the target, thus mistakenly aiming rather than pointing. In either case, it isn't the gun's fault. Some of the best long-range hunters of all time used side-by-side 10- or 12-gauge Magnums.

One cause of this pointing problem with a side-by-side may come from the way hunters first encounter the gun, which is generally in a non-hunting situation. Be it in a sport shop or a friend's den, the hunter handling a side-by-side for the first time concentrates on the gun during dry firing, in which case he perforce sees the barrels standing out boldly and, perhaps, blotting out some of the field. To gain the correct impression of a side-by-side, however, one must always focus beyond the gun at a target and let hand-to-eye coordination bring the piece to bear without an undue fixation on the gun. Thus, a side-by-side's broad barrels can be a detriment to fast, accurate pointing if you develop faulty gun-handling habits and don't use your eyes properly. But when your head is down tightly on the comb of a horizontal double, the rib gives the same single-line pointing plane as any over-under, pump, or auto.

When compared to the over-under, a side-by-side has a shallower barrel opening angle, which makes load changing and reloading easier in the cramped confines of a blind, pit, or skiff.

One subtlety of the side-by-side is its trim profile which slices through the wind for a smooth swing free of buffeting. An over-under, on the other hand, presents a deep barrel assembly to the wind, and both hunters and trap shooters have felt air pressure shoving on the tubes.

If side-by-sides have any drawbacks for waterfowling, they are twofold. Models built for magnum loads and heavy recoil are robust and, to varying degrees, muzzle heavy. They lose some of their famed spirited handling qualities. Moreover, side-by-sides send raw recoil into the hunter's shoulder when powerful loads are used. This pair of drawbacks must be considered when selecting a side-by-side for waterfowling, and the hunter should balance gun weight and responsiveness with

potential recoil. Absorbent recoil pads are a necessity. For most hunters, a standard 12-gauge with 28- or 30-inch barrels will do splendidly. Hefty 10- and 12-gauge Magnums can weigh down an average hunter, impeding his movement and coordination.

Today's leading offerings from U.S. suppliers are the Browning B-SS, Winchester Model 23, Savage-Fox Model B, and Stevens Model 311. There are also many side-by-sides available from foreign manufacturers for those who want to shop around.

Of course, not all duck guns must be long-barreled. When ducks pass close or work to the blocks, upland guns will kill cleanly and be more effective than the longer, more tightly choked waterfowl specials. If a hunter can restrict himself to shots inside 30–35 yards,

If one gets his head down properly on a side-by-side, the broad barrels disappear and he sees only the rib, as is the case on an over-under or repeater.

When ducks work to the call and decoys, a dynamic double bored IC&M, such as this
Winchester Lightweight Model 23, is a delight to use.

a side-by-side bored improved cylinder and modified can be mistaken for a magic wand. Some of the best scoring I've yet done on mallards came with Winchester's English-gripped 12-gauge Model 23 and its open-bored, 25½-inch tubes. Few hunters would consider that a bona fide duck gun, but when birds break close and one must swing through his arc swiftly, the upland-type double can't be beat.

There is a standing theory, backed by scientific evidence, that a side-by-side kicks in the direction of the barrel being fired. Technicians call this a resultant force, produced because the bore and the stock do not have the same center line. This point of physics is often mentioned in any pro and con discussion of doubles, but, in reality, few

The highest-quality over-under ever made in the United States was Remington's Model 32.

people ever notice it under actual field conditions. I have patterned and hunted with everything from a .410 side-by-side to several 10-gauge Magnum doubles without detecting the phenomenon. Those who read further into doubles and come upon the topic again should therefore be skeptical of its importance.

OVER-UNDERS

The subject of recoil lines and forces is a convenient place to slide into a discussion of over-unders. While not as racy and trim as the side-by-side, over-unders still have excellent handling qualities, aesthetics, compact mechanics, and effective dynamics. Of primary interest here, however, is the speed with which an over-under can drive in its second pattern. Indeed, single-triggered O-Us have the potential for delivering the fastest second shot in shotgunning. The reason rests with recoil energy, force lines, and barrel positions. An over-under's lower barrel not only sits in coaxial alignment with the stock, but it is also depressed below the stock's comb line, and these characteristics give what is commonly termed straightline recoil. If the gun comes straight back instead of jumping and/or kicking off to one side, the shooter can retain control easier during recoil and can regain alignment quicker thereafter. It is this feature that endears over-unders to champion clay target and live pigeon shooters, and it can also be put to good use by hunters.

There is one thing that can negate the fast-firing potential of an over-under — excess recoil from heavy loads. No gunner can recover quickly if the ammunition overpowers the gun so that it jumps and whips violently. Common sense in ammunition selection is therefore necessary.

The obvious reason why so many hunters opt for an over-under rather than a side-by-side is the supposedly narrower sighting plane. As explained before, however, this is often based on poor technique rather than an inherent weakness in side-by-sides. The side-by-side may block out rising targets, but in high-angle fire on ducks and geese the target is normally seen above the tubes and shouldn't hinder scoring if the shooter knows what he is about. Nevertheless, the narrower barrel segment of an over-under is deemed more accurate by many hunters, and if that feature is needed to give them confidence and visual comfort, more power to them.

During the years that I have been writing about guns, I have had many opportunities to try consignment guns that were either on the market or about to be announced, and one of the things I found most annoying on over-unders was a rebound (closing slightly) which made it difficult to reload the lower barrel after ejection. I would check every O-U for such rebound before buying; if the barrels bounce back slightly after opening, avoid the model like the plague. Trying to reload vertical doubles like that during periods of fast action is one of the most frustrating things in hunting, and is especially so in cold weather when one's fingers are numb.

Over-unders have been rapped for the way wind can buffet their deep, slab-sided barrel assemblies. I have felt this on a trapshooting field when the wind was 90 degrees to the barrels, but I cannot say I have ever felt it afield. The reason, no doubt, is because a trap shooter stands stationary for a short time with the gun mounted before calling "Pull!" whereas a hunter's gun is generally moving, and continues to move, when it is shouldered. Nevertheless, many current over-unders have

The greater opening angle necessitated by an over-under to load the lower barrel may be a consideration in tightly cramped blinds and pits.

air-flow provisions between the barrels. Some have no ribs between the barrels whatsoever; others have variously cut ventilated slots. The Ruger Red Label has removable side rails.

Perhaps the best of America's early over-unders was the Remington Model 32, now prized by collectors. The gun had totally opened space between the barrels except for the hanger arrangement at the muzzle, and it was considerably trimmer than the bulky, heavyweight Model 3200. Anyone interested in hunting with a shootable collector's piece could do far worse than a Model 32.

Weatherby's line of over-unders is made by SKB in Japan and is the class of the low-priced field, meaning guns below a thousand dollars. Given fancy Claro walnut, generous checkering, and Weatherby/California profiles, they handle well and score to the extent of a

hunter's ability. My own experience with a Weatherby 20-gauge Orion made me a booster of the gun, and patterns with a pet 1$\frac{3}{16}$-ounce 20-gauge magnum reload were excellent from the gun's 28-inch M&F barrels.

Ruger's Red Label is another pass-shooting O-U of promise. Although very trim, the gun has a heavy action body to offset some recoil and to generate some momentum. A 28-inch-barreled Ruger, either in 20 or 12 gauge, fits nicely into pass-shooting. In the future, Ruger plans to make a stainless steel-receivered Red Label.

At the low-priced range of over-unders is Stoeger's Brazilian-made I.G.A. It has the plain features favored by many in a knockabout gun destined to get soaked and dented, and its price is less than that of most autoloaders.

Appropriate waterfowl engraving is found on this massive 10-gauge Magnum double once imported from Spain by Stoeger. (Photo by Gerald F. Moran)

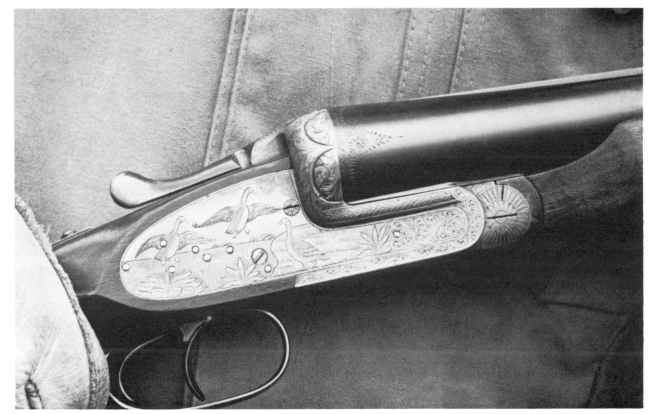

The Beretta S 680 series of over-unders is a nice line of smooth-handling doubles, especially with 28-inch barrels as shown here.

Winchester's Model 101 Waterfowl Gun with blued receiver, full-size recoil pad, and Winchoke-equipped 32-inch barrels is in the traditionalist's camp, and is a workhorse of a modern duck and goose gun.

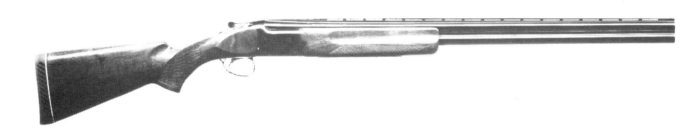

Browning's Citori Field Grade hunting model is a popular over-under.

The great Browning Belgian-made Superposed is being made to honor various species of waterfowl. This is the Pintail Issue; the birds are done in gold inlay.

INVESTMENT-GRADE DUCK GUNS

Those who fancy doubles often get into gun collecting or investing. Aside from engraved Winchester Model 12 pumpguns, this is the field for investors and those who simply appreciate gun art. Getting started involves thousands of dollars, not merely hundreds. Pride of ownership is a motivating force, of course, and hunters specializing in waterfowling can find doubles with specific engraving relating to their sport.

The best known series of waterfowl doubles is Browning's current offering of Belgian-made Superposed guns emphasizing a different species of duck annually. One series is known as the Black Duck Issue; a more recent one is the Pintail Edition. More will be forthcoming, the prices varying with the year. Browning's Grade VI Citori has engraving of mallards inlaid in gold, with the Grade V having the same scenes, sans gold, on the receiver.

Whether it is a knockabout field gun, an advanced grade with improved or specialized features, or a true work of art, the double shotgun fits a waterfowler's world. Owning one is a pleasure; handling one, a delight. And their dynamics are such that a modern sportsman either won't need a third shot, or won't miss it.

6
Beginners' Guns

It is fun to watch a youngster scan the autumn skies, to see him make a few misses, and then proudly hold his first greenhead. Introducing adults to the waterfowler's world is equally satisfying. Both the young and the old will come away from those outings with fond memories, and, besides being etched in their minds, those memories will always be associated with the guns they used. That's why it's so important to use good judgment when selecting guns for beginners, and instructing them in their use. When the sights and sounds and smells of the marsh have faded, there will always be the gun on the rack or in the corner to help bring them back. Indeed, of all the equipment used for hunting, the greatest amount of pride goes into the gun.

Beginners are in a Catch-22 situation. They need a gun that fits them and their sport if they're to do their best; however, because of inexperience, a lack of shotgunning theory, and woefully unsophisticated technique, they don't have the faintest idea of what a gun should feel like in their hands and at their shoulder. Few have ever read on the subject; most beginners plunge in because it looks like fun. And often a know-it-all egotism prevents them from accepting their personal shortcomings. That's where either literature or a knowledgeable father or partner comes in handy.

There are really two categories of beginners: youngsters and adults. They both share some of the same basic requirements, but because of the differences in physical stature, will need different guns.

JUNIOR SHOOTERS

Many fathers have a sadistic way of introducing their sons and daughters to shotguns. They slip a hard-belting, high-velocity or magnum load into a 12-gauge, hand the youngster such a long, heavy gun that he or she wobbles and struggles just to hold it, and then advise, "Hold 'er tight or she'll kick ya good." With teeth clenched and eyes closed in fearful anticipation, the youngster flinches off a shot and gets knocked two steps backward while dear old dad laughs and asks, "There, now do you still want to go along duck hunting?" Such an experience could leave a young person gun shy for life.

It's all so stupid, but it's done every year by fathers who apparently enjoy proving to their children just how macho they really are to stand up to the pounding recoil of big guns. A lot of these fathers are likely to lose the thrill of hunting with their own children by such brutal introductory antics, however. Kids don't get any real enjoyment out of being kicked silly by a shotgun, and neither does anyone else, and if that's what duck hunting is all about, they'll opt for other forms of entertainment, of which there are plenty.

Youngsters should start with shotguns that are scaled down for easy handling, and the gauge and load should generate light recoil. There is no need for big bores, long barrels, and optimum magnum loads. Few beginners have enough skill to hit beyond 20 to 30 yards anyway; therefore, why outfit him or her with a gun and load intended for 60- to 75-yard shooting? In most instances, a youngster is properly outfitted if he has enough gun and load for 35–40 yards. Shooting beyond that range is only a frustrating waste of money. The sensible thing for a father or coach to do is to teach the child something about range judgment — using tree heights, decoy placement, or paced-off yardages — and then instruct him or her not to shoot anything that could be deemed farther away.

The ideal gun for a junior waterfowler is a 20-gauge with stock and barrel dimensions scaled for young hands and bodies. There is nothing wrong with using a .410 bore or 28 gauge for practice on clay targets, as they have low recoil levels that are easy to live with. When ducks or geese are the name of the game, though, leave the .410 and 28 at home and take, as minimum ordnance, a 20-gauge choked modified or full with 1- or 1⅛-ounce loads of 5s or 6s. A modified 20 with such ammo can handle 30–35 yards, and few beginners can score on anything beyond that distance. Number 4s and 2s aren't needed for ducks at this range: No. 5s and 6s carry enough energy and fill out a modified pattern better. If the same discipline is applied to geese, No. 4s will serve for 35- to 40-yard shots and put more pellets into the spread for multiple hits. At this writing, only Federal Cartridge makes steel shot loads for the 20. Both the 2¾- and 3-inch loadings have No. 4 steel shot, and they are quite adequate for 30–35 yards. From what this writer has seen at the patterning board, they will often give full-choke percentages from modified-choked 20s. The 2¾-inch Federal steel load does over 1,400 f.p.s., and the 3-incher tops 1,300 f.p.s. from a 26-inch barrel. If the beginner can lay the patterns with lead or steel shot on his bird, the loads can do the rest.

Youth model shotguns are readily available these days, and they're getting better. At one time, only a few break-action single-shots were scaled down to a youngster's proportions, the classic being Winchester's Model 37. A father who dotes on snob appeal might hunt up a Model 37 Youth Gun for his son or daughter; on the collector's market, it'll probably cost between $150 and $200. The youth-style break-actions of today are priced below $100, and the discount market takes

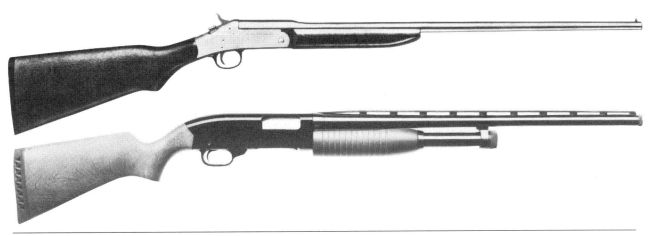

Nobody is a natural shot. Beginners need plenty of practice at shotgun shooting just as they do at baseball, football, or basketball. A ground-mounted Trius trap and a stack of clay targets, plus light-recoiling ammo, are good for starters.

A 20-gauge gun is the lightest gauge recommended for waterfowl. This is H&R's inexpensive single-shot, available in either full-size or Youth style.

U.S. Repeating Arms is making a Youth Slide Action with a short barrel and stock, along with easy-to-reach pump handle, in 20 gauge.

them closer to $50–$60. The foremost makers are Harrington & Richardson and the Savage/Stevens combine. Harrington & Richardson offers a junior-sized Model 088JR 20-gauge single with a 25-inch modified barrel and a 12½-inch length of pull. The gun opens easily with a push-down lever release located on the right side of the exposed hammer. With an overall length of 39 inches and a weight of about 5 pounds, the Model 088JR can be handled and carried easily by any 12-year-old.

There are two youth models listed by Savage/Stevens, both very similar except for the opening mechanism. The Savage/Stevens Model 94-Y has the conventional tang-top opening lever like a double barrel, while the Stevens Model 9478-Y has an action release lever positioned at the leading edge of the trigger guard. Otherwise, both the Model 94-Y and the 9478-Y have 26-inch modified barrels in 20 gauge with 12½-inch lengths of pull and overall lengths of 40½ inches.

Break-action single-shots are entirely legitimate beginners' guns, and their recoil is manageable in the 20-gauge models. Going to a 12-gauge single-shot can be detrimental, as those light guns kick like the proverbial Missouri mule with anything beyond trap loads.

The main problem in coaching youngsters who have single-shots is getting them to swing and shoot with a swift movement. Their tendency is to track each target deliberately and aim the gun, because they want to make their one and only shot count. Such deliberate aiming, along with the concomitant dawdling on trigger pull and slow swinging, is the antithesis of sound wingshooting practice. The beginner must be made to feel loose with a single-shot, and he must be made to realize that he'll score better if his pointing and swinging are dynamic and geared to hand-to-eye coordination rather than riflelike precision. It may take a while for youngsters to overcome the feeling of apprehension and doubt which underlies crisp, rapid moves, but a coach can't let down on theory and permit slow, precise aiming.

The concept of youth-sized guns has been carried into the realm of excellent repeaters. There is no longer any need to saw off a full-sized stock for Junior or Sis. Remington was the early leader in this category, coming up with a shortened version of its popular 20-gauge auto, the Model 1100 Lightweight. The gun is called the Limited and has a 12½-inch length of pull plus a 23-inch barrel that can be had in either modified or improved cylinder chokes. It weighs a mere 6½ pounds and measures 41½ inches overall. This is a great beginner's gun because it has such soft recoil and such splendid stock dimensions.

A year after the Model 1100 Limited was announced, the Remington Model 870 Lightweight pump was also trimmed to match the auto's dimensions. However, the Model 870 Limited 20-gauge weighs only 6 pounds but has a full-sized recoil pad attached for a 12½-inch length of pull and a 41½-inch overall length. Barrel lengths and chokes are the same as for the autoloader.

Remington's move was followed shortly by U.S. Repeating Arms, the company that bought out Winchester's stateside gunmaking facilities. USRA offers a Youth Model slide-action based on the Model 1300 XTR design but made within the economy-priced Ranger line. This gun has a 22-inch barrel that can be had with either a solid modified choke constriction or the screw-in Winchoke feature. It's a plain-barreled gun sans any sort of rib, and is chambered for 3-inch shells (something the Remington Model 1100 and 870 Limiteds lack). It also has a 13-inch length of pull (compared to other youth-style guns with 12½-inches), and a weight of about 6½ pounds. A recoil pad is fitted to the butt, and the gun's overall length is 41⅝ inches.

These three scaled-down repeaters give fathers a chance to outfit their children with guns that have follow-up capacity. There's always a second load ready in the magazine, and that knowledge allows the young hunter to be loose and less concerned about making the first shot count, as is the case with single-shots. This extra insurance brings mental relaxation, which encourages smooth, crisp swinging, pointing, and follow-through.

Undoubtedly, the biggest mistake a father or concerned coach can make is giving a youngster too much gun and load too soon. Children with 25–30 yards of ability (if that much) don't need 60-yard guns. What they need is sound schooling in fundamentals on close-range targets that won't frustrate them, and the learning process should include guns and loads that don't punish them. Shotgun shooting and hunting are sports to enjoy. For a soft-recoiling practice load in those beginner's 20s, try this handloaded recipe:

Winchester 2¾″ AA case (20 ga.)
Winchester 209 primer
14.0 gr. Green Dot Powder
Win. WAA20 wad
3/4 oz. No. 9 shot
Pressure: 10,800 p.s.i.
Velocity: 1,200 f.p.s.

A small wad of newspaper or something similar is needed over the pellets in the shot-cup to take up space and permit a good crimp; 3/4 ounce of shot is a bit sparse.

When coaching a youngster, make certain you yourself are versed in sound wingshooting fundamentals. Too often shotgun coaching is a matter of the blind leading the blind; fathers and friends hand down erroneous advice. Once some shotgun savvy has been implanted, proceed with patience. Educational psychology informs us that a student can only learn one or two things per class session in school, and it's no different in shooting. It'll take time. Remember, you didn't become the great shot that you are on just a few shells. Accept the fact that missing targets is a part of learning how to shoot. Emphasize the basics in a most positive manner. Stay away from the tendency to keep saying, "Don't do this," or "Don't do that." There are a million things a beginner shouldn't do, and harping on them is a poor, depressing coaching method that only clutters the beginner's mind. Focus solely on what the youngster should do, and keep it enjoyable and simple. You're not an NFL coach or a drill sergeant.

Shooting at clay targets thrown from a duck tower such as this will help the beginner — and the seasoned veteran — improve his technique on high, crossing targets.

ADULT BEGINNERS

An adult beginner is pretty much in the same duck boat as the youngster. He lacks experience, has no knowledge of sound wing-shooting theory, and is unfamiliar with shotguns. Often an adult starts duck hunting just to be with the guys.

But the mature beginner differs in two ways from his young colleague. He may be misled by a know-it-all egotism not found in the youngster, and he or she is physically larger than a child, meaning that a full-sized gun is in order.

It's interesting to watch a novice adult hunter handle a lot of guns in a sport shop and set them all aside saying, "Nope, they don't seem to fit me." The fact is that probably all the guns do indeed fit. Most newcomers to shooting simply don't know how to handle and mount a shotgun properly. Gunmakers have spent considerable time and money researching the subject of stock dimensions, and practically all popular field-grade guns today will fit everyone except a seven-foot NBA center on one extreme, and Happy, Doc, Sneezy, and the rest of the Seven Dwarfs on the other. Stock designs are based on the average shooter's needs. About the only adjustment that might be necessary is in the

A youngster holds his first greenhead. The gun is a Harrington & Richardson 20-gauge Youth Model.

length of pull. Taller people, or even average-sized hunters with longer arms, can have that increased by the installation of a recoil pad and/or spacers. Shorter people can have some of the stock sawed off and a pad reattached for the appropriate length. Other than that, an adult beginner can rest assured that experts have analyzed stock dimensions before the tooling was set, and that as he or she develops fundamentally sound technique the initially uncomfortable gun will fit quite nicely. It's a matter of accepting the inexperienced shooter's shortcomings rather than being critical of basic gun design.

An adult beginner probably should buy his first waterfowl gun with the idea of replacing it or supplementing it with a second one later on after he learns more about himself as a hunter under field conditions. Clinging stubbornly to an ill-chosen first gun can take some enjoyment out of the sport.

Some freshmen duck hunters may have had previous shooting experiences in the armed forces, and they tend to apply their expertise with military rifles and handguns to shotguns. That's a mistake. Shotguns and wingshooting are entirely different, and, instead of wasting money, these people should consult a hunter or trap or skeet shooter of known ability and judgment for advice. That sharpshooter ribbon won with an M-16 means nothing when a greenhead goes high-balling overhead at 57 yards with a wind on its tail.

Although adult beginners will select full-sized guns, there are some important points to be made. First, as with the young shooter, optimum long-range potential isn't needed. An adult has no more inherent skill than a teenager; therefore, it'll be a couple of seasons before he or she can handle 35- to 40-yard shots with any degree of skill. Therefore, why select more gun and load than are needed for close- and intermediate-range gunning? The sensible beginner will pick a gun and load

suited to his ability, and stay within his limits. A repeater with a 28-inch, modified choke barrel, or a 28-inch-barreled double bored modified and full, is a good choice. If the hunter disciplines himself to shoot only within his personal effective range, said gun can be in 12, 16, or 20 gauge. Loads can be 1¼ or 1⅜ ounces of hard 5s. It is purely an ego trip or poor judgment on their part when adult beginners pack Long Toms and the most robust magnum loads in stock. Seventy-five yards worth of equipment won't compensate for just 30 yards worth of personal skill.

If anybody needs a lively gun, it is the beginner. Heavy guns and long barrels can weigh him down, causing a slow, labored swing that never gets ahead of birds. Just two inches less barrel, such as buying a 28-inch instead of a 30-inch, can make a difference. The Remington Model 1100, for instance, was designed to balance best with a 28-inch ventilated rib barrel, and sticking on a 30-incher can make the gun muzzle heavy and a noticeably slower swinger for many adults of moderate experience, let alone beginners. New hunters who restrict themselves to sensible yardages can often do beautifully with 26-inch barrels because they move so spiritedly. Doubles bored improved cylinder and modified are excellent over decoys or when the birds work just above the tree crowns for 25- to 30-yard shots. A 1¼-ounce load of hard or copper-plated 6s will suffice for adequate penetration and full clusters for multiple hits into the vital area. No beginner need be ashamed of holding back on birds at dubious distances; that's a desirable sportsmanlike trait, one conducive to conservation because it greatly reduces the number of crippled and lost birds. Moreover, the beginner — adult or junior — who hits a goodly percentage of his shots inside 40 yards will have more than his fair share of the harvest.

7
The Target Defined

It was one of the first geese I'd ever shot at, and only some fuzz from its rump drifted down. The old-timer watched as the bird held its place in the wedge, then said, "Geese may be big birds, but they're awfully small targets." It took a few more hunts, plus time at the cleaning table, before my teenage mind fully comprehended what he was driving at. But once I'd become acquainted with the anatomy of ducks and geese, and saw how patterns registered on the birds, I also began to differentiate between the bird and the target. The old boy did indeed have a point.

If a fully plumed goose is placed on a patterning sheet, it practically fills the 30-inch circle. So do some of the larger ducks. A mature northern mallard with its wings outstretched extends beyond the circumference and covers the 15-inch-diameter core. Just looking at a mallard in flight lets a hunter visualize the approximate size of his pattern. And practically anyone seeing that bird-to-pattern relationship can't help but wonder how birds that large can fly through such patterns without being dropped cleanly every time.

But fully plumed birds, as a whole, cannot be considered the target except in a most general way. The target for a waterfowler is the bird's vital area, which is much smaller. The vital area includes the head, neck, and heart/lung mass directly ahead of the diaphragm. The wing butts can also be included, although breaking them doesn't produce a clean kill; shattering the first wing bone merely brings the bird down immediately. However, the outermost wing bones aren't included as vital spots, as hits there often leave the bird able to glide beyond positive retrieving range.

When a hunter considers his target relative to pattern density, then, he must think solely in terms of the vital area, not the total surface area of a bird. All those pellets that snap through tail feathers and wings, along with those that impact in legs and a few organs (kidneys, liver, and intestines) guarantee nothing in the way of a knockdown. Sometimes the shock of multiple hits to the liver/kidney area can buckle a bird, but don't count on it.

Some of the accompanying photographs illustrate the vital area of a mature mallard. They were made by tracing a late-season drake and coloring the vital area black. The art wasn't undertaken for pattern evaluation, but rather for comparative viewing. If a hunter comes to any conclusion by studying the pictures, it should be that the old-timer was correct: a big bird's vital area does indeed become a small target when compared to the main 30-inch circle, to the bird's outline, and to the 15-inch-diameter core.

A MATHEMATICAL BASIS

British shotgun authority Major Sir Gerald Burrard suggested that a bird's vulnerable area in square inches, on an overhead shot, is 0.88 of its weight in ounces ($A = .88W$). If we establish 42 ounces as the weight of a large duck, the resulting vulnerable area would be approximately 37 square inches. That seems large, but is it? The 15-inch core of patterning sheet contains a little over 176 square inches; therefore, about five vulnerable areas could fit inside the core of a pattern. There are roughly 707 square inches in a 30-inch-diameter circle, meaning 19½ of those areas could be

---

There is a big difference between the overall size of a duck or goose and the size of its vital area. Tracing a bird onto patterning paper and then blackening the vital area can be enlightening.

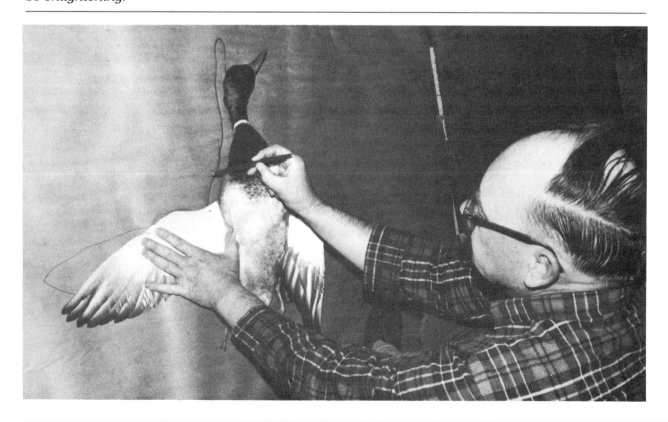

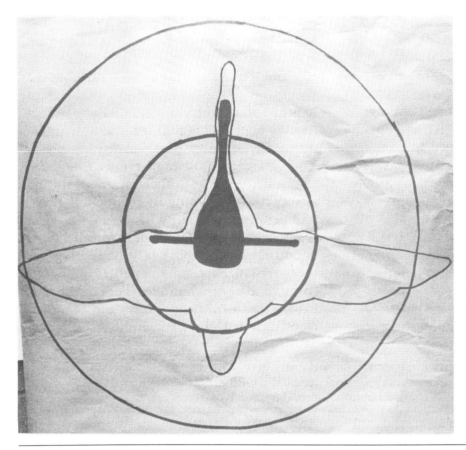

Although a mature mallard pretty well fills out a 30-inch-diameter patterning circle, its vital area takes up only a small portion of the 15-inch-diameter core. The failure of pellets to find these indicated vital areas leads to crippled and lost birds.

squeezed into the overall patterning ring. Finally, an American clay target I've just measured has a 4.40-inch diameter, giving it a surface area of 15 square inches. Thus, although a vulnerable area of 37 square inches seems big at first glance, it dwindles markedly when put into mathematical perspective.

It should be pointed out that Burrard always wrote in terms of vulnerability when he covered this topic, and his concept included the rearmost viscera (liver, kidneys, intestines). My own comments, however, stress the concept of vital area and exclude the parts behind the diaphragm. A more realistic computation, it would seem, can be derived by substituting 0.70 for Burrard's 0.88, giving us an equation that reads: $A = 0.70W$. Applied to the same 42-ounce duck, the revamped equation gives us 29 square inches of area, which comes closer to *vital* than merely *vulnerable*. The reduced figure, of course, means a hunter's pattern must reach an even smaller target within the larger bird, and that pattern density is always desirable for making multiple hits without fail within such a compact area whenever the shooter makes a good swing.

With this in mind, hunters should always try to keep the pattern up front where the vitals lay. Instead of looking at the bird's large body and broad wings, concentrate on the head and neck when pointing and swinging. Look sharply at that outstretched head and bill; make that the focal point of hand-to-eye coordination. If the forward allowance is then a bit on the short side, the pattern can still pick up the bird's wings and body. However, if the forward allowance comes up short when the hunter is focusing on the bird's body, it will be a clean miss or, worse, a gut-shot hit with pellets centering behind the diaphragm. Waterfowl, like upland game, live and die up front. If this chapter can get hunters to understand that and to focus on the head/neck target area, it will have done its job.

CHANGING ANGLES

The Burrard equation applies mainly to overhead shots. When the angle changes, so does the size of the target area.

Reaching the bird's vitals can be very difficult on outgoing shots such as those en- countered in jump shooting when teal or woodies vault from the far side of a pond and buzz away low. The target area then shrinks to about the size of the bird's lateral cross sec- tion. Even for the biggest ducks, that is hard- ly larger than a clay target laid flat on a pat- terning sheet. This puts stringent demands on pattern density *and* penetrating power. The bird's outgoing angle reduces the effec- tive pellet velocity in the amount of its own speed, thus detracting from shocking power and penetrating energy. The head and neck regions are either significantly foreshortened or entirely blocked out by the body. The wing butts are still exposed, but pellets must fight through feathers that offer a curved surface loaded down by air pressure, and there is a chance for deflection. Penetration through the

This photo shows what can happen when a hunter doesn't center his target with a tight-patterning load: the vital area is missed, and the bird would probably be wing- tipped at best. For most hunters, better marksmanship and/or wider patterns are in order.

back is often minimal, as pellets deflect or use much of their energy driving through bone. And to reach the heart and lungs, pellets must fight through fluid-laden tissues, organs, and intestines. Therefore, taking long shots at outgoing birds invites crippling because the true target is hidden. The use of open-bored guns is discouraged here. Putting a lethal concentration of high-energy pellets into such a small target area requires considerable pattern density.

Crossing shots appear to present an ample target area, but, in reality, it is reduced by about one third. The far-side wing butt is protected, and the chest area of a waterfowl is smaller when seen from the side than when it offers a broad overhead chance. If the shot charge reaches a passing bird when its on-side wing is up, the pellets can penetrate the chest to their maximum potential. But if the on-side wing is down, it can serve as a shield of sorts, deflecting pellets and/or making them expend some of their energy before impacting on the body. Many such wing-down hits produce wing-broken birds still capable of movement. No hunter can time his shots to arrive on passing birds when their wings are up, of course. But hunters can understand the shieldlike effect of the on-side wing and take the precaution of focusing on the bird's head and neck so that the pattern concentrates up front rather than on the wing/body unit.

Incoming ducks and geese are perhaps the easiest to drop for positive retrieves. Their incoming speed adds to the pellets' velocity for extra energy. Moreover, practically everything exposed to the pattern is vital area except the wing tips. The head and neck may be foreshortened, but the pellets can get to them easily; and the chest area is broad, although certainly smaller than that of an overhead bird. The wing butts are equally open to the pattern. A mistake often made on incomers is stopping the gun to take a riflelike shot, which can send the pattern high or low depending on the bird's angle, and the result is hitting either the back or breast with fringe pellets.

In summary, whether a hunter is experimenting with patterns or practicing on skeet clays, he must think in terms of (1) vital target areas, not entire birds, and (2) pattern concentrations that will put multiple, energy-laden hits into those smaller spaces. The patterning part will be covered in another chapter. The shooting part requires a learned technique that concentrates on leading the front of a target, not the target in general, so that the pattern mass is concentrated up front where the vital areas are. Cutting rump fuzz from a honker is hardly perfection.

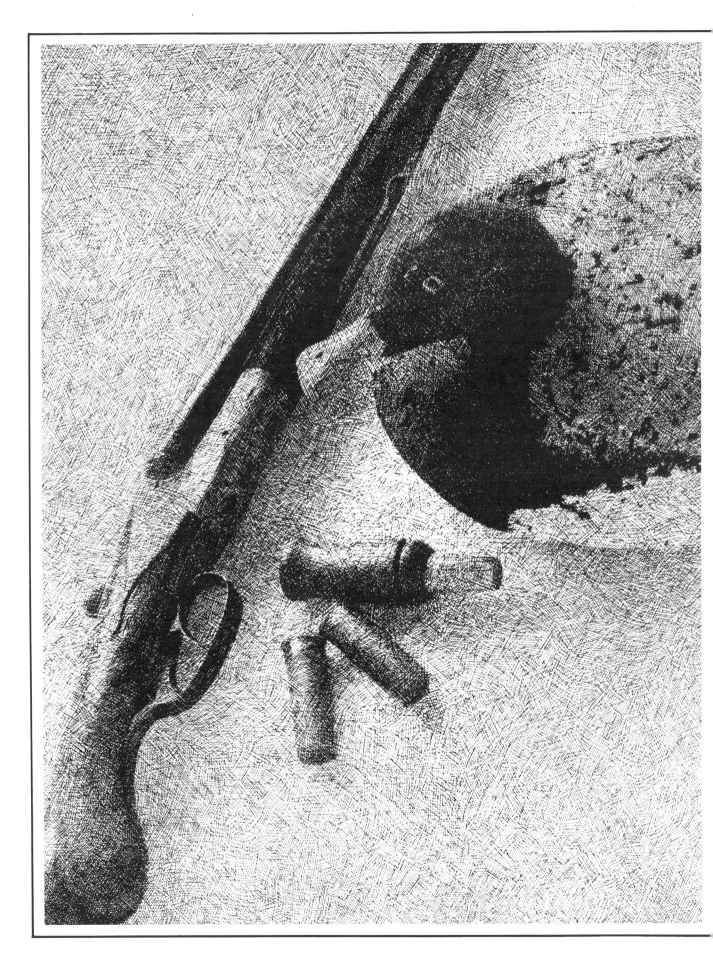

8
Pellet Performance and Selection

Part I: Performance

Pellets are to wingshots what line is to an angler. Both are at the business end of things — where reliable performance is vital. Yet fishermen will buy expensive rods and reels only to compromise on cheap lines and leaders that part under the strain of a lunker or steady casting; while shotgunners will splurge on fine guns and then hunt with economy loads containing low-quality shot that patterns poorly and penetrates inadequately. Indeed, no custom-made stock, gold inlay, engraved receiver, or ventilated rib ever brought down a bird. The pellets do that work. They are the single most important element in successful shotgunning.

Unfortunately, many hunters believe that all pellets are alike — that they are simply lead spheroids. But nothing could be further from the truth. For although lead is a heavy metal which, theoretically, overcomes air resistance well to retain velocity and deliver energy downrange, it is also malleable; hence, it is easily deformed by the setback pressures of firing and by the swaging forces of bore travel. As a rule of thumb, pure lead pellets in modern shotshells (having only enough arsenic content to affect shape during the formation process) will experience at least 45–50 percent deformation. Then, as they encounter air resistance, such deformed pellets will flare from and/or slow down to trail the main shot mass, resulting in long shot strings and low striking power.

The realities of pellet deformation often puzzle hunters who, when they slice open a new shotshell, find the pellets nicely rounded and polished. "They look good to me," is the normal observation.

However, that's before primer detonation and powder ignition. When a shot charge goes from a static mass to a kinetic mass traveling at 1,150 to 1,400 f.p.s. in just 12 to 20 inches, there are a pair of destructive physical forces at work — setback and bore travel. The impact of both upon pellets can be understood if we let our mind's eye visualize steps in a shotshell's blast-off.

Imagine a loaded shotshell in the chamber of a duck gun. The shot charge is packed in a plastic shotcup and is held in place by a tight crimp. When the firing pin falls, it detonates the primer which, in turn, ignites the powder. The burning powder produces a violently expanding gas which is the propelling force. In many respects, this is like exploding gasoline vapor pushing against the piston in the cylinder of an automobile engine (which is why Remington calls its plastic wads Power Pistons). Within just a few microseconds, the powder gases create a pressure that goes from zero to 10,000 p.s.i., give or take a thousand or two in the various gauges and loads. It is this intense pressure rise that complicates shotshell patterning through a condition known as setback.

Setback begins when the shot charge is momentarily sandwiched between the sudden swell of powder gases and the restraining crimp. Moreover, there is always the shot charge's own inertia that must be overcome, something that can also contribute to deformation since the lower layers of shot start moving sooner than the upper layers to cause raw pellet-against-pellet mashing. Thus, with forces applied fore and aft, the pellets find themselves in a pincer-type trap that easily deforms lead regardless of how bright and perfectly round the pellets looked before firing.

Because the crimp yields to permit upper layers of shot to start forward, most setback deformation will take place in the lower half or third of the shot charge. One studious glance at a fired shotcup or plastic shot wrapper will prove this; the lower half of the shotcup or wrapper will show deeper impressions than the upper half or two thirds.

Setback and pellet deformation don't end in the chamber. That's just the start. The remaining trip through a conventional shotgun barrel is an obstacle course for pellets. Beyond the chamber are two narrow passages that require shot charges to swage down abruptly — the forcing cone, and the choke constriction. The forcing cone is a tapered segment that funnels the ejecta from the spacious chamber into the smaller bore diameter; the choke is a narrowing of the bore at the muzzle to influence pellet flight for pattern control. In many mass-produced shotguns, the forcing cone is relatively short and abrupt, and in many typical waterfowl guns, the choke is tight. Accordingly, at both points the pellets are subjected to further mashing as gas pressures drive the wad and lower layers of shot into the upper pellets during the momentary slowing of the upper pellets during the swaging process.

There is also the matter of bore scrubbing, which flattens a pellet as it speeds along in abrasive contact with the bore wall. This happens to the outer pellets, of course, but these can be numerous in the long shot columns found in magnum-length shotshells. This type of deformation has been greatly reduced by protective shotcups and wrappers, but it hasn't been entirely eliminated. A close study of shotcups and wrappers will still reveal some perforations which allowed bore contact. Therefore, although a casual hunter may feel secure with plastic wads and wrappers, plus the glint of nicely polished shot, deformation is still rampant in a shotgun. Setback forces and swaging pressures remain in conventional, unaltered smoothbores of all persuasions.

THE PELLET HARDNESS FACTOR

The main way to reduce or eliminate pellet deformation for improved patterns and penetration is by using hardened pellets. That brings us back to a point made earlier in this chapter, namely, that pellets should no longer be thought of as simple spheroids. Ammunition makers and component suppliers have upgraded pellet quality and there are now several grades of hardened lead shot on the market. All hunters would do well to study these different grades to note their strengths and weaknesses.

Insofar as waterfowlers are concerned, the worst of these is drop shot, otherwise known as soft shot. It is primarily lead with just a pinch of arsenic to prompt form, and it deforms substantially under firing and bore-travel pressures. With drop shot, it is often difficult to reach a pattern tighter than 50 percent even in a true full-choked barrel.

Chilled shot is the next step up from drop shot. For some reason, many shotgunners past and present have attributed greater hardness to chilled shot than it actually possesses. They also tend to believe that it is hardened by some mysterious cold-air process during manufacturing, which isn't the case. Chilled shot is harder than drop shot by the addition of antimony or some other hardening alloy. This addition amounts to 1.75 to 2.0 percent, and that level, despite popular notions, isn't enough to improve performance as much as an average hunter assumes. There is still a potential for 35 to 45 percent deformation in a load of chilled shot, and many bona fide full-choked shotguns will pattern no better than 55 to 63 percent at 40 yards with chilled shot. It is this kind of low-antimony shot that is used in inexpensive promotion loads — Duck & Pheasant, Quail & Squirrel — because it is cheap and keeps the retail price down; however, hunters who buy it as a bargain are long-range losers, because the shot is soft and seldom gives a true 70-percent patterning performance. Deformation-prone chilled shot also

penetrates poorly, and it is one reason why unsophisticated hunters hear pellets rattle on high-flying geese without bringing them down cleanly.

During the last decade or so, magnum-grade shot, alias high-antimony or hard shot, has come on strong with handloaders. High-antimony shot, as its name implies, carries more antimony than chilled shot. It is therefore harder and less inclined to deform during setback and bore travel. In most full-choked guns, high-antimony shot will give a 40-yard pattern of 70 to 80 percent, meaning deformation affects but 20 to 30 percent of the charge. The amount of antimony varies according to pellet size, but is still well in advance of whatever hardeners are employed in ordinary chilled shot. These high-antimony pellets are used in the more expensive lines of commercially loaded ammunition, as antimony is very expensive and drives up material costs.

High-antimony shot has become readily available to reloaders in 25-pound bags from such sources as Taracorp Industries (Lawrence brand shot) and Hornady, both of which market it as "Magnum" shot. The hunter who wishes to stick with black (unplated) shot is being penny-wise and pound-foolish if he picks ordinary chilled shot over high-antimony magnum shot just because "It looks as good and is cheaper." There's a significant difference between chilled and magnum shot when actual results are measured scientifically. Magnum shot wins in both pattern density and individual pellet penetration due to the greater incidence of retained form.

Even more impressive than high-antimony black shot are copper- and nickel-plated pellets. At first glance, one would assume that the plating is largely responsible for the pellets' performance, and that it defends against pellet deformation. However, plating alone won't keep pellets round; the shot must have a high antimony content in the lead core to assist in form retention. It is possible to get plated shot that doesn't have a hard core, and it will also pattern indifferently. However, the combination of a high-antimony lead core and copper or nickel plating will generally bring at least 75 to 80 percent patterns from full-choked guns. Copper-plated shot is distributed by Taracorp but dealers must often be coaxed into stocking it as the demand still seems to be small. The big three among American ammo makers — Federal, Remington, and Winchester — all offer factory loads with copper-plated shot.

Nickel-plated shot is harder than copper-plated, and it is the standard shot for Olympic trapshooting. However, it is also more expensive, and its added practical advantages can be marginal alongside good copper-plated pellets for the average hunter. Handloading enthusiasts who wish to wring every last percentage point out of reloads can find a selection of nickel-plated shot offered by Ballistic Products Inc., P.O. Box 488, Long Lake, Minnesota 55356.

To what extent can one expect pellet hardness alone to enhance the density of any given gun/load combination? It is impossible to give a universal answer, of course, since each barrel is a physical law unto itself. However, as one indication of potential variations caused by pellet quality alone, a test was conducted with the author's 12-gauge Remington M1100 using a Walker screw-in choke tube with a nominal 0.690-inch constriction. Number 2 chilled, Lawrence Magnum-grade, and copper-plated shot were used. Five rounds of each were handloaded as follows:

Winchester 2¾" AA case
Winchester 209 primer
36.5 gr. Winchester 571 Ball powder
Winchester WAA12R wad
1½ oz. shot
Pressure: 10,300 l.u.p. (or p.s.i.)

Velocity: 1,260 f.p.s.

All powder and shot charges were scaled. Shooting was done over the standard 40-yard distance using the 30-inch-diameter patterning circle. Averages for the five-shot strings read like this:

Chilled Shot	58%
Magnum Shot	71%
Copper-plated Shot	78%

The difference between chilled No. 2s and copper-plated duces was a whopping 20 percentage points which, with 1½ ounces of No. 2s, figures out to about 27 pellets per pattern! Even the difference between the chilled and the Lawrence Magnum-grade black shot amounts to roughly 18 pellets per pattern. For the record, here's the average number of pellet perforations per target:

Chilled Shot	78
Magnum Shot	97
Copper-plated Shot	106

Other gun/load combos may not deliver these identical counts, but the disparities will normally show the same trend — the harder the pellets, the tighter a pattern will hold for long-range shooting. Trap shooters learned that lesson long ago in their handicap events where competitors using chilled shot in reloads found they didn't stand a chance against gunners shooting hard, high-antimony shot.

Thus, the shotgun pellet is more than just an insignificant blob of lead. It has become a complex subject that deserves more attention than the average hunter has heretofore given it. Too much game has already been crippled and lost by poor patterns and low energies from badly deformed shot. A truly sophisticated waterfowler will always choose the hardest pellets obtainable. The few extra

Pellet deformation is the bane of all shotgun shooting, especially so for long-range waterfowling. These No. 2s were fired from a 10-gauge Magnum into soft snow and recovered to show how chilled shot deforms due to firing setback, bore scrubbing, and bore pressures.

nickels and dimes spent on high-quality shot pales to insignificance amidst the other costs of a hunt.

Part II: Shot Size Selection
DUCK LOADS

In the earlier part of this century, some writers maintained that individual pellets needed a minimum of 1.5 foot-pounds of energy at the point of impact for adequate penetration on ducks, and that at least four such pellets were needed in a bird's vital area for a total of 6 foot-pounds of energy for a clean kill. These figures have been bandied about in sporting literature, and even today they still find their way into print. But although the four-pellet part of the aged equation is still valid, there has been a modest upward revision in the desired amount of pellet energy. Critical and experienced observers today are more inclined to stress an individual pellet energy of 2 foot-pounds as the minimum effective blow, which brings the aggregate energy to 8 foot-pounds. Barring those lucky one-pellet kills that occasionally occur when a single pellet somehow finds the head/neck region of a bird, this newer energy level is an excellent one to strive for when evaluating downrange gun/load performance. It is the standard by which duck loads will be measured in this book.

Before shot sizes can be judged according to these minimums, however, some considera-

Although not widely known among hunters, there are two grades of black shot available: magnum-grade has a high antimony content for hardness and retained pellet form; ordinary chilled shot is relatively soft and is subject to substantial deformation before it leaves the barrel.

tion must be given to the subject of range. In duck hunting, there are basically three working ranges: (1) close range, (2) intermediate range, and (3) long range. A close-range shot will be inside 30–35 yards. This can occur when ducks either come into the decoys, are somehow stealthily approached by a jump-shooter, or by chance happen to be flying low over a pass or point under certain weather conditions. At this range, an improved cylinder 12-gauge and hard No. 6s can be a lethal team. The only problem with such specialized short-range equipment is that it invites crippling and lost birds if the hunter misjudges range and reaches for farther shots, or if conditions change and the birds stay well out. Indeed, in the long run a modern water-fowler would do well to select his equipment with intermediate ranges in mind, as that would overlap close-range requirements and also provide an extra margin of effectiveness.

The most popular pellet among duck hunters today is the No. 4. But popularity alone doesn't make it right; the public has been wrong before. And for shots out to 45–50 yards, there are both scientific and empirical reasons to select No. 5s over the ubiquitous No. 4s. Stating that 5s split the difference between the density of 6s and the energy of 4s is too vague. Let's look at the actual figures.

Number 5s have a nominal diameter of 0.12 inch as compared to the No. 4's slightly larger 0.13-inch girth. That mere one hun-

The force of firing setback is easily detected by examining the plastic shot wrapper or shotcup: setback pressure builds on the lower layers of pellets, forcing them to dimple the plastic and even perforate it. Such pressure is greatest on the lower layers.

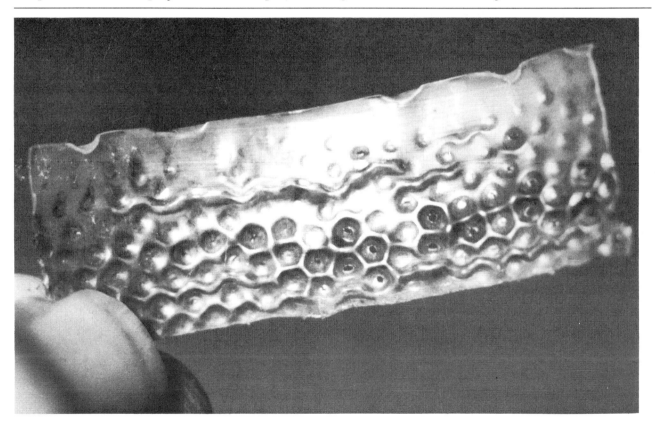

dredth of an inch may not strike average hunters as being extremely important, but it is. By virtue of size alone, the No. 5 pellet has sufficient weight for adequate energy while still being small enough to pack significantly more pellets into shot charges. Here, for example, is how approximate pellet counts stack up for 5s and 4s in common charge weights:

Charge Weight	No. 5	No. 4
1 ounce	170	135
1¼ ounces	215	170
1⅜ ounces	237	187
1½ ounces	258	204
1⅝ ounces	280	221

The No. 5 pellet is, surprisingly, often overlooked by most duck hunters.

In terms of actual patterns, a 12-gauge doing 65 percent at 40 yards with 1½ ounces of No. 5s would put about 168 pellets into the 30-inch-diameter circle, whereas the same performance of 65 percent with 1½ ounces of 4s would put only 132 pellets into the same area. It takes no Ph.D in mathematical probabilities to know that the extra 36 pellets in a cluster of No. 5s gives just that much more chance of finding the target's vital area compared to the No. 4s.

For long-range duck shooting, the long-forgotten No. 3 pellet serves admirably to split the difference between the power of No. 2s and the density of No. 4s. Hard, high-antimony No. 3s are available for reloading, although the commercial ammo makers don't load this size shot at the present time.

Patterns aren't the only measure of pellet potency, of course. The energy requirement of 2 foot-pounds per pellet must also be met, and No. 5s do that for intermediate ranges. Hard or plated 5s that retain their form will carry a full 2 foot-pounds of energy to 55–60 yards with muzzle velocities as low as 1,185 f.p.s., which is about that of commercially loaded 1¼-ounce ammunition for the 3-inch 20. In fact, No. 5s should long ago have become the standard duck pellet in the 20-gauge Magnum, not the No. 4 shot. The following energy figures are for No. 5s at 40 and 60 yards when fired at various velocities:

Muzzle Velocity	Retained Energy	
	40 Yards	60 Yards
1,200 f.p.s.	3.14 ft-lb	2.22 ft-lb
1,255 f.p.s.	3.32 ft-lb	2.32 ft-lb
1,330 f.p.s.	3.56 ft-lb	2.46 ft-lb

Why not use No. 5s for long-range waterfowling out to 60 yards if, as the statistics show, they do have adequate energy? The answer is because there is always the bugaboo of some pellet deformation, plus the myriad variations in air resistance. When distances reach 55–60 yards, the No. 5 becomes marginal and another pellet size must be considered. This judgment is not made on the basis of sheer mathematics, but is instead the result of empirical assessments in the field. It wasn't until No. 5s were stretched beyond 45–50 yards that crippling was observed; inside 45 yards there was a definite tendency toward a very high percentage of clean kills. Thus, for intermediate ranges, the No. 5 pellet, in either high-antimony black shot or copper-plated version, is ideal. Especially is this so in the 3-inch 20, the 16-gauge, and the standard 12 when it is fed 1⅜-ounce short magnums. A modified-choked 12-gauge with 1½ ounces of hard No. 5s is deadly between 30 and 45 yards.

Long-range duck loads are those intended for use beyond 45–50 yards. Most hunters today would be better off letting such high-flying birds pass unmolested, as they do not have the wing-gunning skill to score on them. But, human nature being what it is, the fusillades will undoubtedly continue, and, upon occasion, a duck will be scratched down to encourage the sky blasters. If this sort of ridiculous duck shooting is going to continue, the ammunition should at least be potent enough to drop the bird cleanly when a barrel-stretcher gets lucky.

The best pellet for long-range duck loads is not readily available. It's the No. 3, preferably magnum-grade with a high antimony content or copper-plated. The commercial loading companies haven't turned out 3s since World War II, and finding a bag of this shot size for reloading can itself be quite a hunt. However, Lawrence brand shot is made in size 3, and Ballistic Products also handles No. 3s in both magnum-grade black shot and nickel-plated types.

Number 3s have a nominal diameter of 0.14 inch and count about 110 to the ounce. Number 2s run 0.15 inch and tally just 88 per ounce. Fired at 1,300 f.p.s., No. 2s retain nearly 5.6 foot-pounds of energy at 60 yards, which is excessive. Some of that energy can be sacrificed for increased pattern density, which is where 3s come in. They come very close to the energy of 2s, but, in the same charge weight, they offer a better chance for multiple hits in the vital area. Number 3s deserve revival among waterfowling specialists for long-range duck gunning.

If No. 3s aren't readily obtainable, however, No. 2s are recommended instead of No. 4s despite their surplus energy. It's better to favor the strong side when selecting pellets for this type of hunting. The requisite is a tight-patterning magnum charge to enhance target saturation. Ordinary chilled shot isn't acceptable for such extreme

If a shot charge happens to reach a crossing bird when its wings are down and shielding its body, the pellets need tremendous energy to fight through and reach vital areas. (Photo by Gerald F. Moran)

shotgunning work on tough targets; high-antimony black shot or copper-plated 2s are needed to minimize pellet deformation.

GOOSE GETTERS

Big geese are strong birds, rawboned, heavily muscled, and practically armor-plated by a layer of thick down that absorbs pellet energy. While handling bagged geese, it isn't unusual to have pellets trickle out of the down, proving the need for optimum penetrating energy.

An acceptable rule of thumb among experts indicates that a minimum energy of 3 foot-pounds per pellet is needed at the point of impact for positive penetration, and that five such hits are desirable in a honker's vital area for an energy aggregate of 15 foot-pounds. Hunters who have brought down geese with less than five pellets may cock a skeptical left eyebrow at that stiff criterion, but they are immediately reminded that the goal is a clean kill in midair, not a mere crippling hit that folds a goose but lets it sneak away to be lost in the rushes.

Unlike the earlier discussion of duck loads, there is no place for an intermediate-range concept for geese. Once the range gets beyond 35–40 yards on geese, the heaviest pellets immediately come into play. Thus, there are only two range considerations: (1) short range, implying shots definitely within 35–40 yards; and (2) everything beyond, which is thereby classified as long range.

When a hunter knows his birds wil be inside 35–40 yards, he can do exceedingly well with loads of No. 4 or No. 5 shot; and a modified choke patterning 60–65 percent will expedite matters. At 40 yards, No. 5s with a muzzle velocity of 1,260 f.p.s. still have about 3.33 foot-pounds of energy if they're not deformed, and that satisfies the 3-foot-pound minimum. Number 4s launched at the same speed retain roughly 4.45 foot-pounds of energy per pellet at 40 yards. In either case, both these pellets have sufficient energy for close-range goose hunting while also providing the necessary density for the minimum five-pellet-hit. When this author hunted around Wisconsin's famed Horicon Marsh during times when hunting pressure was light and wedges of geese could be coaxed into decoys set on farmland, the favorite handload in our group was 1⅜ ounces of copper-plated 5s moving at about 1,300 f.p.s. It was a devastating load within its range limitations, delivering multiple hits that anchored geese where they fell.

With 4s and 5s, however, a hunter must discipline himself against taking reckless, skybusting shots. Mathematically derived energy tables may show that 4s and 5s do have slightly more than 3 foot-pounds of energy for another 5 to 10 yards beyond the 40-yard marker, but field observations indicate strongly that such pellets can be gross cripplers when misused. They fall to submarginal energy levels quickly, and, if pattern density breaks down to register less than five hits, a clean knockdown isn't assured.

If a hunter knows he will take shots beyond 40 yards, he should select his pellets with the longest range in mind. The important factors here are pellet hardness for re-

tained form, and pellet size for maximum energy. Ideally, the gun/load combination will give an extremely tight pattern with a high center density evident at 40 yards. In the conventional 40-yard testing, a long-range outfit should do at least 80 percent. Regardless of the patterning ideal, however, we must realize that most hunters don't have the skill to center their birds at long range, and that many hits will fall short of the five-hit standard. Shot string length also plays a role in overall weakness as ranges go beyond 40 yards. Therefore, the emphasis must be placed on individual pellet energy, as the long-range sniper cannot rely on multiple hits for shocking power.

Number 2s are the lightest pellets serviceable for long-range goose shooting to about 60 yards. Starting with a muzzle velocity of 1,260 f.p.s., No. 2s that don't deform retain about 5.5 foot-pounds of energy at a full 60 yards. Given the realities of pattern deterioration, it would take three such No. 2s to reach the recommended total of 15 foot-pounds of energy. Even if No. 2s still had 3 foot-pounds of energy at 70 yards, the thin pattern at that range would be unlikely to deliver this 15-foot-pound total. What is needed are pellets with significantly more individual energy so that fewer hits will still reach, or top, the 15-foot-pound minimum.

This may very well make a tight-patterning load of BBs the most universally sound goose load. With a nominal diameter of 0.180 inch, and packing about 50 pellets to the ounce, BBs are powerhouses. Driven at a muzzle velocity of 1,300 f.p.s., they have about 16 foot-pounds of energy at 40 yards and 12 foot-pounds at 60 yards. A couple or three such BBs will put more than the stipulated 15 foot-pounds into a bird's vital area at 70–75 yards. The main point is that BBs must be hard enough to preserve their form for optimum patterns and exterior ballistics. Consequently, copper-plated BBs are enthusiastically endorsed as the single best shot size for all-round goose hunting.

There are places where No. 4 buckshot is used on high-flying geese. Hunters who congregate around refuges cram the heaviest loads of No. 4 buck they can find into 10-gauge Magnums and then proceed to ventilate the ether. This is pretty much poke-and-hope shooting, as few, if any, hunters have the skill to score on birds 75–110 yards high. There is no consistency in the scoring, but when somebody does get a No. 4 buckshot into a

RETAINED ENERGY TABLE
[Chilled Shot]

MUZZLE VELOCITY	SHOT SIZE	MUZZLE	RETAINED ENERGY [foot-pounds] AT: 40 YDS.	60 YDS.
	BB	34.37	16.27	12.13
	2	19.07	7.98	5.76
1,330 f.p.s.	4	12.70	4.77	3.35
	5	10.08	3.56	2.46
	6	7.61	2.50	1.70
	2	18.01	7.71	5.60
	4	12.04	4.62	3.26
1,295 f.p.s.	5	9.56	3.45	2.40
	6	7.21	2.43	1.66
	2	17.30	7.50	5.45
1,255 f.p.s.	4	11.31	4.45	3.16
	5	8.98	3.32	2.32
	6	6.77	2.34	1.61
	2	16.04	7.13	5.23
1,220 f.p.s.	4	10.96	4.29	3.06
	5	8.48	3.21	2.25
	6	6.40	2.26	1.59
	4	10.08	4.13	2.97
1,185 f.p.s.	5	7.98	3.09	2.19
	6	6.04	2.18	1.52

high bird, there's generally enough energy to bring it down. An unfortunately high percentage of the hits made with buckshot loads do not produce clean kills; most birds are merely crippled or wing-broken and must be run down. But just being able to bombard high birds with a chance of a lucky hit motivates some hunters, and the concept of sports hunting based upon clean kills within reasonable range is foreign to them. Thus, No. 4 buckshot will continue to play a role in goose hunting, although one can't help but ponder the ethics of it all, especially when we know that random pairings of shotguns and buckshot pattern horribly.

Those who fantasize about ultra-long-range effectiveness on geese may find the No. T buckshot interesting as a better balance between pattern density and pellet energy. Actually, T buckshot isn't something new. It was always a part of the listing employed by Tatham & Brothers, early shot manufacturers, whose pellet dimensions pretty much became the American standards. Basically, T buckshot has a nominal diameter of 0.200

inch and counts about 36 to the ounce, whereas No. 4 buckshot has a nominal diameter of 0.240 inch and runs 21 per ounce. The T buckshot pellet is again being made and is being handled as a specialty item by advanced reloading suppliers.

As with all other buckshot, T buck has the potential to pattern poorly from tightly choked barrels. Experiments have shown that, in general, a modified choke handles buckshot better than a full choke. And unless buckshot pellets are made of hard, high-antimony alloy, or unless they are copper-plated, they deform very badly as they swage through the forcing cone, bore, and choke constriction. For optimum patterning efficiency, all buckshot loads should have hard pellets and granulated polyethylene buffering.

For a sportsman who accepts range limitations and the challenge of a hunt, however, BBs are still sufficiently potent for geese out to 75 yards. The problem is that most hunters have difficulty judging range properly.

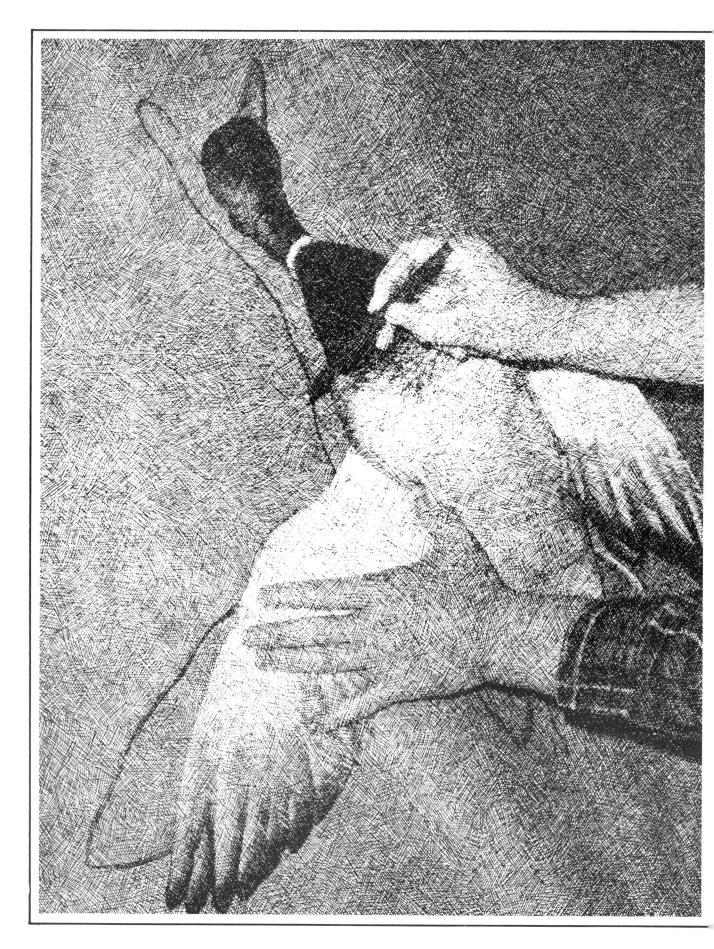

9
Practical Patterning

During my formative years as a high-schooler and college student, I devoured every word I could find about sporting arms and their performances. One of the articles I remember best was done by a writer who, now long gone to his reward, investigated the subject of what constituted a "hard-shooting" duck gun. To begin, he borrowed those guns that had a local reputation for being especially lethal on passing waterfowl. These turned out to be Winchester Model 97 pumps and some of the famous American-made doubles like the Bakers, Smiths, and Parkers. The guns owners and witnesses alike marveled that, "The way those guns drop ducks, they've gotta be shootin' like rifles."

Then the writer borrowed some of the guns that were known locally as cripplers because of the way they feathered and wounded a lot of ducks. Their owners complained that the patterns were too open and that ducks were seldom dropped cleanly.

As I recall, none of the owners had ever bothered to pattern their guns before the writer approached them, their assessments having been pure guesstimates conjured up after field observations.

When the writer came up with his results, there were surprises all around. Patterning with the brands of ammunition normally used by the respective gun owners, he found that the supposedly "hard-shooting" guns didn't reach true full-choke percentages. They averaged around the modified-choke level, meaning 55–65 percent at 40 yards. This was quite a letdown for those who thought their guns were super-tight.

On the other hand, the guns that were suspected of throwing weak, open clusters were found to shoot definite full-choke patterns of 70 percent or higher, and they were inclined to print rather snug center densities. The tests showed that the actual patterns were just the reverse of what the owners had anticipated.

That left a perplexing question: why would guns falling short of their designated percentages be delivering so many clean kills, while the tight-patterning guns did substantial crippling? The answer became clear when it was learned that the hunters were generally overestimating their ranges. Instead of taking mallards at 50–60 yards, as they had bragged, the true ranges were found to be 35–45 yards when measured accurately. At that distance, the guns giving modified patterns from full-choked barrels were impressive for two reasons: first, they were probably giving the hunter somewhat more spread to make hitting easier; secondly, the modified patterns were putting more pellets into the outer reaches of the patterning circle for improved chances of target saturation regardless of where the pattern picked up the bird. This, after all, is the epitome of shotgun patterning theory: to employ evenness of pellet distribution for clean-killing target saturation anywhere inside the 30-inch-diameter circle.

A load's long-range potential is "read" in the 15-inch-diameter core of patterns fired at 40 yards. These will be the pellets remaining in the main mass downrange. Varying the load or some part of it can affect a change in core density. In this case, the reload used chilled shot and put only 28 pellets into the core.

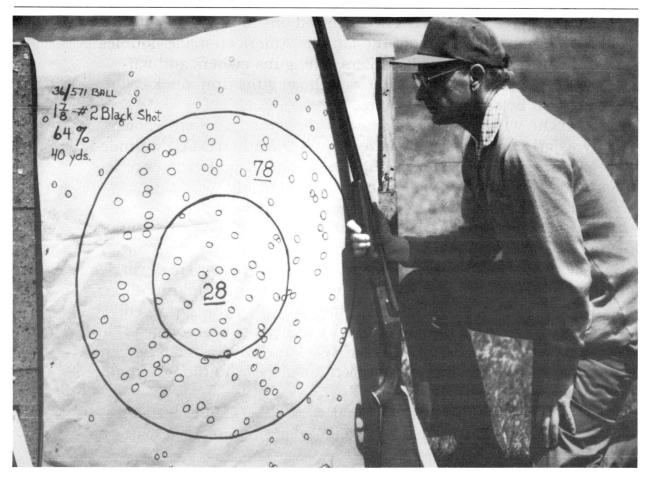

A four-or-five pellet hit from the outer edge of a pattern can look, and be, as potent as a perfectly centered shot. By accident, then, the hunters with supposedly hard-hitting guns were getting exactly the right patterns for their range and skill — only they didn't realize it, and they mistakenly thought they owed everything to much tighter patterns.

The guns tagged as "cripplers" on the other hand, simply gave patterns that were too tight for the ranges involved and for their owers' skills. Truly tight-patterning shotguns can punch their main pellet mass into 24 inches at 40 yards, the fringes outside that two-foot diameter being weak and patchy. Lacking adequate edge and fringe density for certain target coverage throughout the 30-inch-diameter area, such patterns often only nip the target when hunters get close but don't center the mark. It was a classic case of bragging-tight patterns being counterproductive. Had the owners patterned their guns and analyzed their performances for coverage, they could have had the chokes altered for more effective shot dispersion.

Those duck hunters of yesteryear have much in common with today's sportsmen, most of whom don't pattern, either. Talk about

---

Here, the core picked up 46 hits when the handload was given copper-plated pellets. Obviously, the gun/load combo that produced this pattern would be better suited for long-range work.

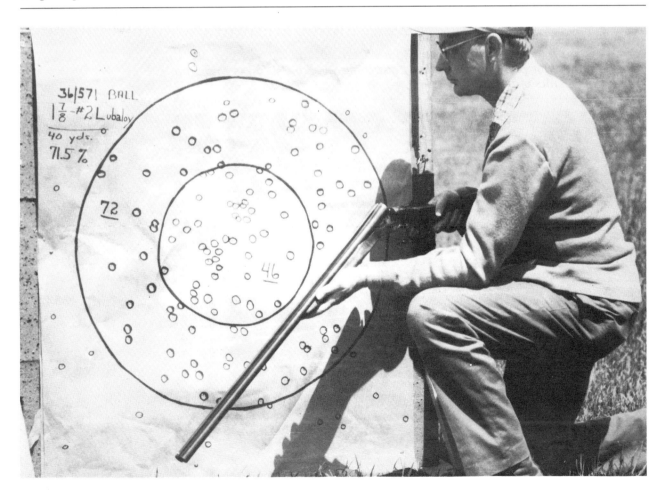

shotgun performance still hinges mainly on empirical factors (field observations), naive testing (blasting into pond water or snow), or a form of egotism born of pride of ownership (the it-patterns-great-because-it's-*my*-gun syndrome). One lucky pellet to the head of a honker causes a modern hunter to pat his gun fondly and proclaim that, "This baby really reaches out!" Totally ignored is the fact that a solo spheroid like that can come from an overall pathetically weak pattern, sheer chance having more to do with the kill than either skill or pattern. Indeed, a goose can be killed at 60 yards with a cylinder-bored riot gun if just one BB or No. 2 from that widely scattered shot string happens to hit the bird's vital head/neck area. But that certainly doesn't justify riot guns and cylinder bores for goose hunting, as the next fifty times that

solo pellet might miss the vitals and only wound the bird. Only patterns on paper will give an indication of whether or not a given gun/load combination can consistently send potent loads of shot aloft.

THE IDEAL PATTERN

What should one see on paper? The ideal pattern will have pellets of adequate energy spread evenly throughout the 30-inch-diameter circle so that, wherever the target's vital area is placed therein, it receives the minimum number of pellets deemed necessary for a clean kill. However, shotguns are less than 100 percent effective. Although great strides have been made to improve pattern density and consistency, perfection has not been reached. That's why this chapter

---

Patterns should ideally be fired into blank sheets of paper. The rings and duck outline used here were for photographic effect. But the important thing is knowing how to "read" the results of patterns.

deals with practical patterning, not ideal patterning. Moreover, the pattern evaluation methods presented here are designed to help hunters get as close to the ideal as possible for their respective ranges without a deep involvement with target-face divisions and intricate mathematics.

A TWO-STEP METHOD

Some writers have argued that, on a practical basis, a shotgun should be patterned over the distance at which it will be used. For instance, if the gun is a 10-gauge Magnum that will be swung on geese 75 yards away, they say, then loads through it should be tested at 75 yards. To a degree, they have a point. But in a more practical approach, the industry standard of 40 yards will suffice nicely for initial testing if the experimenter intelligently applies a simple two-step pattern-reading system. After such introductory and cursory testing has been done, longer-range shooting can be tried to refine one's knowledge of performance. The two-step pattern-evaluation method involves: (1) checking the basic efficiency, or percentage, to determine exactly what choke equivalency is being printed; and (2) comparing the center density to the overall density as a means of assessing range potential. Each step and the procedure for using it, along with an explanation of its importance, will be covered, but first let's set up the sheet and establish the scientific fundamentals.

GETTING STARTED

One of the biggest chores in pattering — and probably *the* main reason why more hunters don't pattern their guns — is finding cardboard or paper of sufficient size. Sheets a yard wide are about minimum; those 40 inches square better. Blasting into yesterday's newspaper or the bottom of a clay target box

is amateur night stuff. Those who pattern a lot should obtain a roll of kraft wrapping paper; those interested in testing just a few rounds can buy some sheets from a local merchant. Cardboard is often available at bicycle shops, as bikes are shipped in wide slab-sided packaging. In any case, make certain the sheets are broad and clean for easy viewing and pellet-hold counting.

Do not draw the 30-inch-diameter circle on the paper before shooting. A dark aiming point is okay; however, in shotgun testing the circle is inscribed only *after* the paper has been plastered. The shooter then locates the center of mass by examining the entire perforated sheet and swings the circle around that point. A transparent overlay works perfectly, because it allows one to remain in visual contact with the center of mass while the circle is being drawn. For most casual patterning, however, the easiest method is tying a felt-tipped marking pen to a string representing the 15-inch radius. Then the end of the string can be held at the center of mass as the circle is drawn. Placing the center and inscribing the circle after the shot thus evaluates the main mass despite potential firing inaccuracies and/or vibrations that would have caused off-center impact in a pre-drawn circle.

After the 30-inch-diameter circle has been drawn, use the same center point to draw a smaller 15-inch-diameter circle. This will henceforth be known as the core of the pattern, and it will be used as a means of comparing pellet distribution within the pattern to determine range potential.

The testing range of 40 yards means from the muzzle to the target, not from the shooter's toe to the target.

Shooting can be done from the sitting position, from a benchrest, over the hood of a pickup, or from the standing position. The only matter of importance is getting the cluster centered as closely as possible. For those who can manage it, the standing (off-

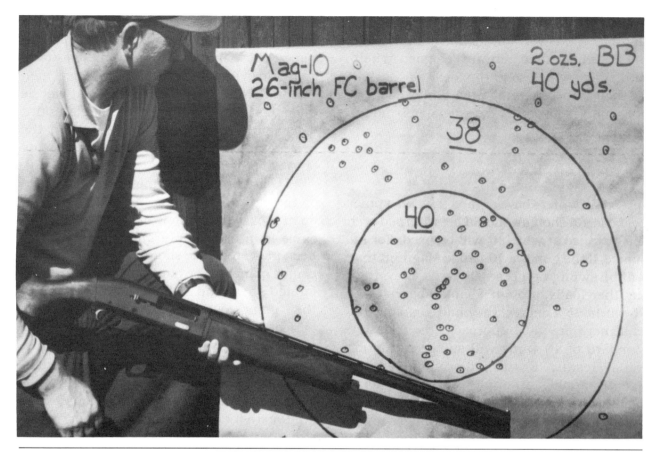

Do short-barreled guns give adequately tight patterns for long-range waterfowling? Apparently so. This 26-inch-barreled Ithaca Mag-10 gave a 3.0 thickening rate with a 2-ounce load of copper-plated BBs.

hand) position is best with heavy loads, as the upright body is supple and can absorb recoil better than it can when scrunched or hunkered down stiffly.

Once the shot has been fired and the circles drawn, the pellet count begins. Begin by counting those in the 15-inch-diameter core, marking or circling them with a felt-tipped pen to ensure an accurate tally. When the total is known, write the figure in the core. Then repeat the counting for the outer ring, which is often called the annualar ring by shotgun technicians. Again, write the total on the paper for continued reference. With these numbers established, we can get on with step one and learn how the gun/load combination

is performing in relation to its designated choke.

FIGURING BASIC PERCENTAGES:
Step One

To determine a shotgun's efficiency (percentage), add the number of hits in the core to those found in the annular ring and divide that total by the number of pellets originally in the unfired shotshell. If a standard full-choked 12-gauge using 1½ ounces of chilled 4s put 50 pellets into the core and 74 into the annular ring, for example, the total for the overall 30-inch circle would be 124. That tally is then divided by 204, which is the industry's approximate number of chilled 4s per 1½ ounces. (See chapter 8.) The quotient is 60.78, which means the load is patterning at 61 percent efficiency. What does that tell us about the gun/load combination's performance? Once the efficiency has been calculated, a hunter can judge for himself by comparing his patterning results to this choke efficiency table:

Extra Full	80% or higher
Full Choke	70% to 79%
Improved Modified	65% to 69%
Modified	55% to 64%
Improved Cylinder	45% to 54%
Skeet Choke	35% to 44%
Cylinder Bore	34% to 44%
Cylinder Bore	34% or less

Regardless of the full-choke designation on our hypothetical 12-gauge, then, the gun is only delivering modified choke efficiency with the equally hypothetical load. Before it could move into the full-choke category, it would have to place 142–143 pellets into the overall 30-inch circle. Any hunter who patterns his equipment and finds that it is not reaching his expectations need not be surprised or frustrated. Such variations happen all the time; a lot of guns do not give their designated percentages with certain loads, especially when soft or chilled shot is employed. The first recourse should be patterning with other ammunition with harder shot. A second move is having the barrel regulated or refined for better patterns, which is the subject of a later chapter.

Because patterns vary from shot to shot, an average of ten patterns from the same gun/load combination is recommended for better accuracy. However, few hunters have the patience for such involved testing and counting, and the procedure can be reduced to just two or three patterns if the hunter understands that his results can be off by 5 percent or so, plus or minus. Thus, when a final average based on two or three patterns is approaching, say, 69–70 percent, the average after ten patterns might be anywhere from 66–67 percent to 72–73 percent. That may not seem like a big difference in print, but in actual shotgun performance it's the difference between mediocre modified and honest full choke. And you'll never know in which direction that variable factor will go unless a few extra patterns are shot to establish a trend. Using just a single pattern to evaluate a gun and load is being sloppy.

Do patterning percentages alone tell us anything? They do, but only as indicators of range potential. The higher the percentage, the more remaining pellets there will be to find the target's vital area. Guns that throw skeet or improved cylinder percentages, for instance, generally have enough density to handle ducks and geese inside 30 yards and, in some cases, as far as 35 yards, but beyond 35 yards their widely scattering shot strings no longer ensure multiple hits to the vital area. Between 30 and 45 yards, the higher percentages of a modified or improved modified choke are more likely to provide such density while also providing a little extra pattern width for easier hitting. As ranges start pushing past 40–45 yards, true full-choke percentages are needed for their densities if the four- or five-pellet minimums are to be placed in vital spots, and beyond 50 yards the concentrated shot strings of extra-full-choke are best. If a hunter does no more than apply these criteria to his patterning results, he's already gone a long way in assessing his equipment's actual — not envisioned or guesstimated — performance.

As a tangent result of patterning only for percentages, a hunter will learn if his gun is indeed shooting directly to the point of aim. This quality is normally taken for granted by casual sportsmen, but there are a lot of guns around that do not center their patterns. This can be especially true of the less expensive doubles.

One year I received a new 3-inch 20-gauge side-by-side just days before the goose season opened, and didn't have time to pattern. But I took it on good faith that the barrels had been influenced properly, and I used the gun with loads of copper-plated shot that had patterned well in most 20-gauge Magnums I had tested previously. Early into the season I had a pair of easy shots that should have been clean kills, but in each case the birds were only wing-broken and had to be run down over corn stubble. The gun also crippled a few mallards and woodies that normally would have folded cleanly, so after a morning hunt I set up some huge cardboard sheets and fired from 40 yards at a black aiming point centered on each sheet. Eyeballing those patterns told me immediately why I was only crippling on pushover chances; the right barrel was placing its pattern 15 inches to the left of the aiming point, while the left tube was barely nipping the right side of the sheet. That double's barrels were so out of alignment that shots were crisscrossing far short of 40 yards, and so off-target as to cause clean misses at 50 yards if the hunter pointed dead on. To center an oncoming goose with the right barrel, I had to swing through his left wing tip! Needless to say, the manufacturer got that gun back in a hurry.

Although most choke devices are installed accurately, it doesn't hurt to check them for fit. A prudent move with screw-in tubes would be firing through each at least once to check their individual accuracy. Modern machinery does work to tight tolerances, but the machinist who worked on your chokes could have had a terrible Monday morning.

Don't expect a shotgun to shoot slugs and birdshot to the same center of impact. Barrels vibrate differently with slugs than they do with shot charges, and the slugs often strike well away from the pattern's normal center. Thus, you may very well miss that big buck if, on the opening morning of deer season, you slip slugs into the duck gun and take to the deer woods without having done some preliminary sighting-in work with slugs.

The vibrational differences between normal hunting loads can also cause some shift in the center of impact as one goes from one type of powder and shot weight to another, but the variation is nowhere near as great as that between slugs and shot charges from the same tube.

READING LONG-RANGE POTENTIAL:
Step Two

The second step of practical pattern reading, if taken properly, helps one expand his knowledge of gun/load performance for long-range waterfowling while still using the same patterns shot at 40 yards. This is where the importance of the 15-inch core comes in, because its 40-yard density indicates what the shot charge will have left at 50 yards and beyond. For the pellets that appear in a patterning circle's annular ring at 40 yards have already begun to angle away from the mass, and they will shortly be leaving the main 30-inch cluster. Somewhere around 50 yards, the only pellets remaining in the 30-inch circle will be those that were either in the 15-inch core or very near to it at 40 yards. The rest will have dispersed. Tests have shown that beyond 40 yards patterns break down variously at the rate of 7 to 25 percent for every added 5 yards of range, the actual breakdown depending on the specific choke load, and pellet hardness (form) factor. These variables will be covered more fully in chapter 10. The point here is that the core of the pattern at 40 yards holds the key to *estimating* downrange potential without extensive test shooting. It isn't exactly precise, but for practical purposes it's far better than sport shop guesstimates.

The pattern's long-range prowess is estimated from an arithmetic comparison of the core's density to the annular ring's density at 40 yards. It is an easy comparison. Before it need be undertaken, of course, the prior check of overall efficiency should have proved that the gun/load duo was indeed doing true full-choke percentages (70%) or better at 40 yards with legitimate waterfowl loads. If a gun doesn't deliver at least this much pattern efficiency, there isn't any reason to apply this second step, because there aren't enough pellets to be concerned about.

When a gun does print 70 percent or better at 40 yards with potent loads, its added range potential can be measured by the aforementioned rating system based on comparing the pattern's core density to the annular ring's density. That might sound complicated, but it's really very easy: multiply the 40-yard pattern's core density by three and divide the result by the number of hits in the annular ring. If we use the same hypothetical core/ring densities from the earlier example of a 1½-ounce load of chilled 4s — which put 50 pellets into the core and 74 into the ring — the equation would look like this:

$$3 \times 50 \div 74 = 150/74 = 2.0$$

Now, what does that 2.0 figure mean in terms of pattern suitability for long-range gunning? It means that that particular pattern is barely marginal for extended ranges, because in this rating system, anything below 2.0 lacks the core density needed for positive long-range density. A 2.0 rating is marginal and, at best, can handle 50 yards with adequate target coverage when heavy shot is used. The best long-range patterns will have a rating of 2.5 to 3.0. Those are the ones that, with heavy shot, can retain density and have the best chances of getting multiple hits into a target's vital area.

Finding a gun/load combination that will do 3.0 is difficult, but reaching 2.5 is entirely within reason using today's sophisticated shotshells with their buffered payloads of copper-plated pellets.

Don't be misled into believing that patterns averaging 70 to 80 percent are automatically long-range performers. If they have already opened up at 40 yards to put a high percentage of their pellets into the annular ring, thus dropping the rating below 2.0, they can be cripplers beyond 40 yards due to their rapid pattern dispersion.

If a hunter doesn't care for a rating system, he can apply a simple ratio to determine a load's long-range suitability. This ratio suggests that the core have at least two pellets for every three found in the annular ring. Such a 2:3 ratio is essentially what the 2.0 rating involves, and it is deemed acceptable, albeit marginal, for shots past 40 yards. Whenever the ratio gets below 2:3, the patterns become dubious for longer range. For instance, a 1:3 ratio is very weak, such a pattern having very few core pellets to fill out the cluster beyond 40 yards.

Once a load is found to give a dense core rated at 2.0, or preferably higher, some added patterning can be done at longer ranges to expose the amount of pattern breakdown. The important thing is knowing how to read 40-yard patterns so that extended-range testing can be minimized, and that only the most promising loads need be tried. And by the time a practical hunter carries his load testing and analysis this far, he may well have been bitten by the patterning bug, as it is a fascinating study. For such newly sophisticated shotgunners, the following chapter will take a further in-depth look at pattern development and breakdown, and other shot string dynamics that affect performance on game.

10
Shot String Dynamics

Reading patterns according to the criteria set down in the preceding chapter is, in effect, a study in plane geometry. Everything is viewed in terms of a sheet of paper placed perpendicular to the gun's bore axis. And although that type of patterning and reading can tell us a lot about potential downrange performance, there's more to it than meets the eye.

Remember that in-flight shot charges have three dimensions — (1) width, (2) height, and (3) depth or length — not just the two (height and width) that we see on the vertical plane of a patterning sheet. And it is that third form factor, depth, that forces us to consider solid geometry concepts as well, because in the air patterns aren't flat. A concern for the role of depth, or tailing, in shot string dynamics is especially important for successful long-range waterfowling, as the farther away a target is, the more chance a shot string has to expand both laterally and longitudinally, and the result of such continuous expansion is progressive weakness. Knowing what to expect in terms of weakness from various chokes and loads makes one a wiser judge of his equipment's capabilities; therefore, this chapter will cover the fundamentals and vicissitudes of shot charge expansion with a mind to giving some rule-of-thumb guidelines for reading and strengthening each load's potential.

LATERAL EXPANSION

It is commonly believed that patterns open in a linear, conelike manner with the main mass of round pellets bunched up front and the deformed ones trailing behind in ever-decreasing numbers. If this were true, an ice cream cone with a scoop of pistachio would indeed represent the form of an in-flight shot charge.

But that's not the way it happens, unfortunately. The solid object more representative of the in-flight shape of a shot charge is a trumpet's flared bell. The flare occurs for two reasons. One is that when air resistance overcomes a pellet's velocity and forces it vari—ously; deformed pellets obviously are affected sooner than healthy round ones. Secondly,

pellets that take on a spin, or "English," simply curve off of their own volition whenever their rotational velocities create boundary vortices intense enough to carry them away. In any case, pellets leaving because of deformation and/or spin tend to do so in an abrupt flare rather than a gradual, linear, shallow outward angle.

What this means to the hunter, of course, is that loads that pattern tightly at 35–40 yards can deteriorate disastrously in only ten

This photo sequence illustrates how a gun/load combination that seems to be shooting very tight inside 40 yards opens thereafter. At 35 yards, the rig did at least 85 percent with an extremely high center density, and a casual shooter might jump to unwarranted conclusions.

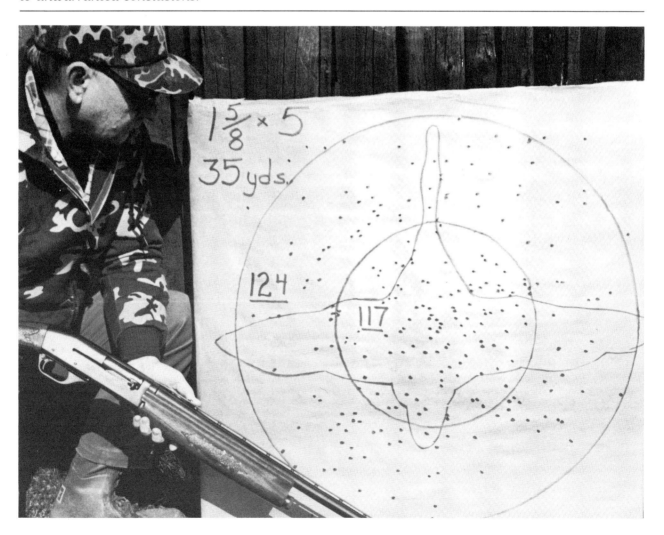

more yards of flight even if their 40-yard efficiencies were 70 percent or better, and their core ratings were 2.0 or higher. At the crux of the problem is pellet condition; shot loads that are easily deformed and/or caused to spin by barrel vibrations or the precessive influence of the choke taper will suffer from earlier, more abrupt flaring than will loads using pellets that retain their shape and are bedded to resist spin. This all goes back to the need for hard shot and emphasizes the importance of buffered shot charges.

The accompanying series of four photos illustrates how quickly a pattern can weaken when pellet flare occurs with relatively soft, deformation-prone chilled shot. The gun was a 3-inch-chambered Ithaca Model 51 12-gauge Magnum, which, with the following reload, averaged 71 percent at 40 yards:

Federal 3″ plastic case
Federal 209 primer
39.0 gr. Blue Dot powder
Win. WAA12F114 wad
1⅝ oz. chilled 5s
Pressure: 9,900 p.s.i.
Velocity: 1,300 f.p.s.

No buffer was used to cushion the pellets, and, all things considered, the 40-yard patterns were excellent. As the first photo shows, the 35-yard core density was extreme. In the second photo, however, the core has already lost over 30 percent of the density it had at 35 yards, although the overall count is still enough to class the pattern as a bona fide full-choke effort. Also noteworthy in the second photo is the fact that there is no significant increase in the number of pellets in the an-

---

Just five yards farther on, at 40 yards, the same outfit put fewer pellets into the core, although overall the patterns were still around the 71 percent level to confirm it as a true full choke.

Notice that at 45 yards the shot mass has broken apart considerably, and the pattern is at 55 percent, which puts it on the borderline between improved cylinder and modified.

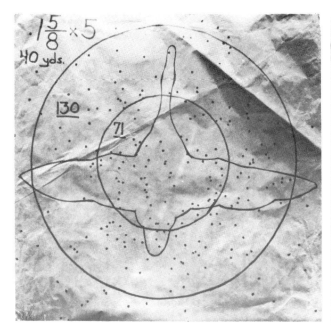

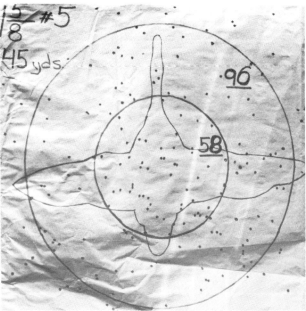

nular ring, which would indicate a sudden flare.

By 45 yards, as the third photo shows, the overall pattern is down to just 55 percent, and the core has lost about 20 percent of the pellets it had at 40 yards. The annular ring has weakened substantially, dropping from 130 pellets at 40 yards to just 96. Rated on the basis of choke nomenclature, the 45-yard pattern is on the dividing line between weak modified and strong improved cylinder, meaning it lost a full degree of choke in just 5 yards.

The 50-yard results are indicative of radical flare. Half the pellets that were in the

Finally, at 50 yards the pattern is down to about 33 percent, or a nominal cylinder bore performance. If one subtracts another 10 percent of the pattern from 40 through 50 yards for tailing weaknesses, the actual field effectiveness would be assessed even lower. Thus, patterns fired at short range must be analyzed carefully to determine their true, not estimated, long-range potential.

Shot charge tailing can weaken the pattern as ranges get beyond 40 yards.

core at 45 yards have strayed, and the annular ring is down to just 68 pellets. The overall efficiency is only 33 percent, making it the equivalent of a cylinder bore pattern. The pattern has gone from full choke to a crippling cylinder bore in just ten yards! An example such as this should convince hunters that they can't jump to any conclusions about a load's long-range suitability just by blasting into a discarded paint bucket at 15 yards and proclaiming, "Wow, does she ever hold 'em tight!" As range increases, the trumpet-bell flare takes place to give an entirely different pattern every five strides. In this particular test, density fell by 20 to 30 percent for every 5-yard increment.

How can a hunter minimize the amount of pattern-weakening pellet flare past 40 yards? One answer is to use hard, high-antimony black shot or copper-plated pellets, preferably in buffered loads. Such hard pellets don't deform as readily as soft or chilled shot; hence, their better aerodynamics will keep them on line longer, whereas deformed ones are thrown off line when their flat sides strike the ether. And buffered loads, which have pellets nestled in granulated plastic, reduce the possibility of pellet spin as well. For example, a simple switch to copper-plated 5s in the aforementioned control reload reduced flare. They gave patterns averaging 80 percent at 40 yards, with an average of 85 pellets landing within the core and 139 in the annular ring. But that increased density alone isn't the point. At 45 yards, the overall pattern was only down to 73 percent, and there were still 68–71 pellets showing up in the core. By 50 yards, the overall percentage was 62 percent, or a solid modified, plus about 45 pellets in the core. In rough terms, that's twice the pattern that chilled 5s produced between 40 and 50 yards, and all the credit goes to retained pellet form.

As a rule of thumb, then, patterns fired with soft or chilled shot will break down faster

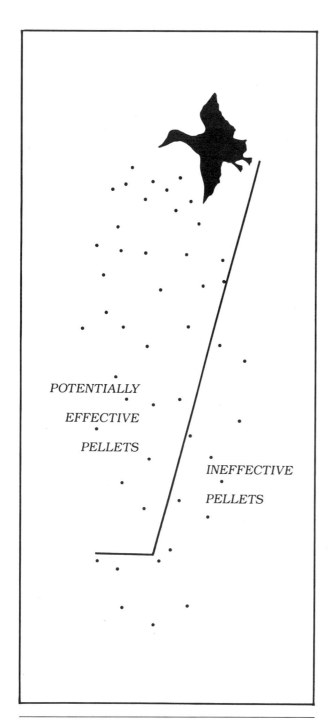

POTENTIALLY

EFFECTIVE

PELLETS

INEFFECTIVE

PELLETS

Although the pellets in the above shot string would all register on paper, those to the right of the diagonal line would be ineffective on a moving target. They would arrive late, thanks to in-flight tailing, and would thus weaken the pattern by their absence on target.

beyond 40 yards than will those made by harder pellets. Hard and plated pellets may suffer a pattern density loss of 7 to 15 percent for every 5 yards beyond 40 yards, while softer shot can easily experience a breakdown of 20 to 30 percent for each extra 5 yards. These obviously aren't precise figures, but hunters who don't pattern can usc thcm to calculate lateral expansion past the standard 40-yard test distance.

LONGITUDINAL ELONGATION

Photographs of shot strings in flight, along with patterns fired into sheets attached to moving targets, prove that pellets do indeed string out variously. The longer the range and the greater the deformation, the longer the string will be. When experiments were first conducted to verify evidence of pellet stringing, deformation-prone soft and chilled shot were still common, and the results pointed toward shot string lengths of 10 feet at 40 yards and 15 to 17 feet at 60 yards. There is no reason to alter those figures, because soft pellets deform as much today as they did then.

The subject of shot stringing is of prime concern to long-range waterfowlers, for it injects an unseen — and normally unexpected — weakness into the pattern. Birds that pass at long range are generally flying at over 40 m.p.h., and if the shot string is very long, there is a good chance that not all of the pellets will arrive while the target is still in the main 30-inch effective area. The potential effective pattern density, then, is reduced by the number of late arrivals. Essentially, this weakness begins to appear only when the range begins to exceed 35 to 40 yards and the target's speed surpasses 30 m.p.h. Inside those close-range and low- to moderate-speed parameters, it seems unlikely that a target can outfly the trailing pellets of a well-placed pattern.

But when targets are 50 to 75 yards out and moving fast, they apparently can outfly the tag-end pellets of a long shot string. Estimates are that stringing can amount to an approximate 10 percent loss of the density seen on patterning sheets for the same gun and load. If the 50-yard performance of a given gun/load combination is 60 percent, for example, the 10 percent loss due to stringing brings it down to 54 percent; consequently, the pattern that shows up as modified on paper is only a strong improved cylinder on high, speeding game. Pellets that register on stationary paper sheets, however late they get there, don't always arrive on time to contact high-flying ducks.

On a purely theoretical basis, it seems that stringing does more to weaken the annular ring area than it does to reduce the clean-killing potential of the core. The core is populated by round, healthy pellets that retain their speed and direction quite well in the face of air resistance, and the hunter who can center his birds still stands the best chance of dropping them decisively.

Unfortunately, however, even the best shotgunners can't center every bird, and when they find the target's vital area only with the annular ring or fringe of the pattern, the weakness comes into play. Wounded birds are the likely result. Thus, every conservation-minded hunter should make an attempt to use loads that reduce stringing so that optimum densities get to the birds' vital area regardless of where they are in the pattern.

What practical method can a hunter use to estimate the pattern he will have in effect at long range? He can shoot patterns at 50, 60, 70, or 80 yards and simply reduce the total pellet count by 10 percent. As the range nears 75–80 yards, he may want to use a 15 percent factor.

These reductions of 10 to 15 percent can make patterns look sick, which may be a blessing in disguise if it makes hunters more cognizant of the scattergun's limitations as a clean-killing firearm.

The goal of every long-range wingshot should be short shot strings for greater concentrations of pellets on distant birds. Only by increasing the on-target tally can one expect to find the vital area with multiple hits. The best way to reach that goal is with buffered loads of copper-plated shot. Some experimenting should be done with a variety of such loads and reloads, as their performances can vary from gun to gun; and in the interest of optimum long-range density, only the tightest-patterning loads should be chosen for extended ranges. Here, again, pellets that don't deform and/or spin will flare the least and will retain similar velocities for a bunched, rather than stretched out, arrival.

Even from a practical standpoint, then, the in-flight shot charge must be viewed as a dynamic, constantly changing mass that can vary in its flare and length depending on the state and stability of the pellets. Most full-choke patterns look good when slapped into a quiet pond at 30 yards, but in the air the pellet mass' breakdown past 30 yards demands attention and consideration. Come to think of it, the only way to be practical about patterns is to become reasonably scientific.

11
Estimating Range More Accurately

Viewed from the side, the mallard was obviously skimming no more than five to seven yards above the tree crowns. And since the trees in that flooded woodlot were no taller than 60 feet, the bird was less than 30 yards high. The hunter I was watching missed with his first shot when the bird was an incomer, then folded it almost directly above him. Once the retrieve was made, though, the distance grew longer with every minute. "Must have been at least forty-five yards," the hunter beamed as he held the bird aloft for us to see over the rushes and cattails. By the time we splashed back to the cars that evening, the shot had stretched into a 55-yarder, and the hunter speculated that it might even have been 60 yards.

That waterfowler isn't history's sole example of a hunter who tells fish stories. Just a few weeks before writing this chapter, I had a phone call from a goose hunter who nonchalantly told me he had taken only a dozen geese last season — all of them between 90 and 110 yards!

And then there was the hunter I happened to meet in a sport shop. He was buying a shotshell reloading press because he wanted to assemble the stiffest magnum load possible. "I hunt with a couple of hotshots," he explained, "and if I want any birds I've got to get 'em at 70 or 80 yards. Otherwise, my partners have everything dead at 60 yards." A short time later, I learned that he and his partners hunted on the channel of a marsh so narrow that a grade-school girl could have tossed a softball across the water underhand.

It would be wrong to say that such grandiose claims about long-range shooting are pure fabrications. Most hunters don't intend to be liars but they do tend to exaggerate.

Making mistakes in estimating waterfowling ranges seems to be a universal affliction innocently contracted. For although people have reasonably good concepts of what constitutes a foot, yard, or meter along the ground, they have never developed the same sense of distance on a vertical basis. Some years ago, for example, there was a newspaper article in which the reporter told of a man who had fallen off his house while repairing the roof, and he wrote that the man had "miraculously escaped injury in the 50-foot fall." The carpenter who had built the house thereupon added that there was more to the miracle than the man's well-being, since the highest part of the house was just 18 feet!

OPTICAL ILLUSIONS

Judging ranges accurately in high-angle wingshooting is complicated by optical illusions, and the results are normally gross *overestimates* in distance, and gross *underestimates* of target speed.

One of the upsetting optical illusions is that objects viewed against the sky appear smaller than they do when observed horizontally when the distances are identical. This phenomenon is generally conceded to be caused by light refraction, and it seems to be somewhat less acute, although still present, on a cloudy day than on a sunny, bright day. A British shotgun enthusiast, Sir Ralph

Tempting — but are they in range?

Payne-Gallwey, lent credence to the illusion with a simple experiment which he detailed in a book, *High Pheasants in Theory and Practice.* A pheasant may not be a duck, but since the same optical factors apply to both species, Payne-Gallwey's work fits our discussion perfectly. Using a caliper attached to the muzzle of his side-by-side, he measured the apparent size of the same dead pheasant, which was stretched out by means of a wire, when it was placed both horizontally and diagonally. The horizontal measurement was taken with the bird 20 feet above the ground and 40 yards out; the diagonal measurement was taken with the bird tethered to a kite flown 40 yards above the gun muzzle, the altitude being regulated by a plumb line rather than the sagging kite line. Given the inclusion of a minor amount of triangulation on the diagonal measurement, the "flying" pheasant startlingly measured about one third the size of the same bird when checked horizontally. Applied to waterfowling, Payne-Gallwey's findings mean that a duck whistling by at just 40 yards can appear to be 60 yards high or more to a hunter who doesn't know about the optical trickery.

It is interesting to note how the size of an apparently high bird increases almost immediately when it is buckled and dropped by a well-placed pattern. In the first few yards of its downward arch, the bird already seems considerably larger than it appeared in flight.

The second optical illusion involves target velocity. The farther away something is, the slower it appears to be moving. Think in terms of a gigantic Boeing 747 jetliner making a landing; if you're back on the airport's observation deck, the 747 seems to float down gently and ever so slowly, touching down like a feather. The aircraft hardly seems to be moving as it comes in with its flaps down,

---

A lot of ammo is wasted each year, and a lot of birds are crippled and lost, because hunters misjudge range and either don't lead properly or shoot beyond the effective range of their gun and load.

emulating a cupped-wing mallard settling into the decoys. But if you happen to be at the end of the runway when that same 747 passes overhead, you'll realize that there's nothing slow about it. The airplane still has substantial air speed, well in excess of 100 m.p.h., and it was only the distance that made it look slow. Thus, geese that seem to be hanging directly above the blind, and ducks that appear to be loafing along, are actually carrying more air speed than the hunter perceives; and if he doesn't take this distance factor into account, he can easily miss well behind the bird by failing to swing fast enough.

When combined, these optical illusions can cause mind-boggling misses for the hunter who doesn't know the phenomena exist. In fact, they can be difficult to cope with even when a hunter understands their impact on the picture his brain sees. There is no way of overcoming the optical illusions with perfect precision. The best one can do is accept the fact that high targets are closer and faster than they appear. After that, only experience and recall will help a hunter judge the amount of gun speed and visual forward allowance needed on a given shot. Hence, repetition and memory also play a role.

There is an interesting adjunct to this matter of optical illusions. Even the camera's eye has difficulty defining objects sharply when they are against a clear sky and the photographer has not employed a filter. Try taking pictures of flying birds or airplanes some day with just a naked lens, and then note how the resulting prints leave the subject's outline indistinct. Perhaps a hunter could judge range and speed better if he wore sunglasses to overcome some refraction.

PHYSICAL RELATIONSHIPS

Although optical illusions do interfere with accurate range and bird-speed judgments, a savvy hunter can sometimes establish improved, albeit still rough, range estimates by comparing a bird's height to that of a tree. This leaves room for error, but it also gives one a closer idea of the range than does simple by-guess and by-golly blasting without forethought.

In many areas, especially flooded regions where waterfowl are hunted, trees don't get too big. A 60-footer is about normal, and that figures out to just 20-yard skeet range when the birds pass directly overhead. Birds moving 10 yards above those crowns are still only 30 yards up, or about where a modified

Although this bank building in the author's home town is just short of 40 yards high, most hunters cannot judge its height and say birds coming directly over it are too high. For any given distance, a vertical object against the sky looks smaller than one viewed horizontally.

choke is beginning to reach its effective spread. When they are cruising twice as high as the trees, they are 40-yard shots; three times as high as the trees puts them at 60 yards. Given the effect of optical illusion, however, mallards not gauged by tree heights seem to be a hundred yards distant when they start topping double the tree heights. In certain situations, hunters termed skybusters are actually trying for birds definitely within the effective range of tight-patterning guns with lead shot; the odious epithet is applied by people with no concept of range judgment. But when the supposedly out-of-range birds are compared to tree heights, they are still in the ball park.

Before anyone can improve his sense of range judgment afield, he must become accustomed to seeing vertical structures of known heights so that he can make comparisons. This can be done by learning the heights of buildings and statues as well as trees. In my home town, for example, there is a bank building that the fire department can almost, but not quite, top with its 35-yard boom. Firemen say the building is 38–39 yards high, and a duck skimming its roof would, for all practical purposes, be a 40-yard shot to anyone standing at the building's base. Yet, when I hear local duck hunters talking about their consistent 75- to 100-yard shots, I casually ask how high that particular bank building is — and thus far only one hunter has come within 5 yards of being correct! He was a construction worker who took time to figure it out by counting the floors and ascribing a certain amount of floor-to-ceiling space for each. All others failed to apply any concept of foot, yard, or meter to the building; they eyeballed the top and guessed it considerably taller than it is.

One hunter, who swats ducks mercilessly at 75–100 yards whenever he leans against a gun shop counter, said he wouldn't even move his gun on a duck coming over that

A football is about the size of a mature mallard's body. Viewing a football being tossed at known distances on a gridiron is one way of learning to judge range better, as it applies to a duck in the air.

bank because it would be too far away even for a full-choked magnum. Other hunters who told smashing tales of bagging their limits at 70 yards (at least!) reacted in the same way, believing the top of the bank beyond sensible scattergun range. The humor, of course, is that if such hunters view the top of a 38- to 39-yard structure to be out of duck gun range, we can only imagine how close their "long-range" kills really were.

I have always wanted to hang stuffed ducks and geese from the roof of that bank so that hunters could visualize birds up about 40 yards, but I'm sure the building's management would frown on such an educational program. As an alternative, however, a hunter with time on his hands — or a desire to improve his concept of range — can hang around the building for a while and watch pigeons, crows, and seagulls as they circle it and sit on the top. Pigeons aren't the size of mallards, but they do give an idea of how quickly a bird becomes a mighty small object as it gets beyond 20 yards vertically or diagonally. Crows, on the other hand, have wings as big as a mallard's, and a good size comparison can be visualized. Seagulls also have a considerable wingspan, and noting the way they suddenly become smaller illustrates the way the same optical effect influences the apparent size of big ducks and all species of geese.

There will probably never be a stately bank building in the midst of a duck marsh or stubble field to give us a clue to the birds' height. But a serious hunter can learn something about this optical game in any city during lunch hour by comparing bird sizes to the known heights of buildings, chimneys, or antennae. Most building superintendents know the dimensions of their structures, and a quick inquiry will provide the facts. From then on, all one need do is watch carefully and let the sizes of birds sink into his mind. That's what is meant by establishing a physical relationship between the target and an upright structure of known height. Such impressions can then be recalled later in the field.

TRIANGULATION

There is always the problem of overall range, of course, as opposed to sheer height. Unless a bird passes directly overhead, some triangulation is necessary when the subject changes from vertical to diagonal. Range multiplies quickly when triangulation is involved. This diagonal distance can be figured using the famous Pythagorean theorem we all learned in high school geometry: it states that the square of the hypotenuse of a right triangle is equal to the sum of the squares of the other two sides. In wingshooting, the hypotenuse is the diagonal line from the hunter's eyes to the bird, while the other two sides of the right triangle are (1) the horizontal distance to the point under the bird, and (2) the vertical measurement to the target above a point directly under it. Obviously, a hunter isn't going to work that type of geometry when ducks are streaking past high and to the right. But a prior consideration for the math behind triangulation can give one a new appreciation for overall range judgment, thereby also assisting in estimating correct forward allowances. Here's an example of how triangulation and the Pythagorean theorem apply in wingshooting.

Suppose a duck is passing 30 yards to the hunter's right and is 30 yards high. Those figures become the sides of the right triangle. We know the square of 30 yards is 900, and that the sum of the squares of both sides is 1,800. That sum of 1,800 thus becomes the square of the hypotenuse as well, and it represents the diagonal line between hunter and duck. By checking a table of squares and square roots, we find that 1,800 falls directly between the numbers 42 and 43, meaning the duck is 42½ yards away.

The distances of 30 yards out and 30 yards up were used because a hunter can see these same dimensions on a big-league baseball diamond, and from that he can visualize hunting situations. It is 90 feet to first base from home plate. And the distance from first base to third base, which represents the diagonal or hypotenuse, is 127½ feet, or 42½ yards. By standing on first base, a hunter can look over to third base and get a feel for 40- to 45-yard ranges. If somehow we could stand on first base while third base was swung 90 feet above home plate, we'd have a better idea of vertical ranges.

A football field is another place to learn range judgments. Most gridirons are marked off in 5-yard increments, and a football is roughly the size of a mature mallard's body. Stand on the goal line and have a kid walk out to the 50-yard midfield stripe and throw the ball 25 yards straight up. That's a mean toss, but if he does indeed get it 25 yards straight up, the Pythagorean theorem tells you you're looking at the size of a mallard's body on approximately a 56- to 60-yard shot.

If you want to visualize what a mallard's body looks like at 100 yards, have the kid walk down the field and hold the football over his head while standing on the opposite goal line. Even without the complications of optical illusions, it looks mighty small.

Thus, there are ways in which waterfowlers can improve their concept of range. It means they must comprehend the impact of optical illusions and combine that with the problem of triangulation. Nobody will become perfect at it, but conscientious awareness of the factors involved plus an effort to observe bird sizes against structures and trees of known heights can eliminate the ridiculous errors that are now so common among hunters who measure with their ego rather than a yardstick or range finder.

Handloaded short Magnum for the standard 20-gauge took these mallards in Manitoba's pothole and grain stubble plains country.

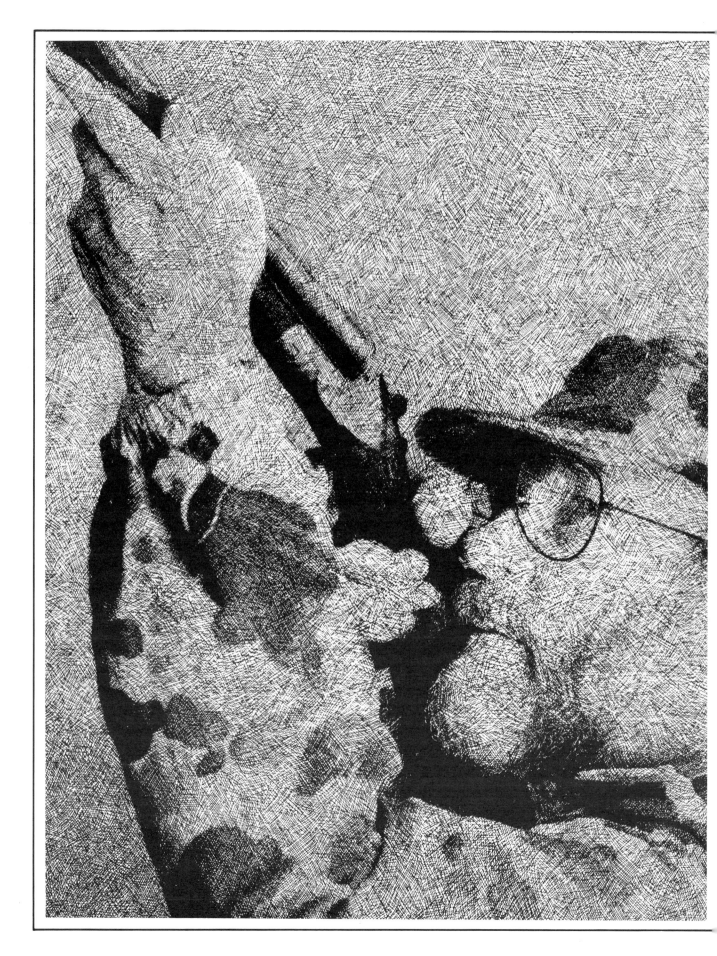

12
How Far
Do You Lead 'Em?

A beginning skeet shooter invariably asks the same question when he tries his first round. As he steps up to each station, he'll turn his head to the veterans and say, "How far do I lead these targets?" It is the intelligent thing to do, because it expedites learning. If somebody weren't told that he needed about 3½ feet of lead on the high house clay from Station 4, he might need dozens of practice rounds to come by that forward allowance through trial and error.

When it comes to actual field shooting, however, that same question isn't asked as quickly or as regularly. Tell a weekend hunter that he's shooting far behind his ducks or geese, and he'll often resent the inference that he doesn't know what he's doing. "Hell, I'm leading 'em!" will come the reply. "I've got the muzzle out in front," but seldom is there any mention of how much in terms of feet, yards, meters, or bird lengths. There is just the bland concept of lead, of seeing some daylight between the muzzle and the bird. The question of how much lead isn't addressed from scientific and mathematical bases, although that's very important because distance magnifies the need for increased forward allowances well beyond what an inexperienced or unsuccessful wingshot deems realistic with modern magnum, high-velocity loads, and long-barreled guns.

The problems here are threefold: one is that shotgun pellets slow markedly when launched into the face of air resistance; a second is that high-winging game is generally moving faster than it seems to be flying; and third is that many hunters misjudge range badly. The last two problems are dealt with in other chapters. Our purpose in this chapter is to explain leads according to the in-flight times of variously sized pellets fired at different velocities. These calculations will be known as *mathematical leads,* as they can be figured according to established time/distance values. The answers will tell us how far ahead of a given target the pattern must be launched if it is to intercept the mark, and that will give us some valid concepts about actual leads.

Since much waterfowling involves passing or overhead shots, our equation that determines mathematical leads will pivot on a perfect 90-degree (full deflection) shot. The forward allowances are developed by converting the target's speed to inches per second (i.p.s.) so that we can compare the target's movement relative to the pellets' in-flight time, which is stated in tables in terms of fractions of a second. The equation looks like this:

$$T^V \times P^V = L \div 12'' = \text{lead in feet}$$

The T^V equals target velocity in inches per second; P^V is the pellet's in-flight time over a given distance stated in fractions of a second. The resulting L is lead in inches, and it is converted back to feet by dividing by 12.

As an introductory example, let's say a duck is high-balling past the hunter at 60 miles per hour (m.p.h.) a full 60 yards from the gun. Such a target is traveling at 88 feet per second (f.p.s.) or 1,056 i.p.s. (88 x 12 = 1,056). From our ballistics tables we learn that it takes a No. 4 lead pellet about 0.1193 second to fly 60 yards if it left the muzzle at 1,330 f.p.s. and remains round for optimum aerodynamics and exterior ballistics. If the pellet is deformed it slows quicker, but we can't calculate that; it remains an empirical factor subject to individual situations. All we can say is that deformation doesn't decrease in-flight time, and we stress, once again, the use of hard shot. For the sake of our work here, we'll assume perfectly round pellets. And putting these known figures to work, the equation becomes:

$$1{,}056 \times 0.1993 = 210.46 \div 12$$
$$= \text{about } 17\tfrac{1}{2} \text{ feet}$$

Not many casual hunters would guess that a high-flying mallard or skimming canvasback with wind on his tail needs a lead longer than the family rowboat! It must be emphasized immediately that the 17½ feet of forward allowance *only* compensates for the pellets' in-flight time! To this must be added such variables as the individual hunter's reaction time, swing speed, and trigger pull, along with other delays affected by primer detonation, powder combustion, and the load's bore travel. Thus, no precise lead can be set down, because each human differs, as do the lock times and accelerations of different guns and loads. What the equation has established, then, is just the minimum amount of forward allowance geared to the pellets' in-flight time; nothing the hunter or gun does can reduce those initial 17½ feet of basic lead, they can only add to them. Moreover, since some amount of deformation and shot stringing is possible with lead loads, a savvy wing-gunner should think on the long side of 17½ feet.

If all the above figures remained constant except the bird's speed, which dropped to 40 m.p.h., the lead would shorten some. Forty miles per hour is equivalent to about 720 i.p.s., and the equation becomes:

$$720 \times 0.1993 = 143.50 \div 12$$
$$= \text{about } 12 \text{ feet}$$

That's still the length of a rowboat, and it becomes longer when the human/mechanical delays are added. On the basis of bird lengths, the forward allowance for the faster duck would be at least six mallard or canvasback lengths, and for the slower duck it would be a minimum of four lengths. If it were a smaller duck, the number of bird lengths would increase according to the exact species, of course.

You don't trust the equation? To prove its validity, let's apply it to the 90-degree crossing angle of skeet's high house clay from Station 4. Skeet targets emerge at about 88 f.p.s., but they lose velocity because of air drag and gravity and are doing, say, 55–60 f.p.s. when they cross the stake at the middle of the field, which is about a 20-yard shot. Skeet loads of No. 9 shot fired at 1,200 f.p.s. need about 0.0615 second to go from muzzle to target. So we convert the target's speed to inches (60 x 12 = 720) and run the equation:

$$720 \text{ x } 0.615 = 44.28 \div 12$$
$$= 3.69 \text{ feet}$$

The accuracy is thereby proven as practically all skeetmen who apply the sustained lead on Station 4 high house clays acknowledge the need for about 3½–4 feet of lead, with the slower swingers using 4–4½ feet.

What about waterfowl leads at closer ranges? If we bring the mallard and canvasback in to 40 yards, but still give them 60 m.p.h., the mathematical lead will shorten, for it simply takes less time for the shot charge to cover the distance. In the case of No. 4s started at 1,330 f.p.s., the in-flight time drops to 0.1187 second, and the equation does the rest:

$$1,056 \text{ x } 0.1187 = 125.35 \div 12$$
$$= \text{about } 10\frac{1}{2} \text{ feet}$$

That's a lot less than the 17½-foot minimum lead needed at 60 yards, but it's still about four mallard lengths when all the various other lag times are factored in. Indeed, from my own field observations, a 40-yard shot at a target no faster than 40–50 m.p.h. is the limit for an average hunter's mixture of skill and luck. If we cut that duck's speed to just 40 m.p.h. at 40 yards, the lead drops to just 7.9 feet for the high-velocity loads of

---

Determining the lead is puzzling for beginners such as this young man after a pair of passing mallards. A mathematical approach based on pellet in-flight times can help provide one with an idea of forward allowance, although after that the individual shooter's swing speed also becomes a factor.

4s, and that seems to be within the average shotgunner's capability; he can swing the gun fast enough to maintain the lead, and his and the gun's built-in time lags aren't as detrimental because in-flight time is still reasonably swift. But go beyond 40 yards and 45 – 50 m.p.h., and an unpracticed hunter's technique falls far short of the long leads required. Simply visualizing spanning leads while trying to swing with or faster than the target is a difficult task, proved by the millions of misses chalked up annually be waterfowl hunters.

PELLET SIZE INFLUENCE

Pellet size can change the leads somewhat, because heavy shot retains its velocity better than light shot. For the sake of comparison, let's change the No.4 pellet in our examples to No. 2s and 6s, and *assume* that they will remain perfectly round. A No. 2 fired at 1,330 f.p.s. takes about 0.1908 second to cover 60 yards (whereas the No. 4 took 0.1993 second). Working the same equation for the 60-yard duck at 60 m.p.h. gives us this:

$$1{,}056 \times 0.1908 = 201.50 \div 12$$
$$= \text{about } 16\tfrac{3}{4} \text{ feet}$$

With No. 6s, which should not be used over 60 yards but are discussed here merely to establish a comparison, the in-flight time would be 0.2108. The equation becomes:

$$1{,}056 \times 0.2108 = 222.60 \div 12$$
$$= 18\tfrac{1}{2} \text{ feet}$$

Thus, increasing or decreasing the pellet's size can alter the mathematical lead. What it all means in the end is debatable, however, as not many humans can be accurate, both in pointing and in timing, to within a foot or a fraction thereof over 60 yards with a scattergun. Far more important is the overall concept of a generally long overall lead and a fast swing.

MUZZLE VELOCITY FACTORS

Obviously, muzzle velocity is also a contributing factor to lead lengths at long range. Faster pellets carry more energy than slower ones of the same size and shape: hence, the faster spheroids will overcome the deadening effect of air drag better. This can be readily shown by comparing the difference between the 12-gauge No. 2 high-velocity load (1,330 f.p.s.) used in the example and the 3-inch 20's 1¼-ouncer which has a muzzle velocity of around 1,185 f.p.s. Again, let's use No. 4 shot and project it to the duck 60 yards distant. The 20's load would require a minimal in-flight time of 0.2159 second as opposed to the high-velocity load's in-flight time of 0.1993 second. Give the greenhead or canvasback 60 m.p.h., and this is how the 20 stacks up:

$$1{,}056 \times 0.2159 = 227.99 \div 12$$
$$= \text{nearly } 19 \text{ feet}$$

That, of course, is a mathematical lead of 1½ more feet than the same pellet size at 1,330 f.p.s. Couple that added mathematical lead with a hunter's lag time and the gun's lock time, and it might explain why weekend hunters fail with the sweet-swinging 20 at long yardage; they aren't setting off 20-foot leads!

By employing this equation, then, anyone can calculate the mathematical leads required to compensate for the in-flight time of pellets over various ranges at various muzzle velocities. Given here are some of the shotshell muzzle velocities for various loads of commonly used pellets, and they are accompanied by the in-flight times of those pellets over fundamental hunting ranges. The reader must contribute the estimated speed of his target to complete the raw material to work the

The forward allowance needed to hit waterfowl at long range is often much greater than hunters imagine. The birds have a lot of air speed.

calculations. Determining a target's speed in inches per second is easily done. Multiply the speed in miles per hour by 1½ and, in a second step, multiply that product by 12 to obtain the answer. For instance, 60 m.p.h. is 88 f.p.s. If one were to multiply 60 by 1½, he would arrive at 90 f.p.s., which is close enough for wing-gunning work. Multiply either 88 or 90 by 12, and the product is a near-enough inch-per-second figure to obtain a reasonably accurate lead picture. They may not be precise to the exact inch, but the forward allowances stipulated mathematically give waterfowlers a fair idea of what they need in the way of lead, usually to their surprise.

Passing ducks against the sky tend to appear smaller and slower than they do when viewed horizontally, but a long, fast swing stroke and a concept of necessary forward allowance are necessary for successful scoring.

STEEL SHOT DIFFERS

One final point – the tables herein apply only to lead shot. Steel shot is an entirely different entity. It does not have the same density as lead, nor does it deform. Thus, while the same equation can be employed to figure leads with steel shot, the in-flight times will differ. Steel pellets start faster than lead, retain velocity better over the short range due to retained spherical shape, but then lose velocity faster than lead as they near 35 – 40 yards. This subject is discussed more fully in chapters 22 and 23.

TABLE OF PELLET IN-FLIGHT TIMES
[Chilled shot]

MUZZLE VELOCITY	SHOT SIZE	PELLET TIME [Sec.] TO	
		40 YDS.	60 YDS.
	BB	0.1107	0.1815
	2	0.1148	0.1908
1,330 f.p.s.	4	0.1187	0.1993
	5	0.1210	0.2047
	6	0.1238	0.2108
	2	0.1173	0.1944
	4	0.1211	0.2030
1,995 f.p.s.	5	0.1235	0.2083
	6	0.1262	0.2145
	2	0.1201	0.1902
	4	0.1240	0.2074
1,055 f.p.s.	5	0.1264	0.2128
	6	0.1292	0.2189
	2	0.1230	0.2029
	4	0.1268	0.2115
1,220 f.p.s.	5	0.1292	0.2169
	6	0.1319	0.2230
	4	0.1297	0.2159
	5	0.1320	0.2210
	6	0.1384	0.2274

13
Long-range Wingshooting

Anyone who has read about the basic wingshooting techniques knows that there are three traditional methods of setting off the forward allowances needed to intercept flying targets: (1) the spot shot or snap shot; (2) the sustained lead; and (3) the swing-past system.

Unfortunately, however, none of those techniques, as they have been described in so many books and magazine articles, is the ultimate method for truly long-range wing-gunning. Take the snap shot, for example. This is nothing more than pointing to a spot ahead of a moving target and firing with a static gun. There is no swing or follow-through. It is a pure guesstimate, totally unscientific and woefully inconsistent. At its very best, the snapped shot will score only upon occasion over short upland ranges when luck smiles on the hunter. Thus, although every chapter and verse about shotgunning mentions the snap shot, this poke-and-hope method plays absolutely no role in successful long-range shooting.

The swing-past method, alias the fast swing, has also been questioned as a legitimate technique for long-range work. In the swing-past method, a hunter starts his muzzle *behind* the target and generates gun speed as he overtakes it. According to traditional teachings, the mental command to pull the trigger is given just as the muzzle passes the target. If the gun then continues to swing faster than the target flies, the forward allowance will be built up during the time lag needed for the shooter to carry out the mental command, for the trigger to yield, for the hammer to fall, and for the load to ignite and travel through the bore.

While the dynamics of a swing-past move work to perfection on targets inside 40 yards, however, they generally come up short on

The basic swing-past method begins with the gun being brought up behind the target (Step A). It is then swung through the target, with the trigger pulled just as the muzzle passes the target's front end. The speed of the swinging gun then carries the muzzle well ahead of the target to establish a forward allowance during the shooter's reaction time, and while the hammer falls and the load moves through the barrel. Unfortunately, most hunters cannot swing fast enough to set off the long leads needed on long-range shots where the forward allowance can be 10 to 18 feet! The basic swing-past method is good mainly for close- and intermediate-range shotgunning.

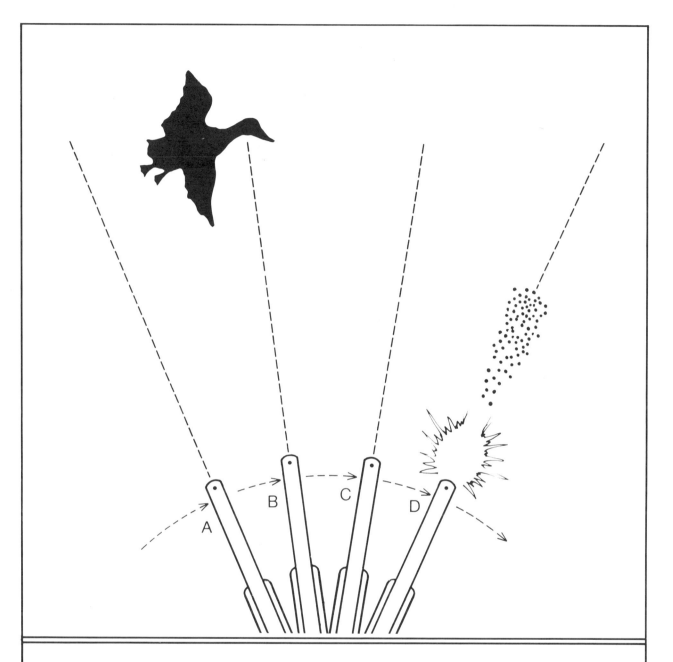

The elements of an extended swing-past method begin with the hunter bringing the the gun up from behind the target (Step A) and, with accelerating gun speed, swinging through and passing it (Step B). Unlike the basic swing-past method, however, the hunter does not pull the trigger as the target is being passed, but instead delays the trigger pull until obvious daylight appears between the target and the muzzle (Step C). This delay accounts for reaction time, lock time, ignition, and bore travel and permits the gun to swing farther ahead of the target (Step D), at which point the shot charge emerges. The shooter's main task thereafter is continuing into a positive follow-through without losing gun speed.

more distant targets. The reason: virtually no one, not even the most expert shotgunners, can swing fast enough to set off those tremendously long leads needed on passing targets at 50 to 60 yards if he follows the conventional tenets of the swing-past system.

Because writers through the ages have seen the swing-past system's shortcomings for long-range shooting, they have tended to advocate the so-called sustained lead for long-range waterfowling. In recent years, though, the sustained lead has also become suspect among critical scattergunners. Essentially, the sustained lead utilizes a moving gun that is pointed and swung a calculated distance ahead of the bird. If a hunter determines that a certain duck requires a 6-foot lead, for instance, he gets his gun pointed that far ahead and continues to swing with the target while the forward allowance is locked in. When the gun is tracking smoothly ahead of the target at the estimated distance, the trigger is pulled as the gun retains its speed and flows into a positive follow-through still the stipulated distance ahead of the bird. The daylight between muzzle and target represents the shot charge's in-flight time. The sustained lead, then, has been recommended for long-range wing-shooting simply because the forward allowance is definitely established and an ultra-fast swing isn't required to build up the lead. By all theoretical judgments, it should be perfect.

But despite its theoretical strengths and the long-standing emphasis placed upon it by past and casual writers, the sustained lead has also come under criticism among sophisticated shotgunners. It has at least a couple of inherent flaws that hinder its effectiveness, neither of which are readily understood or assessed by typical hunters. One of these flaws rests with gun speed. To use the sustained lead properly, the lead must be set up with the gun tracking at the target's speed. However, birds passing at 50 to 65 yards always seem to be moving slower than if they were just 20 to 30 yards away, and the hunter invariably tracks too slowly, too deliberately. The second flaw — and perhaps the major one — is that the relatively slow swing mistakenly used by most hunters doesn't carry them into a positive follow-through. There is a self-defeating tendency to stop and to aim the shot as the trigger is being pulled. Therefore, although most hunters are oblivious to it, their gun becomes static at that extremely important moment of the swing when it should be totally dynamic. The deteriorating swing thereupon becomes nothing more than a version of the ineffective spot shot.

This inherent tendency to stop and to underlead is especially common when swinging on high-flying geese. Distance creates an optical illusion of slow target speed, and the illusion lulls hunters into commiting the sloppy mistakes of swinging slowly, setting off short leads, and stopping on the trigger pull. The subject of optical illusions is treated fully in chapter 11. Rest assured that the birds are *indeed* carrying the mail with impressive air speed.

To improve his long-range success on waterfowl, then, a hunter must accept the presence of the illusion and overcome its effect by applying more forward allowance through greater swing speed and a positive follow-through. In most cases, however, this isn't going to happen if a hunter clings to the pure sustained lead method; for hunters are human, and humans fall back into their bad habits.

THE EXTENDED SWING-PAST SYSTEM

If the spot shot, the basic swing-past, and the sustained lead don't get the job done for long-range shotgunning, what does?

The best answer is a variation of the swing-past method, which, for want of a better term, we will call the *extended* swing-past system. It is unquestionably the best technique for generating the gun speed needed to establish the long leads and positive follow-throughs required for birds beyond 40 yards.

The extended swing-past system begins like the basic swing-past approach discussed earlier, namely, with the hunter starting his gun behind the target and accelerating it through the bird. However, the trigger is *not*

Swing speed and follow-through become important in applying the extremely long forward allowances needed on high, fast, passing birds.

pulled immediately as the muzzle passes the target as in the basic swing-past sequence. Instead, the trigger pull is delayed a split instant while the muzzle moves far enough ahead of the target to "daylight" the bird. This added distance compensates for the lack of adequate swing speed, and it will vary somewhat from hunter to hunter depending upon individual reaction and movement times. I find I can center the highest birds within legitimate shotgun range by seeing about 1½ goose lengths before pulling the trigger of a rapidly swinging gun. Only time and experience will teach each hunter to visualize his own extended swing distance, but, once recognized, that extended distance will help improve results significantly.

One reason why the extended swing-past method benefits typical hunters is because the accelerating gun develops its own momentum and actually forces a follow-through. With the tendency to swing a shotgun slowly in the sustained lead, such momentum generally doesn't build enough to overcome a shooter's inclination to slow or stop at the time of trigger pull.

There are two vital elements in becoming consistent with the extended swing-past method. One is gun speed. It must be quick and crisp; it must accelerate through the target, race steadily ahead even when daylight appears between the muzzle and target, and keep moving forward along the target's projected line of flight. Any hitching or dawdling as the muzzle works ahead will hinder or completely disrupt gun speed and momentum.

The second point is learning to groove

Whether it's a clay target or one with feathers, the same basic shotgunning techniques apply, as illustrated by this skeet shooter who swings nicely ahead of an incomer simulating a mallard or woodie coming over the trees.

The disc is centered cleanly and the shooter continues his follow-through, just as he should in the field.

The crossing angles of a skeet field offer some of the best practice for waterfowling, especially if one backs off the regular stations by 10 to 20 yards to create a 30- to 40-yard distance.

one's swing speed so that trigger timing can also be established. Timing is, after all, the most important part of any swing-past move. For it is the swinging gun that creates forward allowance during trigger, lock, and bore time, and unless the trigger pull jibes with target velocity and swing speed there will still be extensive missing regardless of an apparent lead. Swing fast and delay the trigger pull, and there can be too much lead. Swing slowly and pull the trigger quickly, and the gun won't have a chance to streak far enough ahead for the appropriate lead before the load exits. A good rule of thumb is to swing as rapidly as possible within your personal physical and neurological parameters while still retaining control and coordination. Don't be reckless or impulsive. Long-range shotgunning demands controllable speed that can be duplicated on successive shots.

The place to develop a sound swing-past technique is on the skeet field. Unfortunately, many hunters scoff at clays. "If I can't eat 'em, I won't shoot," they'll say. More's the pity, because skeet is filled with enthusiastic hunters who make great off-season companions. Also, skeet offers the crossing and incoming angles offered in actual waterfowling, and a serious hunter can work out his problems or groove his swing. Therefore, he'll feel more comfortable with his gun on opening day.

There is some unwarranted criticism of skeet because its range is just 21 yards, which is hardly like the 60- to 70-yard distances common to long-range waterfowling. But one must always remember that the goal in skeet is improved gun handling and swinging so that the proper technique will be applied afield; consequently, the swing's the thing, not the overall distance. The same basic move is used on a 21-yard crossing shot as on a 65-yard passing bird; the only difference is the amount of daylight needed to set up the correct lead.

Where space permits at a skeet club, shooters can back off stations 2, 3, 4, 5, and 6 by 10 to 20 yards for a testy game that gives crossing shots at 30 to 40 yards. With clays leaving the skeet houses at 50–55 m.p.h., which is about the speed of a crossing teal or a mallard streaking downwind, long-range skeet can be a true off-season challenge for duck hunters, and the extended swing-past method fits this game beautifully.

There are some clubs with elevated traps known as duck towers. Unfortunately, few such layouts involve truly long ranges, as it is difficult to set a trap much more than 25 yards above the ground. But while a duck tower is indeed better than no form of practice, long-range skeet does more to teach the extended swing-past method. Don't ignore the skeet field as a practice site for waterfowl gunning. Contrary to some negative thoughts that some hunters hold regarding the clay target sports, the wingshooting techniques are identical whether the targets are clays or quackers. Don't let anybody tell you otherwise.

14
Footwork for the Overhead Shot

The high incomer is a frequent shot in modern waterfowling. Hunters who dot the perimeter of refuges may get no other angle as they try for birds leaving or returning. But although the high incomer is a common mark, it is still missed a great number of times each season. Anyone who has parked near the firing line of refuges or has watched gunners on an upland pass comes to that conclusion in a hurry as he hears a barrage of three-shot salutes ring out every time the birds cross — but seldom does he see so much as a solitary feather come drifting down. True, birds are taken, but the ratio of shells expended for every bird bagged cleanly would make Annie Oakley wince, and ammunition manufacturers smile.

There are two good reasons why high incomers are missed. One is that, because of their altitude, the birds appear slower than they really are. This topic has already been covered in the chapter on range judgment.

The second reason focuses on shooting technique, especially the footwork employed for swinging freely on those long, lofty shots that demand the ultimate in human performance. Unfortunately, most typical waterfowlers don't understand their own physical role in making this sort of swing and shot: the birds come over, high and looking slow; the hunter brings up his gun, aims it a bit in front of the apparently easy target, and pulls the trigger. The birds fly on, unscathed, and the hunter, bewildered, wonders if he needs a new gun or if he should change his brand of ammunition.

But the fact is that, if the birds were indeed within legitimate range, the miss was made by the hunter, not the gun or load. Before anyone can improve on the high incomer, he's got to accept the blame and not use some mechanical object as a scapegoat. This may be difficult for a lot of hunters to do, because one's ego gets in the way. Nobody wants to admit he's a bum shot, not even to himself.

For those of a humble nature, however, there's hope. It lies in learning to apply a British footwork technique to waterfowling. One of the most frequent and challenging shots presented to British wingshots, you will recall, is the high, incoming pheasant that beaters drive over the guns. And although the driven pheasants of England do not approach the extreme heights at which Americans and Canadians snipe at waterfowl, the technique is nevertheless applicable.

But before taking a look at the British technique, let's point out some faults in the typical hunter's method of trying for high birds. Most of these shots are missed because of a slow shotgun swing and a deliberately aimed effort. What isn't as clearly understood is why such shooters don't generate more swing speed. Another flaw is that the follow-through arc and speed are severely restricted, which also prompts one to ask why the swing

High incomers are common chances in waterfowling, and improved footwork can help your success ratio.

and follow-through are slow and ineffectively abrupt on overhead chances.

The answer seems to lie in footwork and leg drive — a typical waterfowler doesn't employ either. Instead, most hunters on our side of the Atlantic tend to stand flat-footed for the overhead shot, and this lack of assistance from the lower extremities denies a wingshot the flexibility of his body. In fact, much American shotgunning theory is predicated upon placing a majority of one's weight on the leading foot, which actually becomes a deterent by negating smooth, crisp, continuous upward movement. What a hunter needs for greater gun speed and a longer stroke on overhead shots is foot and leg participation for an extended up-and-over motion.

The British technique for taking high, overhead birds emphasizes a rockerlike use of footwork and leg drive to assist in supplying the energy for a longer swing, added muzzle speed, and a positive follow-through. The movement also helps free the upper body for a rearward tilt that increases swing arc while still keeping the shooter's shoulder and eye squarely behind the gun. The sequence goes like this:

When the target is sighted and the gun is being thrust to it, the hunter (shooting off his right shoulder) comes up on the ball of his right foot as he stretches to the target. At this point, the leading left foot is still flat as a balance point. Raising the right heel counters the typical flat-footed stance.

As the target nears and the swing increases, the right heel settles back to establish a new balance point while the gun elevates and the shoulders rotate backward. For many gunners not schooled in the British technique, this would be the final move; everything thereafter would be done from a flat-footed position, which stifles further rearward shoulder rotation.

In the British technique, however, there

The writer demonstrates the footwork and leg drive method used by British wingshots. By pushing upward with the off-side foot and knee, the shooter generates added assistance in rotating his body upward and backward for a smoother and longer swing arc.

Practice on clay targets will help establish the rhythm and coordination useful in hitting a higher percentage of high overhead incomers

When the birds pass overhead, one's swing speed and arc must be maintained, something that a hunter standing flat-footed often cannot manage perfectly because his technique negates suppleness at the top of the stroke. The foot and knee drive technique extends the arc by pushing the body.

is a third step that makes all the difference in the world. Rather than remaining flat-footed for the duration of the action, British instruction has the hunter lift the ball and toes of his left foot, thereby generating a leverage factor that virtually pushes the otherwise stiff and restricted torso backward, freeing it for the added shoulder rotation that contributes to a smoother, faster, longer swing and positive follow-through.

A MODIFICATION

British coaches can be quite athletic about this rockerlike movement. A typical duck or goose hunter needn't go to tippy-toe extremes, however. The important thing is remembering the principle of getting the body into the overhead shot by pushing off with the leading foot. This can be done in leaky waders or leather boots. One doesn't really have to start with the upward push of his right foot, although it does help create body momentum. Indeed, there are many times in practical waterfowling — when ankle-deep in the mud or scrunched in a cramped blind, for instance — that a hunter simply can't negotiate the entire routine.

As a modification of the British system for taking overhead shots, the waterfowler can merely remember to push upward with his booted leading foot to assist in shoulder rotation. This may not be the classic British move in every respect, but it works a lot better than the restrictive flat-footed stance employed by those who aim big-bore shotguns like rifles at high-winging ducks and geese.

15
Gun Handling in Cramped Quarters

The morning sky might be limitless on a bluebird day, or the dark November clouds might seemingly roll on forever. The marshes spread for miles. And grain or corn stubble can start at your feet and flow over the horizon. But for all that space in the great outdoors, the waterfowler's real world is often so cramped that it borders on the claustrophobic. The hunter is imprisoned by a narrow blind with a low canopy, is immobilized in a wobbly skiff that threatens to capsize, or is wedged into a damp pit hardly bigger than a fat gopher's hole. And if waiting, freezing, and getting soaked in such meager confines isn't trying enough, swinging into action from them — or attempting to swing into action from them — can be positively frustrating.

We often hear hunters complain, "They came out of nowhere, and I couldn't get on 'em until they were past the blocks and out of range." Or that other sad lament, "I didn't get my gun up. The butt got caught under my armpit."

Sometimes these things happen because of conditions, and no amount of human planning will prevent them. They are the things of which fond and humbling memories are made.

But that doesn't mean the situation is hopeless, of course. Guns and gun handling techniques can be selected to minimize such frustrations. Take the matter of gun handling, for instance. There is no real reason why a shotgun butt should get hung up in a shooter's armpit if he uses the right mounting movement. Indeed, the simple act of sliding the butt upward along the clothing is wrong! It invites improper gun placement and hang-ups.

The most efficient gun-mounting system is known either as the thrust-out or the push-away method, and it combines hand-to-eye coordination with a forward thrust of the gun to clear the armpit. Both fundamentally sound and easily mastered, the thrust-out method emphasizes bringing the gun to the face, not the face to the gun (as is mistakenly done by so many hunters). It will work perfectly in a cramped goose pit or a layout boat, as well as on the high passes or in jump shooting. Here's how it's done.

When a target appears, the hunter should focus his eyes on it and *keep them there*. This is the most fundamental point — and necessity — in wingshooting. A shotgun is made to be pointed, not aimed. There are no sights on a smoothbore for precise alignment. If you're taking a squinty-eyed aim with a shotgun — using the matted receiver top as a rear sight and the front bead as a front sight — you're doing it wrong! In sound wingshooting theory, the muzzle end of a shotgun is the front sight and the shooter's eye is the rear sight. Get the gun mounted so the eye is squarely behind the receiver looking right down the barrel or rib over the muzzle, and you've got all the alignment needed for shotgun accuracy. The problem, of course, is getting the gun mounted for an eye/comb juxtaposition that establishes alignment and maintains it throughout the swing and follow-through, which is what the thrust-out system is intended to do.

Once the hunter's eyes are focused on the target, his second step is getting his head into shooting position to receive the gun. In effect, he is bringing the rest of the gun to the rear sight.

With his eyes on the target and his head in shooting position waiting for the gun, the hunter's hand-to-eye coordination comes into play. A human's hands will work nicely with his eyes if he lets them flow naturally to where the eyes are focused; however, most hunters make the mistake of overcontrolling the gun with deliberate moves more common to riflery.

As the third step in the thrust-out method, the hunter extends his hands toward the target, which means the gun is pointed to where the eyes are focused without any downward glances toward the gun's upper surface. This not only gets hand-to-eye coordination rolling, but also carries the gun butt away from the body to clear the armpit region. When the gun enters the hunter's field of vision, it should be seen only as a blur; looking back at the gun's rib, receiver, or bead at any time during the mount-swing-follow-through sequence is a mistake, because it detracts from natural hand-to-eye coordination and eye-to-muzzle-to-target alignment. If the eye needs a reference point, let it be fuzzy as the focus remains sharp downrange.

Aside from the hands, the initial contact between gun and shooter is at the cheekbone where the comb slides in directly under the eye. At this point in the thrust-out-move, the gun is still forward and away from the shoulder. It is, as mentioned, a matter of bringing the gun to the face for immediate alignment. In other words, eye positioning comes first; shouldering comes last! This is just the reverse of what many hunters do when they concentrate solely on slamming the butt against their shoulder, or sometimes mistakenly getting it well out on the upper arm; for that slam-bang gun handling still leaves them without the correct eye-to-comb juxtaposition, and they invariably must waste time fighting for alignment by stretching their necks, scrunching, or going through other contortions that impede smooth swinging and continued alignment.

Only after the comb is directly under the shooter's eye should the gun be drawn back into the shouldering hollow. This is discussed in detail in chapter 16. Thus, the thrust-out method is predicated almost essentially on establishing positive, immediate

Gun handling technique for cramped blinds and overall wingshooting situations is sometimes called the thrust-out method. It begins with the arms being extended towards the target as the gun comes up. As illustrated here, such a move brings the butt forward and clear of the armpit area where guns can get hung up, especially when hunters wear bulky clothes.

The first contact point is the shooter's cheekbone. This is known as bringing the gun to the face. The hunter's arms are still extended here as the comb nears the cheek and the butt is still well out from the shouldering pocket between the deltoid muscle and the collarbone.

Only after the comb has come to the cheekbone to establish eye-to-muzzle-to-target alignment is the butt finally brought back into the shouldering pocket. The hunter's left arm is now bent since the gun has come backward. By learning the thrust-out system, a hunter can get on target quickly, accurately, and smoothly no matter what his situation or clothing.

Even when the quarters allow total freedom of movement, the thrust-out system of shotgun mounting will help clear the armpit area and prevent hang-ups. (Photo by Gerald F. Moran)

alignment by having the hands work to the eye. To recapitulate, the gun is pushed away from the body toward the target while, at the same time, being elevated for comb-to-cheekbone contact. Only then is the butt brought back to the shoulder. It is an out-and-back move which, although it may sound laborious in print, is actually very easy to master with a little practice.

The thrust-out system can be used for all hunting, of course, and is quickly learned on the skeet field or with hand-thrown clays in a gravel pit. It is especially effective in those cramped places where a waterfowler's first — and often only — move is upward, such as in narrow blinds, stubble field pits, and layout boats or sink boxes. In general, the gun-mounting direction of most waterfowling is upward, anyway, and for that the thrust-out method is perfect.

This young man took his woodies with an early Winchester Model 1911, which had good pointing qualities but was known for stock splitting.

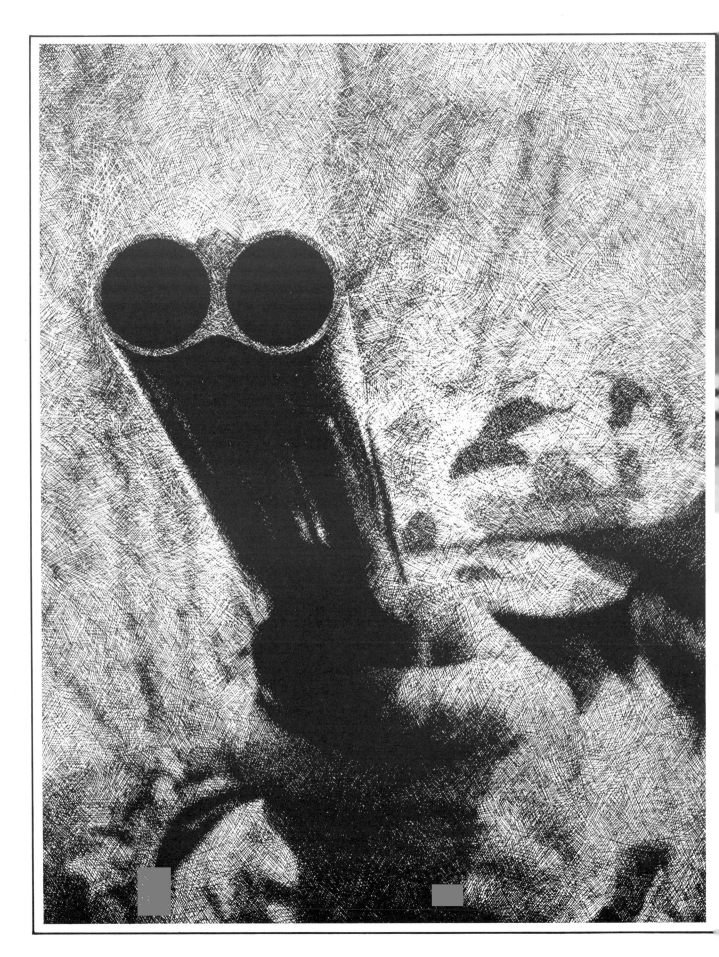

16
Giving 'Em Both Barrels

Waterfowling has always been a multiple-shot challenge. When a flock of teal buzzes the decoys, we come up trying for a double or a triple. Few thrills in hunting equal that of folding a pair of late season greenheads; few shots are as demanding as those on divers skimming the breakers as a thundering nor'easter drives them south. And after a long day's wait in a cold pit we invariably try to pick our limits from the first wedge of honkers that passes within legitimate range. Either that, or we just plain miss the first shot and need to keep hammering if we want the makings for a duck dinner. In any case, few waterfowlers are satisfied with single-shot guns and/or single-shot attempts.

The multiple-shot nature of waterfowling is actually what helped kill off many of the fine old American-made side-by-sides. When pumpguns came along with their capacity of five to seven rounds, followed by autoloaders that spat out five fast patterns, the hunters of yesteryear — both market hunters and weekend sportsmen — set aside their nicely balanced doubles in favor of sheer firepower. Eventually, of course, federal laws mandated the plugging of magazines for a three-shot limit for waterfowl hunting. And if one looks closely, he'll see that the delightful doubles are making a comeback as sportsmen become less meat conscious and more interested in the finer points of gunmaking and wingshooting.

But regardless of whether a hunter uses a pumpgun, autoloader, or double, there's always the matter of understanding and applying a solid technique for follow-up shots. Neither the slickety-click mechanisms of repeaters nor the spirited dynamics of a double will get the job done by themselves. Indeed, hunters who think there's nothing more to rapid repeat shots than a continuous flexing of the trigger finger are totally wrong — as proved by the many ineffective three-shot salvos that echo across marshes, potholes, and stubble.

Bringing off consistently successful follow-up shots requires a concern for both the mental and physical elements of wing-gunning technique. The biggest problem lies in the transition period between shots, a time when (1) recoil can upset alignment and overall gun control, and (2) when the shooter's curiosity about the preceding shot's result can disrupt head position and swing speed. Here's how it happens to many hunters who haven't developed a smooth mental/physical transition.

THE MENTAL ASPECT

Let's say a big greenhead mallard is coming over or passing just a bit to one side — a pushover. "This one's in the bag," our hunter tells himself. He brings the gun up confidently, swings ahead to establish some lead, and pulls the trigger while moving into a follow-through. So far, so good. He fully expects the bird to fold.

But imagine how our hunter's jaw sags as he watches the mallard speed up after that first shot misses. So sure of himself was he that he made no mental preparation for a second or third shot. And as the duck streaks away, our hunter must start all over again. A mental error at the beginning suddenly costs him time and smoothness; he focused on the first shot alone, leaving him with no continuity of mind-to-muscle commands. Before he can start his swing again, he must issue an entirely fresh set of mental commands.

The most important step in becoming a better multiple-shot wing-gunner is always assuming there will have to be a follow-up shot. Don't think in terms of a series of single shots delivered in herky-jerky fashion, but instead key the action by one mental command that carries smoothly and continuously from one shot into the next. Neither the shooter's mind nor body should pause; let each successive shot be a smooth extension of the earlier one. Thus, for optimum speed and effectiveness on follow-up shots, a hunter must begin with a mental command ordering his body to stick with the bird and to keep swinging briskly between shots.

Other mental errors are (1) anticipating a hit, and/or (2) too much determination to "Get that bird!" Excessive anticipation causes a shotgunner to ignore technique. So hopeful of hitting the bird is he that, upon trigger pull, he lifts his head and slows his swing to watch the bird fall. This not only ruins the follow-through of the first shot, but it generally finds the gun becoming static while head position and alignment are lost; then, if a follow-up shot is needed, the hunter must fight back into position and overcome gun inertia before another reasonably good swing can be made. Thus, popping one's head up to view the results of the first shot merely contributes to a poor shot-to-shot transition. Whether lightning flashes or thunder rolls, keep that head down and that gun swinging.

An obsession to score is a terrible mistake. It generally causes a muscular tightness that detracts from overall smoothness. And if there's one key to good shotgunning, it's smoothness.

The cure for anticipatory head lifting and tightness is intensified concentration on proper technique. Purge the brain of thoughts that clutter the purity of wingshooting fundamentals. Don't let greed ("I gotta get my limit!"), doubt ("Wonder if I'll ever hit one?"), desire ("Hope I make this shot!"), or any other emotion overpower concentration and the execution of solid technique. Clear the mind of everything but how you're going to make the swing. It may be a thrill to have a clear view of that big drake folding and falling, but that thrill won't happen very often unless you stay down on the comb, retaining alignment and gun speed, and working into a positive follow-through. That word *work* is especially appropriate, because the ability to concentrate solely on technique when other emotions are boiling does require a large measure of self-discipline.

PHYSICAL FACTORS

Important though the mental game may be to successful second and third shots, there are some disruptive physical factors that de-mand attention. Among waterfowlers, the most obvious of these is recoil. High-velocity and magnum loads generate recoil energies which, even in gas-operated autoloaders, will kick the shooter's head up and cause the loss of original alignment. When shotguns don't have rubber recoil pads that grip and hold, or when hunters don't mount the gun properly, recoil will invariably cause the butt to shift on every shot. A slippery butt is especially disastrous on high-angle fire, and recoil from a gun pointed diagonally or vertically will hammer the gun downward so that it slips lower for each shot and, upon occasion, slams the

---

This photo shows an empty shell being ejected, and a fresh round being fed into the chamber. Making good on the second and third shots requires an understanding of both mental and physical technique. There's more to it than just pulling the trigger quickly.

shooter's thumb painfully against his nose! Such recoil-induced gun action will obviously upset the shot-to-shot transition even if a hunter keys his mind for the correct flow of mental commands; hence, minimizing recoil and controlling gun jump are vital to smooth, coordinated follow-up shooting.

One easy answer to reducing recoil annoyances is going to lighter loads. If a 12-, 16-, or 20-gauge gun throws good patterns with 1¼ ounces of hard No. 5s, there is really no need for anything more robust out to a full 40–45 yards. Many hunters estimate ranges on the long side and think they need

magnums when their shots are in fact well inside 50 yards. But if magnums are the order of the day, other steps must be taken to dampen recoil.

The very least a hunter can do is to have a full-sized or magnum-grade rubber recoil pad attached to his shotgun. The pad should have a bearing surface that clings to the shirt or jacket so it won't slip, even with robust loads, and the length of pull should be adjusted for fast and easy mounting when heavy clothes are worn. For most typical hunters, a 14-inch pull is maximum on a waterfowl gun, and many makers and custom stockers wisely

To be good on follow-up shots, a hunter must learn to handle recoil and get back into alignment and a continuing smooth swing despite the recoil that can cause a looseness between the shooter's cheek and the gun's comb, as is seen here.

whittle that down to 13¾ or 13½ inches. These shortened stocks may not feel right when the hunter is in shirt sleeves, but they jibe nicely with woolen shirts and bulky jackets. And the shortened stocks make it much easier for shooters to regain their proper head position on the comb after recoil energies have subsided, thereby improving alignment and recovery for a quick follow-up shot.

Rearward recoil movement isn't the only aspect of "kick." Muzzle jump is a part of recoil dynamics, and it may be more disruptive than the shoulder-felt recoil. For it is the muzzle jump that pounds one's cheekbone and lifts the gun sharply above the target's line of flight, thus inflicting potential pain and requiring the hunter to fight the gun back into alignment. Too, this upward thrust of a shotgun can be unsettling to the eye-to-target concentration. Indeed, most critical shooters who take an in-depth look at recoil believe that muzzle jump is more troublesome than simple rearward recoil.

Modern technology has made it possible to eliminate the severity of muzzle jump by using gas-escape ports in the upper portion of the barrel. Larry Kelly, who developed the

Recoil, especially muzzle jump, which causes the comb to rise sharply and batter the shooter's cheekbone, can be reduced markedly by a Pro-Port modification. These holes release powder gases upward to help hold the muzzle steady. It's the action-reaction principle, and it works.

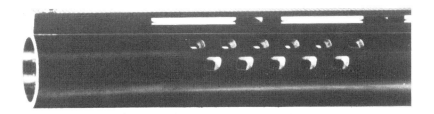

Shooting clay target games such as skeet or trap doubles will condition a hunter to make coordinated second shots count. Note how this trap shooter has elevated his shoulder for better control, something hunters can also do.

Mag-na-port system, is the foremost practitioner of this approach to recoil and jump reduction. Using the EDM process (electrical discharge machining), Kelly cuts a series of elliptical perforations set at a 20-degree rearward slant to the bore axis. These ports invite an upward and rearward exit of powder gases, which in turn puts the action-reaction principle to work; for although the escaping gases spurt upward, they actually supply the power to help hold down the muzzle and drastically reduce muzzle jump. This system is called Pro-Port by Larry Kelly, and it is employed widely by trap and skeet shooters for its effectiveness in reducing gun jump. Pro-Port Ltd. is located at 41302 Executive Dr., Mt. Clemens, Michigan 48045.

Now becoming available are some scientifically designed recoil pads that do more than absorb recoil energy. Experimenters have arranged the slots so that, upon compression, the pad will pull the comb down and away from the shooter's face. It not only eliminates cheekbone pain, but it also makes recoil recovery quicker because one's head isn't knocked skyward. The initial pad of this type was developed by Jack C. Seehase, 1200 Osceola Ave., Winter Park, Florida 32789.

In theory, the over-under can deliver the fastest second shot in wingshooting because the lower barrel generates a straightline recoil that is easily controlled, unless the gun is too light for the loads. The gun is a Spanish-made Laurona O-U with tasteful roll-on scroll.

Gas-operated autoloaders make good follow-up shooting possible by extending the recoil time for less kick and quicker recovery. This is the economy version of Remington's famous Model 1100, the Sportsman 12 Auto.

Similar types of pads are rumored to be available from additional sources, and others are likely to follow.

CORRECT SHOULDERING

One final physical consideration is where a hunter places his duck gun's butt on his shoulder. If it is placed on the upper arm (biceps) or rounded shoulder muscle (deltoid), it is already so far from the face and eye that a shooter must stretch his neck too far for retained alignment. Moreover, both those surfaces are rounded and conducive to slippage. Thus, recoil-induced movement and/or the normal swinging motion can easily cause the comb and cheek to pull apart, and seldom will good alignment be reestablished for successive shots after such poor, untenable form on the first shot.

Shotguns should be mounted closer in so that eye-to-comb contact can be established and retained without undue strain on neck and shoulder muscles. If a hunter must scrunch down or stretch his neck muscles uncomfortably to see squarely down the barrel, he's made a mistake in his gun-mounting fundamentals.

A shotgun's butt belongs in that flat, hollow spot that develops between the deltoid muscle and collarbone when the elbow of the shooter's triggering arm is elevated. Anyone can locate his hollow by placing the flat of his other hand between his shoulder and neck before lifting the elbow of the triggering arm. As will be noticeable, the hollow becomes a relatively flat spot compared to the actual shoulder and upper arm, and guns tucked in here are less inclined to slip or shift from recoil energy or hand action and body movement. But perhaps more importantly, the hollow is closer to the face, and putting the gun's butt there almost automatically positions it comfortably close to the on-side eye. The higher one's elbow rises, the deeper and flatter this hollow becomes, making it more receptive to a shotgun's butt. A hunter need not tilt his elbow abnormally high, however, to shoulder the gun butt properly.

Casual hunters as well as dedicated waterfowlers can improve the position and stability of their mounted guns by applying these subtleties of gun-handling technique; the vaunted firepower of slick repeaters and lively single-triggered doubles is virtually unusable otherwise.

17
Improvements in Ammunition

The premium ammunition bought by modern waterfowlers has very little in common with over-the-counter loads of the first half of this century, but few hunters except the most nostalgic have any regrets. The old-fashioned loads left much to be desired. They had paper cases which, though waxed, were hardly waterproof. Their wad columns were built of nitro cards and pressed-fiber fillers that swelled up when moisture got to them, and, even in good condition, the wads were dubious gas seals.

The soft pellets then in use deformed badly, and the overshot wad employed with roll-crimped shotshells helped disrupt the shot charge. One important fault, albeit one not widely understood by the general public, was the role of the card/filler wad stack on pattern development. Being heavy and having no "air brake" feature to slow it abruptly on exit, it was often shoved like a battering ram into and/or through the emerging shot charge by gas pressure and its own momentum. This battering ram effect from the card/filler wad stack caused blown or donut patterns more regularly than the suspected overshot wafer which pellets could bump out of the way.

There were only two notable advances in shotshell technology before WWII. One was the development of progressive-burning powder; the other was the introduction of copper-plated shot.

The first progressive-burning powders are said to have originated in Germany, but it apparently wasn't long until the American powder makers duplicated the process. Such propellants generated lower chamber pressures for any given velocity than did the former fast-burning fuels, and the lower pressures (or more gradual pressure rises) got the payloads started with a shove instead of a sharp jolt. The supposedly gentler acceleration caused less pellet deformation, according to theory, and Winchester-Western turned the theory into an advertising campaign stressing the "short shot string"; for if there are indeed fewer deformed pellets because of a less violent setback factor, there will definitely be fewer pellets slowing down and trailing the main mass. It was this theory, nothing more, that underscored much advertising of the 1930s and 1940s.

Progressive-burning propellants also permitted the use of more powder for higher velocities with heavier shot charges. The immediate benefactor was the 12-gauge, whose 1¼-ounce loading was quickly taken to 1,330 f.p.s. in the hot-selling high-brass case. The availability of constantly improving powders also made possible experimentation with the 3-inch 20-gauge Magnum and the 10-gauge Magnum. These extra-length magnum shotshells have been refined, however, even today there is still some work left to be done on them.

Copper-plated shot was a Winchester development urged by John M. Olin, dedicated sportsman and high-ranking executive of the Olin-Matheson Chemical Corporation which bought Winchester when the company fell into bankruptcy during the Depression years. Patented under the tradename Lubaloy, copper-plated shot reduced the amount of deformation considerably and made a significant contribution

The shotshells of pre-WWII vintage left much to be desired for waterfowling. Their paper cases, cardboard and fiber wads, roll crimps, and relatively soft pellets hardly delivered long-range effectiveness, despite advertisements to the contrary.

to pattern improvement for long-range waterfowling.

Lubaloy shot and the 3-inch 12-gauge Magnum were championed by Nash Buckingham, a widely read outdoor writer of the period, but, as the old saying goes, the load was apparently ahead of its time. Hunters ignored it, either because of its price or because they didn't understand its importance. Consequently, insofar as the general public was concerned, we entered the decade of the '40s with shotshells not much different from those of the turn of the century. On a conceptual basis, little had been changed except the powder.

POST-WAR PROGRESS

While technological advances stemming from WWII crash programs helped advance shotshell manufacturing and performance, the pace was anything but swift. Improvements came piecemeal. The folded, or pie crimp, came first. Winchester and Remington were using it broadly by the late 1940s, but Federal continued for several years with a "frangible" top wad that was said to disintegrate when it struck air resistance at the muzzle.

Hunters praised the changeover, believing that the absence of a top wad now ensured tight patterns. What they didn't realize, of course, was that the interior wad column was still the same as it had always been, and that it still applied the battering ram effect. Since few hunters ever pattern their guns, the idea of a folded crimp boosted their morale.

If duck hunters did see an improvement in their patterns after WWII, it probably was due to another factor; the ammo makers began using a harder form of black shot known as chilled shot. As explained elsewhere in this book, chilled shot was an alloy made of lead, arsenic to maintain form, and antimony to serve as a hardener. It is doubtful

that the antimony content ever exceeded two or three percent, but even that was a giant step beyond drop shot which had no hardener at all. Patterns made with chilled shot can run 10 to 20 percentage points higher than soft-shot patterns from the same duck gun. But typical hunters at the time never considered the quality of shotgun pellets, and they attributed the better pattern density to the new folded crimps.

The first plastic shotshell bodies were introduced in 1960, a full fifteen years after WWII. Waterfowlers greeted them with glad cries, as it meant the end of swollen wads and cases. Plastic shotshells held their shape, were quite waterproof, and cycled nicely through repeaters.

The modern shotshell is scientifically advanced, having features that give consistent ballistics, considerably improved patterns, generally moisture-proof construction, and slick feeding because of self-lubricating plastic cases. This illustration shows the interior of a Remington Premier shotshell with granulated polyethylene buffering in the shot charge.

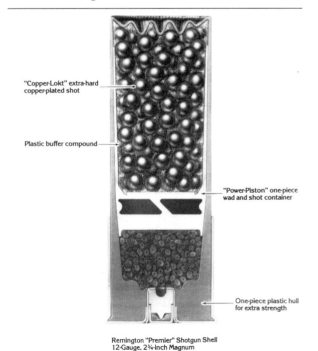

"Copper-Lokt" extra-hard copper-plated shot

Plastic buffer compound

"Power-Piston" one-piece wad and shot container

One-piece plastic hull for extra strength

Remington "Premier" Shotgun Shell
12-Gauge, 2¾-inch Magnum

Of more importance to downrange performance, however, were the various plastic shotcup wads that soon followed. Plastic shotcups guarded against bore scrubbing and, in that way, helped retain additional pellet roundness. Theoretically, reduced deformation put more shot into the pattern *without* reducing pattern diameter. But the public overestimated the productivity of shotcups and assumed they automatically tightened patterns by (1) protecting pellets against deformation, (2) holding the shot charge tightly packed even after bore exit, and (3) adding to the choke constriction. The industry never stated anything of the sort; they merely advertised more pellets in normal-sized clusters. True, shotcups did improve patterns, but generally not as much as fanciful thinkers believed. Indeed, it was my misfortune to meet a dealer who, in pushing the sale of then-new shotcup wads for reloading, claimed that cylinder-bore riot guns would deliver full-choke patterns when fed cupped shot charges! Of such salesmanship are myths created.

Plastic wads with slit shotcups improve patterns by a more subtle means than most hunters visualize: they don't ram into the exiting shot mass the way card/filler wad stacks do. When a slit shotcup wad hits air resistance as it clears the muzzle, its elements, or "petals," lay back and, in this peeling procedure, expose more surface area so the air slows the wad abruptly. This lets the pellets escape without an uncouth smack on the fanny, and without having interior pellets

---

Federal Cartridge Corp. has recently embellished its line-up of modern shotshells with a 1⅜-ounce Heavyweight loading for the standard 12-gauge (left), and a whopping 2-ounce load for the 3-inch 12-gauge Magnum (right).

bumped to the fringe by rear-end wad impacts. Thus, thanks to the air brake effect of slit plastic shotcups, such wads seldom shoot into and/or through shot charges nowadays.

That plastic shotcups automatically tighten patterns is a very debatable topic. The oft-heard remark that plastic wads tighten patterns by one full degree of choke must be ignored. My own patterning has not found it valid. Improved cylinder chokes still deliver improved cylinder percentages despite plastic wads, and modified chokes still shoot modified patterns. The hunter who thinks his modified choke suddenly turns into an extra-full choke whenever he chambers a round with a shotcup wad is deluding himself. Everything must be proved and established for each individual gun and load.

BUFFERED SHOT CHARGES

Every top-of-the-line factory waterfowl and buckshot load today has some type of plastic buffering media in the shot charge. Popular thinking is that the buffer cushions the pellets against deformation; however, a full explanation involves additional complexities, and the bland concept of cushioning is, in reality, a misconception

Buffering material helps improve patterns significantly in three ways: (1) it helps prevent pellet deformation; (2) it helps coarse pellets slide more fluidly through the bore and, especially, through the choke constriction; and (3) it reduces or eliminates pellet spin.

Buffering media works against pellet deformation by filling the spaces between shot

Practically every shotshell manufacturer now supplies long-range loads with a buffer in the shot charge to reduce pellet deformation and to improve patterning.

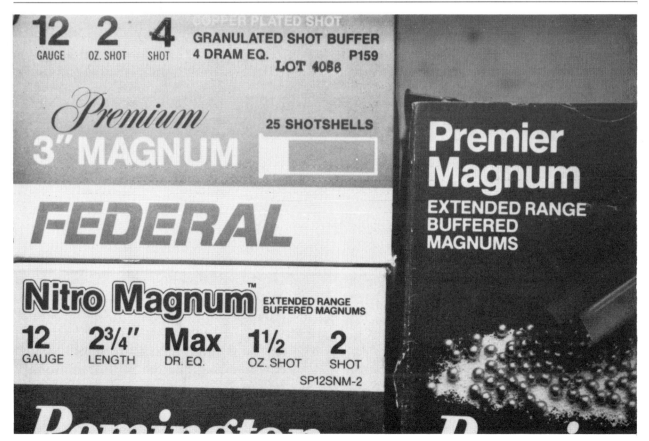

The people at Federal have been leaders in applying advanced concepts to shotshells for significantly improved field performance. From left to right: their 10-gauge 3½-inch Premium Magnum with pellet buffering and copper-plated shot; the 12-gauge 3-inch Magnum, also with buffer and copper-plated pellets; the standard-length 12-gauge Hi-Power Magnum; and the standard-length 20-gauge Hi-Power with hard shot.

so that, when the payload compacts under the force of firing setback, the pellets have no place to go. By denying pellets deformation room, tightly packed buffer practically traps the pellets and forces them to remain spherical. This, then, is not a cushioning act per se, because there is no softness about it; the buffer also becomes hard and compact when setback occurs. A more suitable way of explaining the role of buffering media, it would seem, is an encasement that supports original form. It's not like babying eggs in a styrofoam box, as the buffer also compresses to lose whatever cushionlike quality it had prior to setback.

Experimentation indicates that the fine, high-density buffers excel because they trickle into those tiny spaces between pellets better than coarse buffers. Filling the voids between pellets is especially important with black shot, which should be supported for their entire circumference. A coarse buffer, or a partially buffered load, can work with copper-plated shot, which is tougher and more deformation-resistant on its own, although the results may not be optimum. The ideal seems to be reached when every nook and cranny of the shot charge is filled with fine buffer encasing and supporting the form of every individual pellet. Handloading tends to accomplish this better than commercial buffered loads, because a conscientious reloader can vibrate the media into place and carefully work it to the bottom of the shot charge where setback pressures are the most destructive. Commercially buffered loads, on the other hand, throw metered charges or plop the buffer on top and let it settle by itself — which it may never do. This writer has cut open some factory rounds and found the buffer still on top, a place where it does the least amount of good. Getting the most from store-bought buffered loads seems to require a trick: hold each one with the crimp pointing up and touch the brass rim to an electric shaver so that the top-sitting buffer trickles downward due to vibration to fill the spaces between lower pellets.

The solid, sluglike state of a buffered shot charge under the compressive force of acceleration also helps prevent pellet spin. Both birdshot and buckshot loaded without a confining buffer can begin rotating during their trip through the bore, and once they clear the muzzle that rotation becomes a spin that carries the spheres away from the bore axis like so many tiny curve balls. The technical term

---

The improved performance of buffered payloads is illustrated in these photos of Federal's new Premium buckshot loads. Note how the pellets retain their roundness and stay in line rather than spreading out as in the standard buckshot load; the shot string is already developing at just 6 feet, a subject dealt with in chapter 10. Although these photos show coarse No. 00 buckshot, the same results can be expected with No. 4 buckshot and all sizes of birdshot.

Premium™ Buckshot

 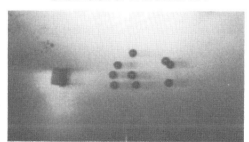 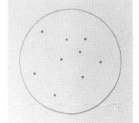

At 1 foot from muzzle shot pellets and buffer emerge from shot cup.

At 6 feet from muzzle minimum dispersion of pellets and superior sphericity are apparent.

Typical 15″ circle pattern at 40 yards from full choke shows density achieved by Premium™ brand 9-pellet 00 buckshot.

Standard Buckshot

 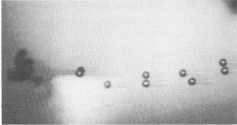 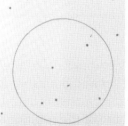

One foot from muzzle

Six feet from muzzle

Typical 15″ circle pattern at 40 yards from full choke with standard 9-pellet 00 buckshot.

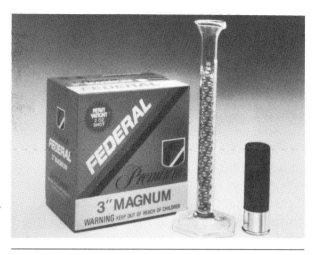

With its load of 2 ounces of copper-plated BBs, Federal's 3-inch 12-gauge Magnum, which is made possible by modern slow-burning powders, is the equivalent of most 10-gauge Magnums and permits the use of a lighter gun for easier swinging.

Buckshot usually comes in less expensive and handy five- or ten-round packs. Shown here is copper-plated No. 00, buffered with granulated polyethylene in a 3-inch 12-gauge Magnum hull.

for this phenomenon is precession and the heavier pellet and buckshot sizes are especially affected because of their greater mass and weight. Some of the rotation is caused by barrel vibrations, a condition known to mechanical engineers as the Magnus effect of

circulation on rotating spheres; the rest can be attributed to the spheres' roll up the choke taper. Hunters may find it hard to believe that their shotgun barrels vibrate, but oscilloscopes prove differently. With pellets or buckshot solidly encased in high-density buffer, however, in-bore pellet rotation is seemingly stifled and the precessive phenomenon, alias the curve ball effect, is reduced or eliminated.

Buffered loads can also improve patterning by smoothing pellet or buckshot flow through the choke constriction. Coarse shot pellets fired without buffer invariably suffer further deformation when they must swage down and fight their way through the choke, because pellets bear mightily against each other in those cramped quarters. With buffer in place, though, both birdshot and buckshot can shift about within their masses and take on a more fluid quality when traversing the tight choke segment of the bore. The result isn't only fewer deformed pellets, but also a better load response to the choke's taper.

Even though commercially loaded buffered shotshells may not be the ultimate as of yet, they are the single most noteworthy advance made by the shotshell industry. Hunters who ignore them because of price are being penny-wise and pound-foolish. For long-range waterfowling, they are a *must!*

CAUTION — PROMOTION LOADS

There are certain people who want the cheapest possible shotshells, and the ammunition industry supplies this demand with something called a "promotion load." All things considered, it's a cheapie. Some typical examples include the Mohawk designation, Duck & Pheasant loads, and the Dove & Quail types. Ditto for the Rabbit & Squirrel ammo, plus those loads imported from foreign countries to sell at a very low price compared to premium shells.

What's wrong with these low-cost shot-shells? You can't tell by rolling them in your hand and examining the exteriors because they are generally good-looking hulls. But the innards are what count, and it is here where *el cheapo producto* shotshells falter. The main problem rests with pellet quality. Promotion loads contain soft shot pellets which deform badly. Seldom do they shoot patterns higher than 60–62 percent even from tightly choked guns. In tests I've run with promotion loads, full-choked 12s never topped 57–60 percent at 40 yards, which is weak modified at best. The reason for using such soft shot, of course, is to hold down production costs; for antimony, which is the standard pellet hardener, is very expensive today, and using any amount of it would automatically jack up the price of each box. Velocities with promotion loads are also slower than they are with premium ammunition, although some customers are gullible enough to believe that the high brass head on a promotion load implies speed and power.

Obviously, all loads aren't alike no matter how they look on the outside. You still get what you pay for. If anything, promotion loads are a regressive step made to fit frugal wallets rather than to contribute to improved wing-gunning effectiveness. Ask your dealer what on his shelf constitutes a promotion load — and stay away from them.

THE NEW HEAVYWEIGHTS

Slow-burning powders, and the manufacturers' willingness to use them creatively, have brought out some innovations that suit a waterfowler's needs perfectly. For example, Winchester and Federal both roll 3½-inch 10-gauge Magnum loads with 2¼ ounces of buffered BBs, 2s, or 4s. Both also load the 10-gauge Magnum with 54 balls of No. 4 buckshot.

Recently, Federal announced a Heavy-weight offering for the 3-inch 12 that heaves 2 full ounces of copper-plated coarse shot, a payload that was once the sole domain of the Magnum 10.

Of interest to duck hunters who stay within close and intermediate ranges should be the newest Federal Hi-Power entry, a standard-length 12-gauge load with 1⅜ ounces of hard black shot, unbuffered, in 2s, 4s, or 6s. We hope that Federal will soon include hard 5s, as that is a great pellet for the 1⅜-ouncer. The Hi-Power is not considered a true magnum load but merely a heavyweight standard round. However one slices the semantics, the idea is a sound one because the 1⅜-ounce shot charge will frequently pattern better than a 1½-ouncer from full-choked 12s, giving the hunter more density with less recoil and gun stress.

THE FUTURE

What advances can we look for in the future? More emphasis on the No. 5 pellet would be fine. Biodegradable wads and hulls would also be excellent, as plastics clutter up a marsh something awful. Perhaps the smaller buckshot sizes which split the difference between BBs and No. 4 buck should be emphasized for goose hunters, thereby giving added density to avoid the one-pellet crippling hits that occur with No. 4 buckshot. In the main, however, the advances made by the industry such as providing buffered loads with copper-plated shot are state-of-the-art. It's up to the individual hunter to perfect his techniques so that he can take advantage of the vastly improved ammunition now on the market.

18
An Objective Look at Magnum Loads

In Latin, the adjective *magnum* is used to describe something that is large or great. Exactly how large or how great isn't specified by the word alone; it's all a matter of the comparative size and stature of related objects. And as a former high school Latin teacher, this author knows that the Romans weren't overawed by the presence of the word. It was just another adjective to be used properly and intelligently.

But when the word magnum came into the English-speaking shotgunner's lexicon, it mistakenly took on a magical aura of having significantly greater power than standard guns and loads possessed. If the manufacturers called something a magnum this or a magnum that, it sold like crazy. And nothing has changed. Casual sportsmen who buy magnum guns and loads turn from the counter with unrealistic expectations. This ballistics megalomania was best epitomized by the young man who, cranking a rusty, bolt-action 20-gauge along the firing line of a refuge, was asked why he shot at birds that were, figuratively speaking, mere dots against the sky. "Heck," he proclaimed, while extending a high-brass hull, "these aren't ordinary loads — they're magnums!" When told that his vaunted magnums were only an eighth of an ounce heavier than standard 20-gauge loads, he wasn't daunted. "They're still magnums, aren't they?" he asked, as he kept banging away at every duck or goose that came by within 150 yards. Obviously, the term magnum misleads certain hunters into believing they are using far more gun than they truly possess.

The so-called short magnum shotshells that are so very popular today had their inception in the 1950s. Until then, the standard-length (2¾″) 12-gauge shotshell's heaviest load was 1¼ ounces in high-velocity or live pigeon persuasion. The 16 gauge topped out at 1⅛ ounces, and the 20 trailed with an even 1 ounce. The short magnums increased those charges to 1½ ounces for the 12 gauge, 1¼ ounces for the 16, and 1⅛ ounces for the 20. Impressive thought that appears on brightly colored ammo boxes, it amounts to nothing more than an extra quarter-ounce of pellets for the 12 and just eighth-ounce increases for the 16 and 20. On the basis of pellet count, the magnumized loads only put 23 more No. 2s in the 12-gauge load, and put 11 more deuces in the 16 and 20. With No. 4s, the 12 gauge received about 34 more pellets, while the 16 and 20 each got about 17 more. When those shot charges are counted out and spread on a table, the additional pellets aren't terribly impressive. Yet, the fact that they're called magnums often negates common sense. The pellet masses may have been increased by 12 to 20 percent, but hunters blinded to scientific reality by the big letters M A G N U M think the loads automatically extend their effective range by 50 to 100 percent. How just 11 more No. 4s could transform the young man's standard 20 from barely a 40-yard gun into a stratospheric antiaircraft weapon is still a ballistics mystery to those who know anything about shotgun performance; however, each season hundreds of

Magnum guns and loads may *give the hunter an extra edge. This snow goose was taken with a 10-gauge Magnum double over a stubble field in North Dakota. (Photo by Gerald F. Moran)*

thousands of hunters make the same error and attempt to stretch short magnums far beyond their capabilities — or purpose.

The fact is that the short magnums were not developed for significantly longer ranges. Originally, the short magnums were developed to put more heavy shot into each load for greater stopping power over *normal* ranges. The pellet increases were supposed to give greater pattern density to enhance the number of clean kills. It was, in a sense, a conservation move to reduce crippling.

But, alas, the buying public hasn't yet understood that theory. The short magnum's role has been misinterpreted to mean considerably more of everything for long-range gunning, and, instead of being a conservation factor, it has probably led to more crippling because hunters fire at birds well beyond the load's potential. Tragic, but true.

Let's take an intelligent look at magnum loads. Assume the standard 20's 1-ounce load of No. 2s patterns well enough in a given gun to be regarded as a positive 45-yard outfit for goose hunting, which means a pattern of at least 70 percent at 40 yards. If that gun continued to pattern at 70 percent with 1⅛-ounce short magnums (and that's a big *if*, as many randomly selected guns lose patterning efficiency with short magnums), the shot string would be sweetened by only 7 – 8 of the extra 11 pellets at 40 – 45 yards. Now, realistically, how much more range can 7 or 8 more pellets really buy? At best, they would increase the range in direct proportion to their effect on the raw pattern percentage, which would be roughly 9–10 percent. Translated into distance, that becomes 4½ – 5 more yards or, overall, 49 – 50 yards. That's far short of the ranges uninformed hunters expect from said loads.

The fact is that, excluding those chance one-shot head/neck hits that keep encouraging skybusters, the added pellets of a short magnum don't increase a typical shotgun's clean-killing range by much more than the bow-to-stern measurement of a rowboat! The only way to get more range from such loads is to have the gun refined for ultra-tight patterns, a subject to be discussed later. Otherwise, a sophisticated shotgunner will employ gun/magnum pairings for what they were intended — a way to pack more penetrating energy into each pattern over normal distances — not as long-range missiles!

VELOCITY FACTS

The recoil and blast of short magnum loads also mislead hunters into believing they're getting more muzzle velocity as well. One glance at established industry figures will prove that factory-loaded 12-gauge high-velocity charges (3¾ drams equivalent) with 1¼ ounces of shot start out at 1,330 f.p.s., while 1½-ounce short magnums move at 1,260 f.p.s. In the standard 20-gauge, factory-loaded 1-ouncers (2¾ drams equivalent) do 1,220 f.p.s. as compared to 1,175 f.p.s. for 1⅛-ounce short maggies. Considering the heavy pellets waterfowlers use, those lower velocities aren't detrimental; the individual pellets that remain round retain adequate velocity/energy levels for legitimate ranges. The point is that the recoil, blast, and impressive title, *magnum*, can fool hunters.

Handloaders can exceed the above-listed velocities for short magnums, of course, and do so safely with slow-burning powders in lab-tested combinations. Merely pouring the coals to a magnum load doesn't imply success, however. More isn't always better. High velocities can produce poor patterns with magnum charges of coarse shot, and the gas pressures required to attain higher speeds can cause stress to the gun as well as the shooter by heightened recoil and muzzle blast.

The only ways that increased velocity can be beneficial in short magnum reloads are (1) if, by chance, the gun/load combo jibes for excellent patterns, or (2) the barrel is regulated for the specific load. Those two exceptions not withstanding, elevated velocity levels can easily be counterproductive. All the velocity in the world won't help if weak patterns merely cripple the bird, or if the shooter misses because he can't handle the recoil/blast level. Thus, while every fractional foot-pound of energy seems to help bring down birds cleanly, velocity must perforce be blended with patterning considerations and the individual shooter's ability to handle recoil.

In general, then, the short magnum concept has largely been misunderstood, overrated, and misapplied. Such ammunition doesn't turn standard 12s, 16s, and 20s into howitzers. Indeed, more than a few full-choked guns will actually put more pellets into a 30-inch-diameter circle at 40 yards using 1¼-ouncers than they will with the heftier short magnums. Therefore, common sense tells us that a gun/magnum team must be patterned before one can jump to any conclusions of long-range potency.

ASSESSING THE EXTRA-LENGTH MAGNUMS

Modern waterfowlers have three legitimate extra-length shotshells available to them: the 3-inch 20 gauge; the 3-inch 12 gauge; and the 3½-inch 10 gauge. All sport the magnum label. All entice hunters. But they do have their strengths and weaknesses, and a further application of critical examination and scientific standards must be applied.

Don't assume that magnums will extend the clean killing range. You must pattern to find if there is a definite advantage. Sometimes magnum loads pattern poorly and are actually counterproductive.

Hunters often overestimate the added "power" of magnum loads. In reality, the number of extra pellets can't extend the range very much. On the left is a 1½-ounce 12-gauge short Magnum with its charge of No. 2 shot separated to show how many pellets are added to the basic 1¼-ounce load (22): on the right is a 1⅛-ounce 20-gauge short Magnum with its charge of No. 2s also separated to show the basic 1-ounce load and the 11 more pellets added to bring it up to magnum specifications. The addition of just 11 and 22 more pellets isn't all that great and won't turn a 40-yard gun into a 75-yard performer.

THE 3-INCH 20 GAUGE

The 3-inch 20-gauge Magnum was already being tested before WWII, but it wasn't until the post-war years that the novelty gained acceptance and, eventually, popularity. It was given its first impetus when some Winchester executives, wanting guns that were more portable than their Magnum 12s, had Model 21 doubles chambered for the lengthened 20-gauge round. That point about portability is important in any assessment of the 3-inch 20, as it indicates that the originators were thinking mainly in terms of gun-handling qualities with reasonable load potency, not purely beefed-up ammo to shoot to the moon.

Initially, the 3-inch 20 was given just 1⅛ ounces of shot. That was increased to 1³⁄₁₆ ounces for a brief time before chemical advances produced progressive-burning powders that permitted a full 1¼-ounce payload with effective velocity (1,185 f.p.s.) and safe chamber pressures. This is basically where the 3-inch 20 stands today.

A look at the figures will disclose that the Roman candle 20 has not yet been brought to the level of a standard 12-gauge high-velocity load, which does about 1,330 f.p.s. with 1¼ ounces of shot. Despite that comparison, however, the 3-inch 20 has given hunters all sorts of fanciful ideas, and more than a few have launched 3-inch 20-gauge loads at birds they'd deem too far for the standard 12! The scientific fact is that, regardless of gauge, a 1¼-ounce shot charge simply can't do more in a 20 gauge than it can in a 12 or a 16.

If a good scattergun theorist weighed all aspects of shotgun performance, in fact, he could prove that the 1¼-ounce shot charge not only has its weaknesses in the 20-gauge bore, but also that, all other factors being equal, it is somewhat *less efficient* therein than in the larger 12 and 16. To begin, there's the matter of shot string length. To fit a narrow 20-gauge shell and bore, the charge is lengthened. In turn, the longer shot charge produces problems in both interior and exterior ballistics.

There is immediately the matter of pressure/velocity ratios. More gas pressure is needed in a small bore than a larger bore to move a given weight to a specific muzzle velocity, and in some instances the velocities can't be duplicated without causing excess pressures in the smaller bore. This is the case of the 3-inch 20 as compared to the standard 12 gauge with 1¼-ounce loads; even with the slow-burning powders now obtainable, the 3-inch 20 can't move its 1¼-ounce charge beyond 1,200 f.p.s. without reaching or exceeding its pressure limitations. Thus, unless a miracle propellant comes along, the 1¼-ounce 20-gauge Magnum will always trail the standard 12 which, when reloaded judiciously, can top 1,400 f.p.s. safely. Indeed, those who fancy the 3-inch 20 may very well

The ideal is reached when magnum loads put more heavy shot on the target in typical ranges for clean kills and positive retrieves. This goose-sized patterning plate was struck by such a pattern.

find that reloads with 1⅛ or 1³⁄₁₆ ounces of shot deliver more in the way of effective power and pattern, as they can be safely stoked to higher speeds while still patterning as well as or better than the 1¼-ounce load.

There is also the potential for extensive pellet deformation inside the chamber and bore. Setback forces can batter the lower pellet layers as the chamber pressures run high and, because of the load's bulk, there is virtually no wad cushioning between powder pressure and shot mass. Added deformation occurs as the long string wedges into and through the forcing cone, down the narrow bore, and then slams into the choke constriction. It is the same basic situation that instigates the radical difference between the way a .410 bore and a 28-gauge handle the same ¾-ounce load; the 28 invariably patterns better and kills cleaner because it has fewer deformed shot and a shorter shot string.

Once outside the barrel, the 3-inch 20's shot string can lower the effective density by tailing out drastically at ranges beyond 40 yards. Experimenters have proved this by firing at patterning sheets moved by vehicles at game bird speeds and ranges. A pattern fired at a moving sheet generally shows less density in the main 30-inch concentration than appears in a pattern fired by the same gun/load combination at a stationary sheet. Slow and/or deformed pellets that eventually strike within the circle of a stationary sheet trail out on a fast-moving sheet, and that can reduce the main concentration's density by 5 to 15 percent, depending on the range and the type of pellets used.

Therefore, on the bases of velocity, pattern, and shot stringing, the 3-inch 20's optimum 1¼-ounce shot charge is variously inferior to the standard 12's high-velocity loading, also with 1¼ ounces of shot. Even with a highly refined 20 and carefully selected loads with hard or copper-plated shot, a scientific approach tells us that 1¼ ounces of shot

in the 20 can't be expected to do much more, if as much, as the same charge in the 12. The narrow 20-gauge bore is simply too tight for optimum efficiency with a shot charge that long and heavy.

Sensible hunters won't expect more from the 3-inch 20 than they do from the 16 gauge or the 12 with 1¼ ounces of shot. If patterns are indeed tight with No. 4 or 5 shot, ducks can be taken cleanly to about 50 yards, give or take a few yards depending on the actual patterns. On geese, the birds' larger bodies absorb more of the pattern; hence, tight clusters of 2s, 3s, or 4s are positive to about 55 yards, again with slight variations either way. By refining the barrel and matching special loads to it, sophisticated shotgunners have wrung another legitimate 5 yards from the 3-inch 20, but such performances seldom occur in unaltered, over-the-counter barrels and randomly selected ammunition. Therefore, the hunter who does no experimental patterning and doesn't have his 20's barrel refined must think of 45 – 50 yards as maximum ethical range. There is a sensible limit to what one can expect from 1¼ ounces of shot.

The best thing that ever happened to the 3-inch 20 was copper-plated shot. Ordinary chilled shot is a disaster in this small bore, deforming en masse. The skybuster who insists on making a fool of himself with a 3-inch 20 should at least launch copper-plated shot for maximum impact in case he ever manages to hit something.

Although significantly increased range isn't a strength of the 3-inch 20, the round does have one meaningful attribute: it can be teamed with a gun that is easily handled and portable while still delivering adequate energy for reasonable distances. This can be of importance to the hunter who finds himself unable to handle and swing a 12 or 10 gauge effectively; the reduced bulk and weight of a 20 could be just what he needs to get on target faster and to generate more gun speed for the longer leads. Indeed, employed within 45 yards, the 3-inch 20's spirited handling can give waterfowlers the same pleasures it gives to uplanders — but stretch it like a rubber band, and it can be a merciless crippler.

THE 3-INCH 12 GAUGE

The 3-inch 12-gauge Magnum stirred up a flurry in the 1920s and 1930s, thanks in part to the writings of Nash Buckingham. His pair of Burt Becker Magnums built on A.H. Fox actions swung across many pages of the nation's foremost outdoor magazines to provide readers with vicarious excitement and a desire for such wondrous weaponry. A common loading for the 3-inch 12 in those days was 1⅜ ounces of shot, and Buckingham was one of the first gun writers to tout copper-plated shot for its minimal deformation.

The buying public followed Buckingham into the realm of the 3-inch 12 Mag. However, for decades they ignored copper-plated shot. Once they put down their greenbacks for the 12-gauge Magnum, they resorted to penny pinching and bought ammunition loaded with common chilled shot, thereby realizing a very dubious advantage, if any. Deformed pellets from a 3-inch Magnum don't pattern or penetrate any better than do those from a standard-chambered shotgun. And it really wasn't until the late 1970s and the early

Magnum decoys, magnum guns, and magnum loads are an obsession with modern waterfowlers, but does a typical hunter actually understand what it all means?

Magnum loads may seem like logical choices when the birds are offering only long-range shots, but logic and science are two different things. Don't overrate such ammunition simply because of its name and the advertising hype.

1980s, when commercial loading companies brought out ammunition with pellets bedded in granulated polyethylene, that average hunters who did not reload began to realize true range advantages from the 3-inch 12. For unlike the limited-capacity 3-inch 20, the 12-gauge long shell has both capacity and ballistics qualities that give it the potential for long-range effectiveness — when approached critically and scientifically. Merely stuffing more and more giant pellets into a big, receptive hull isn't the best answer to long-range efficiency.

Properly loaded, the 3-inch 12-gauge Magnum is our most versatile waterfowling round. It can handle everything from superswift 1⅜-ounce reloads, through 1½- to 1⅞-ounce loads, to the new 2-ounce charges (which come close to matching the Magnum 10). Perhaps more importantly, the guns chambered for the 3-inch 12-gauge round have about the same proportions and weight as the standard 12s, which makes them easier to carry and to swing than the monstrous 10-gauge Magnums. Thus, a savvy shotgunner who can match his loads to the gun and the game can make a 3-inch 12 do about anything expected of a standard 12 and a Magnum 10. The fact that the 10 gauge's wider bore enhances ballistics and patterning with 2-ounce loads of coarse shot does overshadow the 3-inch 12 somewhat if its bore remains around 0.725 to 0.740 inch in diameter; however, with the slightly lighter loads of 1⅜ to 1¾ ounces, the Magnum 12's normal bore can definitely produce tight patterns at effective velocities for on-target performances equal to those of the Big 10.

For the discerning hunter, there are really two distinctly different ways of viewing the 3-inch 12. One way is perceiving it as an extension of the short magnum concept, namely, as a way to get more heavy, high-energy pellets into the pattern for killing shots at normal ranges. A 1⅝-ounce charge of 5s, for instance, will put as many pellets into the air as will the standard 12's 1¼-ounce load of 6s, which gives the potential for equal density with considerably more per-pellet punch. Hunters who realize they don't have the skill to score beyond 50 yards might wisely adopt this approach and select chokes and loads for maximum effectiveness at intermediate ranges instead of pointing everything toward ultra-long ranges. If I were forced to select one gun and choke for waterfowling, it would probably be my Remington Model 1100 12-gauge Magnum with a 28-inch modified barrel. It gives totally adequate target saturation over intermediate distances, while also throwing slightly greater pattern width than a hard-to-hit-with full choke. If I hit a goodly number of the chances I get inside 45–50 yards each season, I'll have a sportsman's bag and can ignore birds that pass farther out. Moreover, it is often possible to find a load or two that will print full-choke patterns from a modified choke, and merely switching to those loads will handle days when the birds are spooky or hanging high.

On the other hand, a 3-inch 12 can be viewed as a bona fide long-range gun for 50- to 70-yard shooting when the gun/load combo is known to pattern tightly. The hull holds enough heavy pellets and progressive-burning powder to justify such efforts on a per-pellet basis, and our advanced components and sophisticated loading techniques make high performance possible even though the 3-inch 12's normal bore diameter is somewhat small for such massive loads. Handloading procedures, as well as pattern reading methods, are detailed in other chapters. Suffice it to say here that, if the 3-inch 12 is to be a clean, long-range performer, a pellet-bedding compound and hard shot, preferably copper-plated, must be employed. Using ordinary chilled shot in the Magnum 12 is disgusting; deformation robs the shot string of 35 to 45 percent of its pellets by 40 yards, leaving precious little for the next 20 yards. Thus, the versatility and long-range potential of the 3-inch 12 can be realized only if the hunter is willing to pay for it in the form of load testing and quality components for high-performance ammunition.

THE IRON MONSTER

There is no other way to describe the 3½-inch 10-gauge Magnum. It is a gargantuan gun that swallows a fistful of shotshell. It was developed in 1932 at the behest of Charles Askins, one of our early shotgun experts, and was popularized by the late Elmer Keith, another well-known writer who liked guns with big holes in their barrels. Although the Magnum 10 is now widely used, it nearly fell by the wayside between WWII and the 1970s. Hunters shunned it for typical waterfowling. With the advent of the refuge system, however, the 10-gauge Magnum made a rapid comeback; hunters who set up camp along the borders of such places, waiting for overhead shots as the birds came and went, wanted all the gun they could get for the serious (and often silly) long-range "barrel stretching" practiced there.

In theory, the hunters weren't wrong about their gauge selection. Of all the gauges still legal for waterfowling stateside, the 3½-inch 10-gauge Magnum is the one best suited for 2–2¼-ounce charges of coarse pellets or buckshot. Thanks to its spacious bore, the 10-gauge has an expansion ratio that permits relatively high velocities with massive payloads without excess chamber pressures.

The technicians call that an efficient expansion ratio. But whatever the name, the Magnum 10 rates huzzas for its ability to put it all together for optimum long-range performance. Besides the advantageous pressure velocity ratio, a massive shot charge flows more fluidly through the 10's cavernous bore than it does through a normal 12-gauge tube for potentially better patterns.

But that's all so much theory, and things have a habit of changing when put to actual practice by the public. The 10-gauge Magnum is like that: on the basis of size alone, it lures hunters into believing that it is a giant magic wand that nonchalantly strokes geese from the stratosphere with virtually any coarse-pellet load. It's the old "more is better" syndrome which, unfortunately, doesn't take into account the problem of pellet deformation. In an effort to save money — as it is expensive to feed a Magnum 10, be it with commercial ammunition or reloads — hunters tend to buy the cheapest factory rounds or the least expensive bagged shot; and that penny-pinching results in the use of ordinary chilled shot, which is readily deformed even in the massive maw of a 10-gauge. Pellet-against-pellet mashing runs as rampant in a 10-gauge Magnum as it does in the 3-inch 20 and 12. This writer has owned three 10-gauge Magnums and an older Ithaca hammer double with the short chamber, and with chilled shot loaded *sans* buffer, they never printed above 55 to 60 percent at 40 yards, which amounts to nothing more than weak modified choke. At the time, I had a tight-shooting 12 which, with 1⅜ ounces of copper-plated shot, regularly put more pellets into a 30-inch circle at 50 yards than did any of those vaunted 10s with vastly heavier loads of chilled shot. The 10 gauge is a classic example of diminishing

returns unless hard, preferably plated, shot is used. Indeed, why thunder 2–2¼ ounces of shot from a heavy-recoiling, hard-to-handle 11-pound 10-gauge when a lighter-kicking, easier-to-handle 12 will pattern as well or better? If a 10-gauge user is going to experience any significant range advantage over the 3-inch 12-gauge Magnum, he will do so only by employing ammunition with buffered loads of copper-plated shot.

There is nothing versatile about the 10-gauge Magnum. For although the hull can be handloaded down to 1½ ounces of shot with fast-burning powder and built-up wad columns, the guns themselves are so heavy that they virtually obstruct the hunter on close-range birds. This writer once found himself on the Manitoba prairie with 1⅝-ounce reloads in an 11¼-pound 10-gauge Magnum double when the morning's targets turned out to be teal over small potholes, and, despite the lighter loads, I'm glad there was no one behind me taking pictures or keeping score. That Iron Monster simply unwound too slowly for such swift targets.

Thus, the 3½-inch 10-gauge Magnum must be considered only for highly specialized work beyond, say, 60 yards. Inside that distance, a typical hunter is far better off with a 3-inch 12 because of its nicer handling qualities. Remember that the word *magnum* stamped on a shotshell doesn't mean automatic success. It translates into nothing more than a few extra pellets per load, and the main element in success is still the nut behind the butt — the hunter. Unless he uses intelligence in selecting premium quality ammunition, and unless he can handle the gun as well afield as he does in his daydreams, the entire spectrum of magnum guns and loads is only an ego trip.

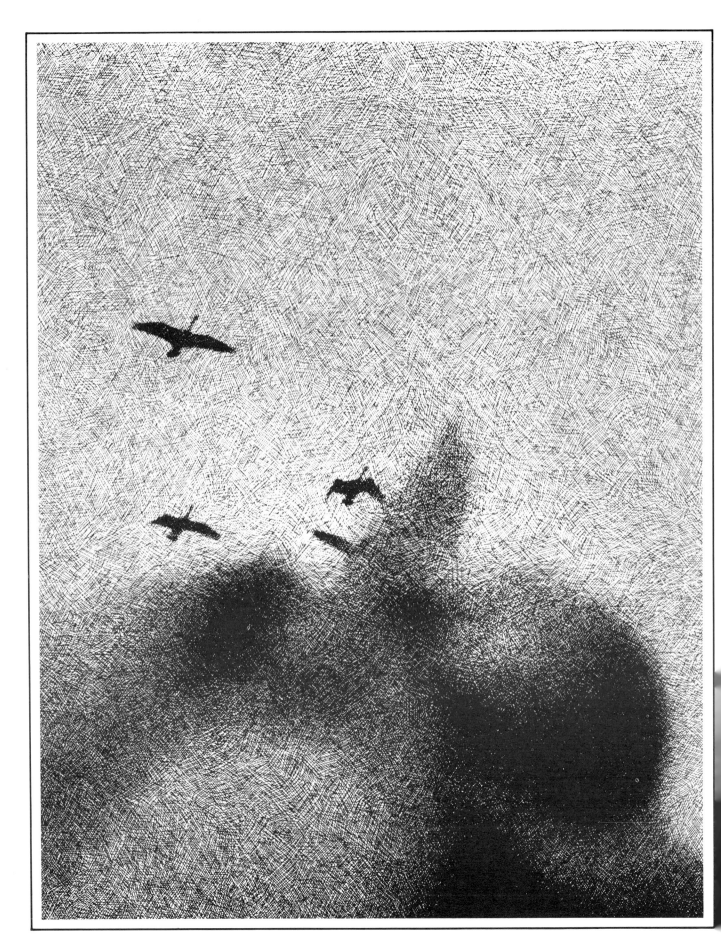

19
Refining the Long-range Shotgun

Deformed pellets and indifferent patterns with large shot sizes are the bane of waterfowlers who strain their skill and equipment for every last yard of range, and their problems aren't solved merely by using heavier and costlier magnum loads. For although advances in the modern shotshell have definitely enhanced the potential for clean kills at considerable range, such features as slow-burning powder, protective plastic wads, copper-plated shot, and pellet-buffering media can't do it all alone. They need help from the gun, specifically the bore.

Before a driver can take over an Indy-type race car, he must hone his personal skill to perfection. But even then his performance will suffer if the pit crew hasn't refined the car's engine. No driver, however great, can get more out of a car than it has to offer. To win at Indianapolis, both the car and the driver must function at their individual best.

The same is true for long-range shotguns: both the load *and* the gun must be refined to reach their individual potential if maximum pattern density and the desirable central thickening are to be achieved for shooting beyond 40–45 yards. Shotshell performance is treated elsewhere herein. This chapter will take an in-depth look at the shotgun's bore and how it can be modified for improved patterning with heavy magnum charges of No. 2s, BBs, and the smaller size buckshot pellets.

CONTRIBUTING FACTORS

A magnum load's patterning potential can be ruined by pellet deformation when the shot charge (1) smashes into the forcing cone immediately after leaving the case mouth, (2) is squeezed and subjected to pressures during bore travel, and (3) slams into the choke constriction when traveling at full speed. Anyone who pushes a tightly fitted cleaning swab through a shotgun barrel can feel those abrupt angles and pressures, and, by using some imagination, can visualize their destructive impact on malleable lead moving hundreds of feet per second. For some pellets, it's like running into a steel wall.

The obvious solution is relieving those bore dimensions and configurations that cause pellet deformation.

FORCING CONE ALTERATIONS

The forcing cone is a short, tapering segment of the barrel just ahead of the chamber. Its purpose is to funnel the ejecta smoothly into the narrower bore as it comes from the generously sized chamber, but, alas, in many shotguns the forcing cone is cut so short that

---

The internal dimensions of a shotgun barrel can be modified so that a minimum number of pellets will be deformed, thus producing better patterns.

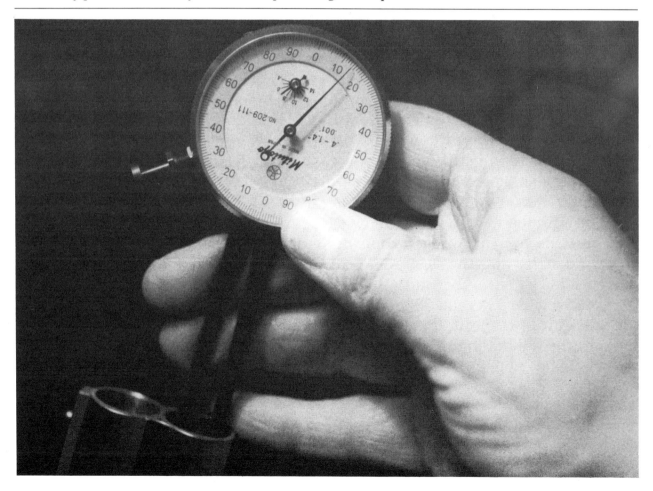

it becomes an abrupt, circumferential impediment. When the emerging shot charge smashes into such a short, abrupt cone, it is slowed briefly and all sorts of pellet-deforming pressures apply. Some deformation occurs when the leading and outer pellets contact the cone's surface; some occurs when the shot mass is compressed as it funnels into the bore; and some is caused by the onrushing wads which, driven by ever-expanding powder gases, continue to exert a rear-end pressure.

The first important step in refining any specialized long-range waterfowl gun is lengthening the forcing cone for a smoother chamber-to-bore transition. Some hunters mistakenly believe that regulating the choke constriction is the primary consideration, but such work can't contribute much if the pellets are still being deformed by a short, steep forcing cone.

Although there is a slight trend to longer forcing cones in today's gunmaking industry, many mass-produced shotguns have cones no longer than ½ to ⅝ inch. A forcing cone of just ⅝ inch can deliver honest full-choke patterns of 70 percent at 40 yards with copper-plated or high-antimony shot; however, reaching those highly desirable figures of 85 to 90 percent or better with magnum loads through such short forcing cones is difficult to accomplish even with buffered loads.

Forcing cones lengthened anywhere from 1 to 2 inches almost invariably help to improve pattern density by funneling the payload more gradually into the bore. A forcing cone of 1½ to 2 inches is appropriate for magnum loads of heavy waterfowling pellets such as BBs and 2s as well as No. 4 buckshot. Practically any good gunsmith can lengthen a gun's forcing cone provided he has the reamers, which are available in 10, 12, 16, and 20 gauge, plus .410 bore, from Brownells, Inc., Route 2, Box 1, Montezuma, Iowa 50171. However, the work is done regularly by Walker Arms Company, Inc., Highway 80 West, Selma, Alabama 36701, whose founder, Ralph T. Walker, was a pioneer in this field. Hunters without any specialized local services available to them can contact Walker Arms for current prices and other information.

Just how much improvement can one expect from a lengthened forcing cone? My own testing indicates that a jump of 10 to 15 percentage points is common, with added density possible if one is willing to spend time in trial-and-error patterning to find a pet load

The forcing cone is a tapered segment between the chamber and bore; its purpose is to funnel the pellets smoothly into the smaller-diameter bore. By lengthening the standard forcing cone from its factory dimensions of about ½" or ⅝" to about 1½" or 2", fewer pellets will be deformed.

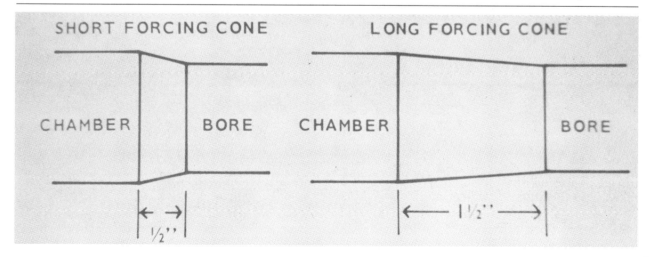

that jibes perfectly with a given barrel. To illustrate, let's consider the before-and-after results obtained by a pair of my personal guns that were given 2-inch forcing cones by Walker Arms. One of the guns was a standard-chambered (2¾″) Remington 12-gauge Model 1100 with a 28-inch full-choke barrel; the other was a Belgian-made Browning A-5 Magnum with a 32-inch full-choke barrel.

Before the longer cones were cut, the Remington M1100 averaged 77 percent at 40 yards using this selected handload:

Winchester 2¾″ AA case
Winchester 209 primer
36.0 gr. HS-7 powder
Winchester WAA12R wad
1½ oz. Lawrence Magnum No. 2 shot
Velocity: 1,265 f.p.s.
Pressure: 10,500 l.u.p.

Seventy-seven percent is excellent performance for a 1½-ounce load of black shot through the ⅝-inch forcing cone of a production gun. But after the forcing cone was lengthened to 2 inches, the very same reload jumped to 90 percent, on the average, with individual patterns going as high as 94 percent! Moreover, the important center density improved to ensure more remaining pellets in the 30-inch-diameter mass beyond 40 yards. With No. 2 shot, this average increase represents an additional 12 to 15 more pellets, which is a meaningful energy increase per pattern.

A shotgun's forcing cone is lengthened by a gunsmith using a T-handle wrench and tapered reamers.

The Browning A-5 Magnum followed suit. It had always been reluctant to pattern well with 1⅞-ounce loads, and with its original ½-inch forcing cone it barely averaged 70 percent using the best reload that testing could uncover:

Federal 3″ plastic case
Federal 209 primer
39.0 gr. Blue Dot powder
Remington RP-12 wad
1⅞ oz. Lawrence Magnum No. 2 shot
Velocity: 1,235 f.p.s.
Pressure: 10,500 p.s.i.

After the 2-inch cone had been reamed, the Browning averaged 80 percent, with some patterns reaching 84–85 percent. On the basis of a 10 percent average gain, the longer forcing cone contributed 15 to 17 more pellets to each pattern. And, here again, the center density was enhanced.

Long forcing cones also improve the performance of factory ammunition. By all theoretical considerations, for instance, Federal's Premium buffered load with 1⅞ ounces of copper-plated BBs should give exceptional patterns for long-range goose shooting; however, those loads averaged on-

---

Screw-in choke tubes, such as these Winchokes in a Model 101 Winchester Waterfowl gun, make it easy for hunters to experiment with different constrictions to find their best patterns.

ly 69–70 percent through the Browning A-5 Magnum while the gun still had its ½-inch forcing cone. When patterned later through the same gun's recut 2-inch forcing cone, the Federal Premium loads rose to an 85 percent average with excellent center density. This puts 12 to 14 more BBs into the main mass, meaning close to 150 more foot-pounds of energy at 60 yards (since a BB fired at a muzzle velocity of 1,300 f.p.s. still carries about 12 foot-pounds of energy at 60 yards).

Thus, the patterning advantages of long forcing cones is obvious with heavy loads of coarse pellets. No waterfowl gun is complete without it if the hunter thinks in terms of optimum pattern density for today's high-flying birds.

THE BACKBORED BARREL

The term backbored is somewhat of a popular misnomer applied to shotgun bores. What it really means is to modify a shotgun by enlarging its bore diameter. A typical American-made 12-gauge, for example, will have a bore diameter of 0.750 to 0.730 inch, and enlarging that to, say, 0.740 inch or more is, in the parlance of the industry, backboring. (At one time, the word overboring was used instead, but it tended to have a negative

The Invector choke system employed by Browning leaves the muzzle with trim, clean lines as the tube fits entirely inside the muzzle.

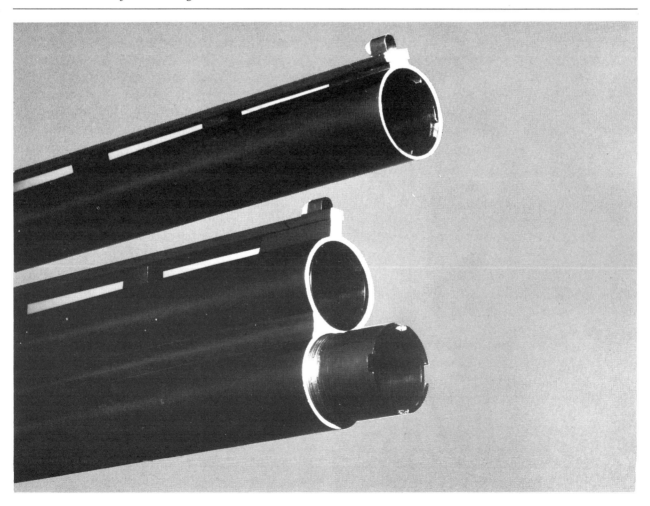

connotation because the public equated the prefix over- with excessive boring and caused them to shy away before learning what it is all about.)

An enlarged shotgun bore relieves pressure on the payload and reduces pellet deformation as well as recoil. There is nothing radically new about the concept, which traces back at least to the 1920s. The reason why it catches so many hunters by surprise today is because they have always taken the smoothbore for granted and have not followed the sophisticated advances in experimentation and performance.

During the 1920s, however, the Ansley H.

Fox Gun Company of Philadelphia offered a waterfowling model known as the Super Fox or HE grade built for the then-new 3-inch 12-gauge Magnum, and these guns reportedly had a taper-bored or oversized bore to accommodate the heavy shot charges. Whether they all were overbored is a moot question. Burt Becker, who worked for Fox on the long-range doubles, also did some independent gun building with Fox barreled actions, and he became famous for the pair of 3-inch 12s with enlarged bores that he made for Nash Buckingham.

Likewise, special overbored barrels were listed for Remington Model 31 and Model 11

This 85 percent pattern was recorded at 40 yards from the Browning A-5 Magnum after its forcing cone had been lengthened to 2 inches. Prior to the modification, the same gun/load duo barely did 70 percent!

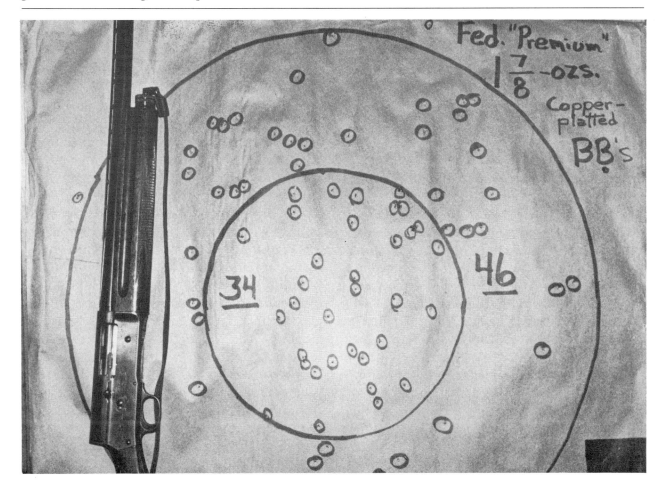

12-gauge shotguns during the middle and late 1930s, apparently to do a better job with the high-velocity, 1¼-ounce duck loads then coming onto the market. Unfortunately, few hunters took advantage of the Remington optional barrel. The point is that backboring isn't a new or dubious shotgun bore alteration. It was merely forgotten by all but a few, and, more precisely, totally unknown to millions who are only now catching up with the concept.

On a technical basis, enlarging a shotgun's bore for today's magnum loads is quite justifiable. The original bore sizes were never intended for such massive shot charges. The practice is especially apropos in long-chambered shotguns like the 3½-inch 10 gauge, the 3-inch 12, and definitely the 3-inch 20. Our current standard bore diameters stem from a time when 10-gauge shells were only 2½ to 2⅞ inches long and held but 1¼ ounces of shot. At the same time, the 12 gauge was just a 2½-incher seldom loaded with more than 1 to 1⅛ ounces of shot, and the 20 gauge measured just 2½ inches and hosted ⅞ ounce of shot. These lighter charges patterned nicely in such bore diameters as a nominal 0.775 inch for the 10 gauge, 0.730 inch for the 12, and 0.615 inch for the 20. As payloads became heavier, however, and as the velocities ran significantly higher due to the introduction of progressive-burning powders, the old bore dimensions seemed too tight to shotgun technicians, and they found that enlarging the bore by 0.005 to 0.010 inch enhanced patterns by allowing a smoother ejecta flow.

The guru among backboring specialists is Stan Baker, of 5303 Roosevelt Way N.E., Seattle, Washington 98105. Baker began by applying the backbore concept to trap guns for less recoil and better handicap patterns, but he has also applied it to hunting guns for significantly improved percentages and tighter core densities with magnum rounds of coarse pellets. One noteworthy example was featured in *Waterfowler's World* (October–November 1983), a magazine dedicated to duck and goose hunters. The episode began with an Ithaca Mag-10, which, with Federal 2¼-ounce Premium loads of copper-plated BBs, was printing very weak center densities at just 40 yards despite an overall efficiency of roughly 82 percent. Baker backbored the barrel to a uniform 0.780 inch diameter and lengthened the forcing cone to 1½ inches. Then, with Baker's own choke tube (0.730 inch diameter) in place, the same Mag-10 and Federal ammo jumped from 82 to 94 percent overall, and the core picked up about 40 percent more pellets. The original gun/load combination had put 64 BBs into the 20-inch-diameter core the experimenter was using, while the refined bore placed 91 BBs from identical loads into the same area. That improvement enriches long-range potential, indeed!

THE AMAZING BAKER BORE 84

Until recently, barrelsmiths took conservative steps in backboring shotgun barrels. A normal 12-gauge bore would be opened from 0.729 inch to 0.740 inch, and anything larger than 0.745 inch was seldom attempted. Hunters and trap shooters feared velocity losses. In 1984, however, Baker took a revolutionary step and announced an amazing *12-gauge* barrel with a basic 0.800 inch-diameter bore. That, of course, is a full 0.025 inch *larger than a 10 gauge's* standard bore diameter, and it represents an enlargement of 0.070 to 0.075 inch over the current 12-gauge bore diameters of 0.725 to 0.730 inch as employed by the sporting arms industry.

At first glance, a hunter is inclined to think the BB-84 is a joke; that powder gases would seep around the wads to lower velocities and ruin patterns. The gun's maw is cavernous, to say the least, especially when one is thinking in terms of the standard 12-gauge. Viewing the barrel from the breech end shows that the bore is little more than an extension of the chamber — there is no forcing cone.

But does performance suffer mightily from the significantly enlarged bore? Not on your life. In fact, velocities *and* patterns are improved!

Personally, I've used a 0.800 inch-diameter Baker Bore 84 barrel to shoot some of the tightest patterns I've ever seen with short magnums. Working with a 30-inch BB-84 on my Remington M1100, I got consistent patterns of 84 percent at 40 yards with Remington 1½-ounce Nitro Magnums filled with black No. 2s, and Winchester Super Double-X loads pushing 1½ ounces of copper-plated 4s averaged 89 percent with some individual clusters topping 90 percent. This patterning was done with a Baker choke tube having a diameter of 0.720 inch, which is about 0.080 inch tighter than the bore. Formerly, such a radical bore/choke difference would have been considered overchoke, but it isn't on the BB-84.

What about velocities? They are amazingly faster in the 0.800-inch 12-gauge bore than they are in the standard bore diameters, strange as that may seem. Loads will put on anywhere from 25 to 50 f.p.s. in the big Baker Bore 84. For example, a Peters 3 drams equivalent load with 1⅛ ounces of No. 7½ shot did 1,241 f.p.s., on the average, for five shots through a standard-sized over-under with 30-inch barrels, but, on the same chronograph setup, shells from the same box of Peters ammunition averaged 1,285 f.p.s. through the BB-84. Short magnums cataloged at about 1,260 f.p.s. in 30-inch barrels did 1,300 f.p.s. from the 0.800-inch tube.

How can we explain this seeming anomaly? By a combination of two factors: first, the powder gases have a wider ejecta base upon which to push. This makes the transfer of chemical energy to kinetic energy more effi-

cient, and it is helped by the flanged, gas-sealing wads so universally employed these days. The old card/filler stacks of yesteryear would be inefficient in the oversized bore. Secondly, the wider bore offers less friction. This reduced friction factor may come into play more importantly during the last half of the ejecta's bore travel than the first half, but the absence of a heavy circumferential pressure on the wad finds gases being used to accelerate the payload rather than having to fight friction.

The backbored, alias overbored, shotgun barrel is getting some attention from advanced shooters and specialty gunsmiths. Its use is spreading in clay target circles. The Remington single-shot Model 870 Competition already has a 0.740-inch bore, and the Perazzi MX-3 competition guns are also coming to these shores from Italy with larger than normal bores. I fully expect that gunmakers in general will start thinking about revamping their bore diameters to suit the heavier shot charges now in vogue. And why not? High-powered automobiles have different cylinder designs than the Model T Ford had. Perhaps one day in the not-too-distant future, magnum-grade hunting guns will come with bigger bores for greater efficiency and less recoil. Until then, specialists like Stan Baker can help wring near perfection from shotguns intended for ultra-long-range shooting.

CHOKE ALTERATIONS

Choke is a word that describes a narrowing of the bore at the muzzle of a shotgun to influence pattern density. The choke constriction does this (at least theoretically) by giving pellets an inward velocity according to the amount and angle of constriction. In general, more constriction means that more pellets will be angled into a narrow, compact cluster, and the less constriction there is, the less likely it is for pellets to remain closely bunched.

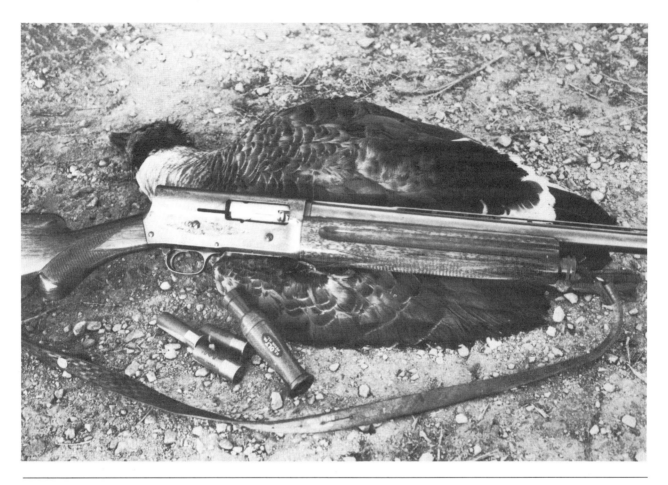

The purpose of barrel modification, of course, is better results in the field. It all paid off on a honker dropped cleanly.

The various degrees of choke used today, along with the percentage of shot they are supposed to put into a 30-inch-diameter circle at 40 yards, are as follows:

Extra Full	80% or more
Full Choke	70% to 79%
Improved Modified	65% to 69%
Modified	55% to 64%
Improved Cylinder	45% to 54%
Skeet Choke	35% to 44%
Cylinder Bore	34% or less

Waterfowlers work mainly with guns choked modified or tighter, and those with full-choke or extra-full-choke constrictions are the most difficult to control. Shotgun barrels are not only individualistic, but the tighter a barrel is constricted, the more such a choke begins to act as another obstruction. Heavy loads of coarse pellets or buckshot don't always respond to them — they have difficulty exiting smoothly. Indeed, a tight full or extra-full choke practically retards the payload, causing jamming, and the abrupt angle can give the pellets excessive inward velocity so that they jostle each other and exit as a jumbled mess. This condition is commonly known as overchoke.

Thus, the barrels with the most constriction, or choke, don't always shoot the tightest patterns. There is such a thing as too much choke for gun/load compatibility. And the unfortunate idea that 12 gauges will shoot like rifles if their muzzle won't accept a dime is sheer nonsense; it leaves no room for considerations of overchoke or gun/load harmony. The only way to determine a gun's actual patterning performance is to pattern and measure the results.

On this writer's rack is an over-under with one barrel choked to 0.680 inch for a constriction of about 0.045 inch. That falls into the extra-full category purely on the basis of dimension, as normal full-choke constrictions for the 12-gauge run between 0.035 and 0.040 inch. Typical hunters swoon when they see that tube and muzzle that "won't take a dime." And the barrel does shoot very tight patterns with trap loads using 1- or 1⅛-ounce charges of fine No. 8s which funnel through like sand through an hourglass. But that same barrel has never done over 60 percent with high-velocity or magnum waterfowl loads pushing coarse shot or the smaller buckshot numbers. Such powerful loads don't squeeze down and flow smoothly through the tight taper, and the pellets scatter due to deformation and/or jamming and jostling.

It has also been argued that pellets take on a spin (precession) as they rumble through a vibrating barrel and up the incline of a choke's taper, and that the spin carries them away from the bore's axis like a baseball pitcher's curve ball. Thus, there is much more to a consideration of choke than tightness.

There are a couple of ways to refine a shotgun's choke influence. One is by matching the load to the choke; the other is matching the choke to the load.

The first method is done by testing a multitude of loads and evaluating them according to the steps in chapter 9. This can involve a lot of shooting, or the very first load tried may do splendidly. It's all trial-and-error experimenting. Barrels are fussy, physical

laws unto themselves, and hunters who have never before done any investigative work with smoothbores are always amazed when they find how much better one or two particular loads will work than all the others.

Many hunters don't enjoy trial-and-error patterning, of course, and they'll reach their goal quicker by selecting a load and having a knowledgeable barrelsmith regulate the choke for better results. In the case of obese magnum loads, this often means having the tight constriction relieved for easier payload passage. When such choke alterations are prescribed, have the barrelsmith remove choke judiciously as you fire test patterns along the way. Taking choke out is easy, but once it's gone, it can't be replaced.

There is a lingering idea that long, tapering, highly polished chokes invariably give maximum long-range patterns. Hunters envision the pellets squeezing together gradually in such a lengthy taper and virtually flowing into a tightly packed in-flight mass. However, barrel specialists, especially those who backbore shotguns, have been finding otherwise. They now believe that a short, abrupt taper does better because the pellets spend less time under bore/choke pressure; hence, there is less deformation. It has also been noted that short, abrupt chokes need less constriction to deliver a given pattern than do long, tapering ones. What finally works to perfection, then, is often not what waterfowlers have traditionally believed to be the best.

The current proliferation of screw-in choke tubes makes it easy for waterfowlers to experiment inexpensively with choke/load combos. By the simple expedient of switching tubes and shooting a few patterns, one can find the most efficient tube for any particular load without incurring gunsmithing expenses. When Winchester announced the Model 101 Waterfowl gun, for example, I received one on consignment and found it came with four

Having a long forcing cone cut into magnum shotguns will normally improve pattern density with coarse, large shot for optimum energy at extreme ranges.

choke tubes: modified, improved modified, full, and extra-full. Initial patterning with the extra-full tube — which is the one most casual hunters would have used without question — showed it did poorly with all manner of 1⅞-ounce loads of 2s and BBs. The patterns had all the characteristics of an overchoke: jumbled pellet distributions with percentages no better than ordinary modified choke. The full-choke tube did somewhat better, reaching 69–70 percent with a higher core density, but there was still a lot to be desired for optimum long-range goose hunting. The breakthrough came when the improved modified tube was used: patterns jumped to a solid 75 percent and the core densities reached a 2.5 rating. By relieving choke constriction a bit, patterns increased by 12 to 15 percentage points over the tighter extra-full tube's output.

Gunmakers are leaping onto the choke tube bandwagon, and it won't be too many seasons before practically all hunting-grade shotguns will have them as either standard or optional features. But what about yesterday's gun, that weatherbeaten old favorite with which you wouldn't dream of parting? Perhaps three quarters of them can be fitted with screw-in tubes as add-on installations. This applies to side-by-sides and over-unders as well as single-barreled repeaters. The 25 percent that shouldn't have screw-in chokes added are those with thin barrel walls as found on some older doubles and lightweight repeaters, plus various frilly foreign guns.

One firm installing screw-in chokes for all gun types is Walker Arms as mentioned earlier relative to long forcing cones. Called the Walker Choke, it can be had in Winchoke-type tubes or Walker's own line of full-thread tubes that fit completely inside the barrel without leaving a knurled gripping ring outside the muzzle. Walker can fit this installation for Walker full-thread tubes to any safe

10-, 12-, 16-, or 20-gauge gun, and the franchise is being extended to certain selected gunsmiths nationwide. Of interest to shotgunners is the fact that Walker full-thread tubes are being cut with the conical-parallel interior rather than just the normal conical taper. In many instances, the short (about half-inch) parallel flat does seem to lend consistency and uniformity to patterns.

Walker also has a service that polishes the bore to maximum smoothness, and this, combined with a lengthened forcing cone and Walker choke system, produces an all-purpose barrel. I had a 28-inch Remington M1100 12-gauge barrel that Walker cut to 26 inches, fitted with a Walker full-thread choke, honed, and reamed for a longer forcing cone. The barrel shoots like a dream, and is one of the few in which an extra-full choke tube patterns as it should.

Other gunsmiths who do quality jobs of installing screw-in chokes of their own design are Stan Baker, who was also mentioned earlier, and Jess Briley, 1085 "C" Gessner, Houston, Texas 77055.

Thus, refining a shotgun's bore for absolutely optimum center density with magnum loads and coarse shot and buckshot means more than just selecting a tightly bored barrel and the heaviest magnum loads obtainable. Although widely done, that bland and unscientific approach may be an average waterfowler's biggest mistake. As I've just been discussing, the reverse approach to barrels now seems to be the way to go. Rather than looking for the tightest bores and chokes, a waterfowler interested in squeezing every last percentage point in pattern density from a shotgun should begin to understand that some cone, bore, and choke relief is more inclined to jibe with the robust magnum loads in use today.

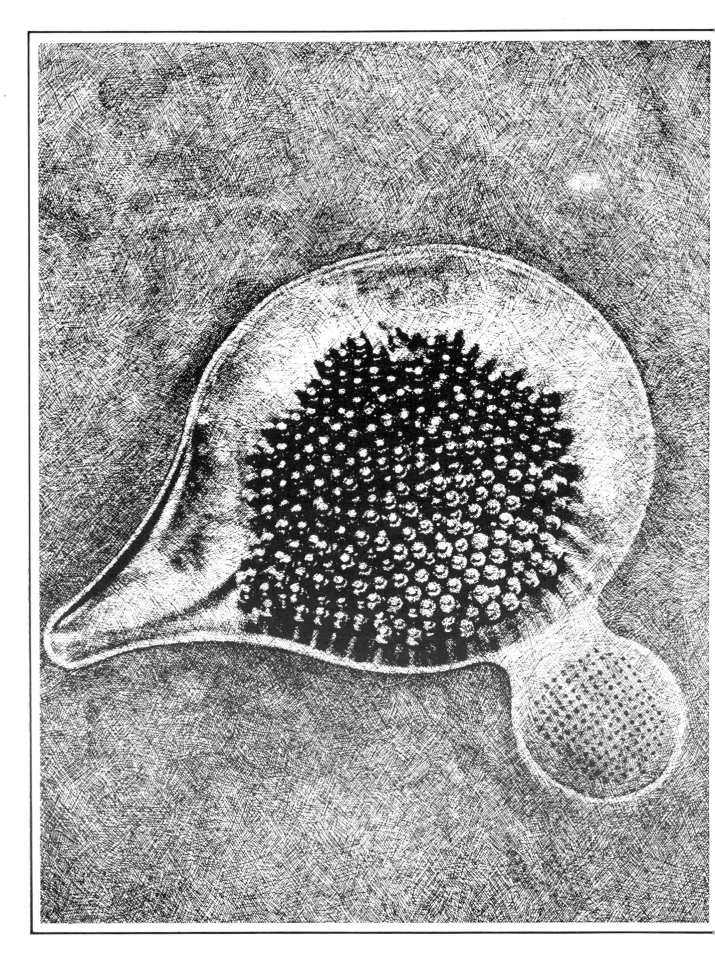

20
Handloads:
Basic Concepts

Hunters often become handloaders to save money. Depending on the local prices of components, which can vary significantly, one can cut his ammunition expenses by 25 to 50 percent per box. That doesn't include the amortization of the press, of course, nor does it include whatever accessories or overhead expenses come into play. All of that must be considered on a long-term basis. What makes handloading pay off is your own labor and simple machinery. What keeps the price of factory loads high are union wages, elaborate machinery, and corporate profits.

Waterfowlers, in particular, can turn handloading to their advantage, saving money while, at the same time, customizing their creations for improved and specialized performance. But while the economies of reloading need no further elaboration, the matter of load selection and assembly do require in-depth commentary. Indeed, one of the first questions a potential or beginning handloader asks is, "What load should I use?" The following information is presented to give some guidance in that direction.

TWO APPROACHES

Handloads for waterfowling can be approached from two directions: one is something we can call the basic concept, meaning utilization of only the simplest methods and a minimum of components and assembly work. The second approach involves subtleties, namely, the sophisticated concepts involving special wads, velocity levels, and buffering. Each is a study unto itself, and, for starters, some experience with the basic concepts is recommended before a further step is taken to more sophisticated recipes. This first section on reloads will cover basic loads and loading.

The idea that the loads and practices to be discussed herein are merely basic or simple need not discourage anyone. They can handle perhaps 90 percent of all modern waterfowling needs. The more sophisticated concepts to be covered in the next chapter are mainly important for ultra-long-range winggunning on geese where optimum pattern density is vital. For the typical duck hunter who doesn't shoot beyond 55 yards or so, there are a lot of highly effective handloads which, easily and inexpensively assembled, will serve admirably.

Essentially, a shotshell's basic components are a hull, a primer, some powder, a wad, and shot. There's nothing fancy about that. However, fundamental though such components are, different combinations produce different performances. Each shotgun barrel is a unique entity, and it can be extremely individualistic about which loads it will handle best. There is no reason to believe that a reload that crumples ducks from your buddy's gun will pattern the same from your gun. Some patterning is always recommended to "see how she shoots."

But a handloader must start somewhere, and the recipes given here are suggested for the respective gauges because they have performed consistently for this writer in a number of different guns.

Several points must be made before delving into specific handloads. One is that nothing is promised if the handloader uses *chilled shot*. Basic handloads contain bare pellets, and the absence of buffering material invites deformation. Too, many heavy hunting loads must perforce use wads with little or no cushioning section, and that intensifies the impact of firing setback on lower pellet layers. Basic handloads that employ hard, *high-antimony magnum black shot, and copper-plated pellets* pay the greatest dividends in improved density and evenness of distribution.

Secondly, many of these loads will have chamber pressures approaching maximum for that respective gauge. The reason is that cold weather bleeds something from ammo, and laboratory tests and field results have shown that shotshells with chamber pressures averaging no higher than 7,000

Every handloader should begin with a scale to make certain of his powder and shot charge weights. For shotshell reloaders, a scale that runs to 1000 grains is suggested, as that gives room to weigh most of the commonly used shot charges.

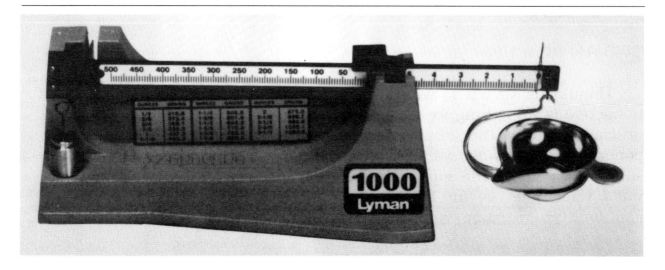

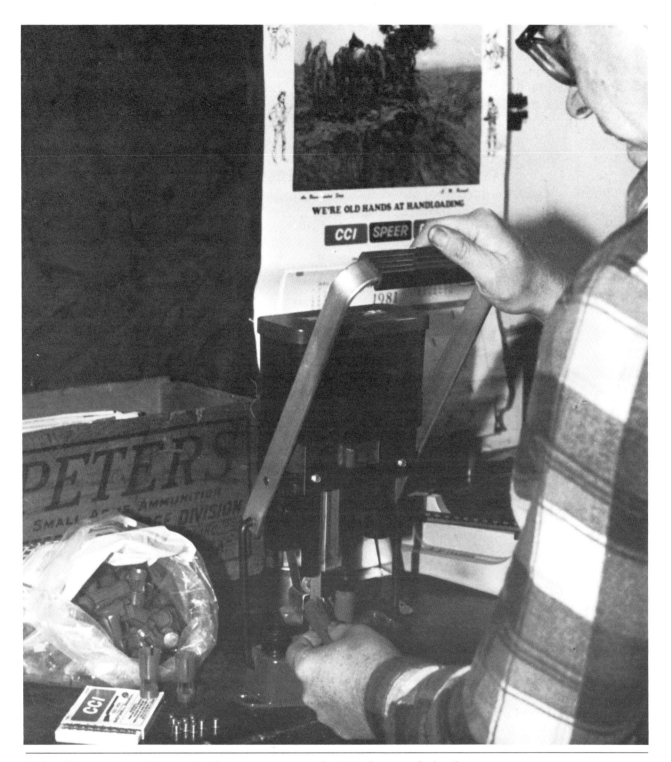

*Reloading ammunition not only saves money, but it also can help the
hunter develop specialized loads for his particurlar gun and hunting conditions.
This handloader is using the inexpensive, but extremely efficient,
LOAD-ALL single-stage press from Lee Precision.*

l.u.p. or 7,500 p.s.i. can give faulty performances such as erratic ignition, wide pressure deviations, and velocity loss when temperatures drop below freezing. Some low-pressure loads will "bloop," leaving wads stuck in the bore — very dangerous! When cold weather becomes a factor, then, maximum or near-maximum chamber pressures promise the least pressure/velocity loss.

The following data, which were run for me at Winchester by M. W. Jordan, prove the reality of ballistics losses under cold conditions. A controlled reload was fired first after being cooled to 0°F and then after being held at 70°F. The control reload was one listed in the Winchester Ball Powder Manual:

Winchester 2¾" AA case
Winchester 209 primer
33.0 gr. 540 Ball powder
Win. WAA12F114 wad
1¼ oz. shot
Pressure: 10,400 l.u.p.
Velocity: 1,330 f.p.s.

After being brought to the respective temperatures by storage, the lab tests gave these results:

At 70°F

Pressure: 10,975 p.s.i.
Velocity: 1,322 f.p.s.

At 0°F

Pressure: 9,375 p.s.i.
Velocity: 1,235 f.p.s.

Thus, going from 70°F (at which temperature many lab tests are run for reloading handbook data) to 0°F caused an average velocity loss of 87 f.p.s. and a pressure drop, also on the average, of 1,600 p.s.i. It's a good argument for selecting cold-weather reloads that have maximum or near-maximum chamber pressures and reasonably swift muz-

zle velocities. They all lose something to cold, but the fast, high-pressure reloads have more left than the slower, low-pressure rounds.

The empty hull's condition is also a factor in ballistics. A good crimp is needed to hold against primer thrust and early combustion so that the proper pressure curve can be reached with the slow-burning powders needed in high-velocity and magnum reloads. If the crimp is weak and yields to primer thrust, the combustion space will be enlarged too rapidly and the heat/pressure peak won't be reached for optimum burning efficiency. This means that fresh, crisp, once-fired hulls are best suited for waterfowling reloads because they still have the crimp strength to resist the initial jolt of primer detonation and early combustion. Hulls with use-weakened crimps, therefore, will often produce lower pressure/velocity levels than once-fired hulls of the same brand with the same components. Therefore, hunters are making a mistake if they reload their old tired hulls for duck hunting and keep the newer stiff ones for trap and skeet. It should be the other way around to ensure optimum ballistics. All data in handloading manuals is compiled with once-fired hulls.

Finally, handloaders must understand that switching components will alter ballistics, sometimes drastically. Going from one brand of primer to another can raise or lower pressures, and, since velocity is a product of pressure, primer substitutions will obviously affect velocities and, perhaps, patterns. Wads also have different pressure-building characteristics, as do hulls. A Federal field-style plastic case, for example, will show lower pressures than a Peters blue target case when all other components are the same. That doesn't mean the Federal field-style plastic case isn't any good, of course. Just the opposite is true: it can be used for many very effective waterfowling reloads because of its spaciousness. The point is that ballistics differ. Thus, if a handloader wants the ballistics for a published reload, he must stick with the stipulated components. Handloading waterfowl loads can be a safe and satisfying hobby, but not when done carelessly.

THE STANDARD 20 GAUGE

The standard 20 gauge is the smallest legitimate waterfowl load. Do not expect whistling-swift velocities from its 2¾-inch hull, as there isn't enough room for generous powder charges, and the small bore diameter restricts gas flow. Nevertheless, by working near maximum pressure levels, the standard 20 can generate enough velocity for adequate penetration with the listed selected data for 2s, 3s, 4s, and 5s at sensible ranges suitable to 1- and 1⅛-ounce shot charges. Ditto for 6s in the modified chokes for 30–35 yards.

This pair of big Canadas fell to 1³⁄₁₆-ounce reloads through a 20-gauge Ruger Red Label over-under.

Don't let the high pressure readings frighten you. The 20 gauge is made for slightly higher chamber pressures than the 10 and 12 gauges to generate adequate velocities in a small bore. Average working chamber pressures of 11,500 l.u.p. or 12,000 p.s.i. are safe in the 20's standard-length and magnum-length hulls:

STANDARD-LENGTH
20-GAUGE RELOADS (2¾")

Winchester 2¾" AA case
Winchester 209 primer
16.5 gr. Herco powder
Remington SP-20 wad
1 oz. shot
Pressure: 10,000 p.s.i.
Velocity: 1,165 f.p.s.

Federal 2¾" field-style plastic case
Federal 209 primer
22.0 gr. Blue Dot powder
Remington SP-20 wad
1 oz. shot
Pressure: 11,000 p.s.i.
Velocity: 1,220 f.p.s.

Remington 2¾" RXP target case
Winchester 209 primer
25.0 gr. 571 Ball or HS-7 powder
Winchester WAA20F1 wad
1 oz. shot
Pressure: 10,900 l.u.p.
Velocity: 1,240 f.p.s.

SHORT MAGNUM
20-GAUGE RELOADS (2¾")

Winchester 2¾" AA case
Federal 209 primer
24.0 gr. 571 Ball or HS-7 powder
Remington RP-20 wad
1⅛ oz. shot
Pressure: 11,000 l.u.p.
Velocity: 1,175 f.p.s.

Federal 2¾″ plastic target case
Federal 209 primer
21.5 gr. Blue Dot powder
Remington SP-20 wad
1⅛ oz. shot
Pressure: 10,400 p.s.i.
Velocity: 1,150 f.p.s.

Federal 2¾″ field-style plastic case
Federal 209 primer
23.0 gr. Blue Dot powder
Remington SP-20 wad
1⅛ oz. shot
Pressure: 10,600 p.s.i.
Velocity: 1,175 f.p.s.

THE 3-INCH 20

While the 3-inch 20-gauge hull offers greater versatility than the standard-length tube, this versatility lies mainly in higher velocities with shot charges lighter than 1¼ ounces. A careful study of published reloading data will disclose that, even with modern slow-burning powders, this shotshell reaches maximum chamber pressures before it generates anything near high velocity with the 1¼-ounce shot charge. To get higher velocities from the 3-inch 20, then, handloaders must use shot charges of 1³⁄₁₆ or 1⅛ ounces instead of the popular 1¼ ounces. Reducing the 3-inch 20's payload by ¹⁄₁₆ to ⅛ ounce isn't all wrong or all bad. Many guns will pattern better with the slightly lighter loads, and that, plus higher muzzle velocities, will enhance

Copper-plated pellets are a boon to improved patterning. Waterfowlers should use them whenever possible in handloads.

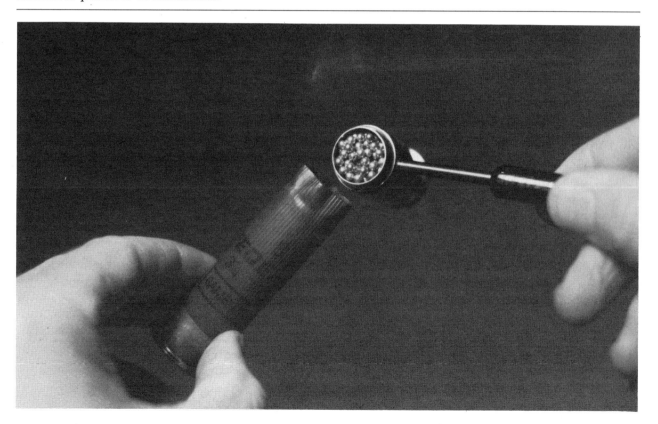

the 3-inch 20's potency with 4s and 5s. The hunter won't sacrifice much, if anything, in the way of density, and he'll gain in pellet speed and energy. Hunters who opt purely for velocity will be interested in the special 1-ounce load heading the following list:

3-INCH 20-GAUGE RELOADS

Federal 3" plastic case (paper base)
Federal 209 primer
26.0 gr. SR-4756 powder
Federal 20S1 wads
1 oz. shot
Pressure: 8,900 l.u.p.
Velocity: 1,315 f.p.s.

Remington 3" Unibody plastic case
Winchester 209 primer
19.5 gr. SR-4756 powder
Remington SP-20 wad
1⅛ oz. shot
Pressure: 10,900 l.u.p.
Velocity: 1,186 f.p.s.

Winchester 3" compression-formed case
Winchester 209 primer
26.0 gr. Blue Dot powder
Remington SP-20 wad
1⅛ oz. shot
Pressure: 10,000 p.s.i.
Velocity: 1,275 f.p.s.

Another of the writer's favorite reloads for the 3-inch 12 gauge: 39.0 grains of Blue Dot powder in the Federal plastic case (paper base) with the Winchester WAA12R wad and 1⅝ ounces of hard, magnum-grade shot. Number 5s are great for ducks in this reload when used through a modified choke barrel.

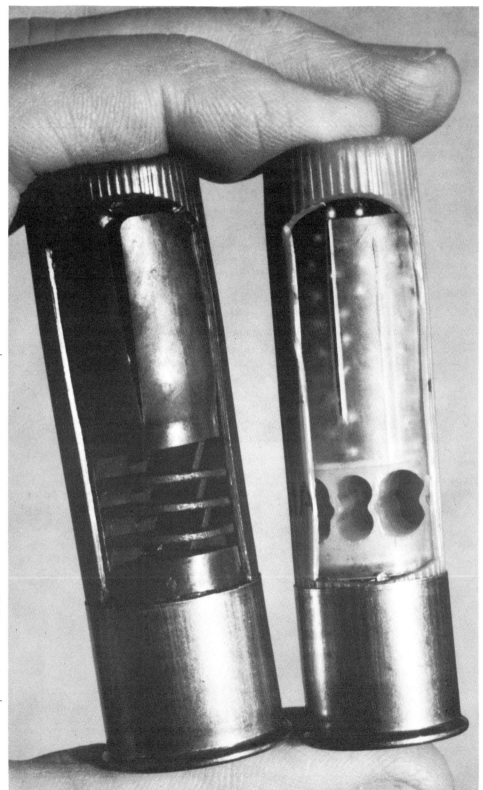

Cutaway views of two hotshot handloads. On the left is a Federal 3-inch 12-gauge Magnum hull with 40.0 grains of Blue Dot powder, the Federal 12S4 wad, and 1³/₈ ounces of hard shot for about 1,350 f.p.s.; on the right is a 3-inch 20-gauge Federal plastic case holding 37.5 grains of Blue Dot powder, a Remington SP-20 wad, and 1³/₁₆ ounces of hard No. 5s for 1,295 f.p.s. Both are hard-hitting loads that pattern well in most full-choked guns with hard black shot or copper-plated pellets.

Federal 3" field-style plastic case
    (paper base)
Federal 209 primer
27.5 gr. Blue Dot powder
Remington RXP-20 wad
1⅛ oz. shot
Pressure: 10,400 p.s.i.
Velocity: 1,285 f.p.s.

Winchester 3" compression-formed case
Winchester 209 primer
27.0 gr. 571 Ball or HS-7 powder
Winchester WAA20 wad
1⅛ oz. shot
Pressure: 11,000 l.u.p.
Velocity: 1,220 f.p.s.

Federal 3" field-style plastic case
    (paper base)
Federal 209 primer
27.5 gr. Blue Dot powder
Remington RXP-20 wad
1³⁄₁₆ oz. shot
Pressure: 11,300 p.s.i.
Velocity: 1,295 f.p.s.

Federal 3" field-style plastic case
    (paper base)
Federal 209 primer
25.0 gr. Blue Dot powder
Remington RXP-20 wad
1¼ oz. shot
Pressure: 10,600 p.s.i.
Velocity: 1,185 f.p.s.

THE FORGOTTEN 16 GAUGE

Although time and technology have ignored the once-popular 16 gauge, its larger bore diameter is more efficient and delivers a shorter shot string than the 3-inch 20. For moderate-range wingshooting, there is nothing more delightful than a 16-gauge side-by-side with 28-inch barrels suitably choked.

Nor are there better reloads than these:

16-GAUGE RELOADS

Federal 2¾" Hi-Power case
Federal 209 primer
19.5 gr. Unique powder
Remington R-16 wad
1⅛ oz. shot
Pressure: 10,800 p.s.i.
Velocity: 1,240 f.p.s.

Winchester 2¾" compression-formed
    case
Winchester 209 primer
28.5 gr. 540 Ball powder
Remington R-16 wad
1⅛ oz. shot
Pressure: 10,300 l.u.p.
Velocity: 1,290 f.p.s.

Federal 2¾" Hi-Power case
CCI 109 primer
28.5 gr. SR-4756 powder
Remington SP-16 wad
1⅛ oz. shot
Pressure: 8,700 l.u.p.
Velocity: 1,320 f.p.s.

Winchester 2¾" compression-formed
    case
Winchester 209 primer
30.5 gr. 571 Ball or HS-7 powder
Remington SP-16 wad
1¼ oz. shot
Pressure: 10,500 l.u.p.
Velocity: 1,230 f.p.s.

THE STANDARD 12 GAUGE

Little need be said to introduce the standard-length 12 gauge. It is the most popular gauge going. And because of that widespread use, handloading data for it abounds. The problem isn't finding good loads, but rather finding some truly outstanding ones like this grouping:

STANDARD-LENGTH
12-GAUGE RELOADS (2¾")

Winchester 2¾" AA case
Federal 209 primer
29.5 gr. SR-7625 powder
Winchester WAA12 Red wad
1¼ oz. shot
Pressure: 10,300 l.u.p.
Velocity: 1,330 f.p.s.

Winchester 2¾" AA case
Winchester 209 Primer
33.0 gr. Ball powder
Winchester WAA12F114 wad
1¼ oz. shot
Pressure: 10,400 l.u.p.
Velocity: 1,330 f.p.s.

Winchester 2¾" AA case
Federal 209 primer
32.5 gr. SR-4756 powder
Winchester WAA12 Red wad
1⅜ oz. shot
Pressure: 10,400 l.u.p.
Velocity: 1,280 f.p.s.

An important part of handloading for cold-weather waterfowling is making sure the load generates enough pressure for adequate downrange performance, positive ignition, and functional reliability in autoloading shotguns. Here, the Benelli kicks out a reload.

Winchester 2¾″ AA case
Federal 209 primer
35.5 gr. 571 Ball or HS-7 powder
Winchester WAA12 Red wad
1⅜ oz. shot
Pressure: 10,500 l.u.p.
Velocity: 1,285 f.p.s.

Federal 2¾″ Gold Medal target case
Federal 209 primer
27.0 gr. Hi-Skor 800-X powder
Winchester WAA12 Red wad
1½ oz. shot
Pressure: 10,800 l.u.p.
Velocity: 1,270 f.p.s.

Winchester 2¾″ AA case
Winchester 209 primer
26.5 gr. 571 Ball powder
Winchester WAA12 Red wad
1½ oz. shot
Pressure: 10,500 l.u.p.
Velocity: 1,260 f.p.s.

THE 3-INCH 12

Handloaders can have a field day with the 3-inch 12-gauge hull. Its versatility extends from super-swift light loads of 1⅜ and 1½ ounces, through medium-weight loads of 1⅝ and 1¾ ounces, to hefty 1⅞-ounces. Although we do not yet have lab data for 2-ounce reloads, that may be just around the corner for the 3-inch 12. However, obese payloads aren't necessarily the forte of the 3-inch 12-gauge hull. Its elongated capacity permits the use of substantially more powder for higher velocities with lighter, albeit still quite adequate, shot charges. With copper-plated pellets that can withstand scorching acceleration without deforming, the 3-inch 12 can add over 100 f.p.s. to the standard 12's muzzle velocities with magnum charges. For example:

3-INCH
12-GAUGE RELOADS

Federal 3″ plastic case (paper base)
Federal 209 primer
43.0 gr. SR-4756 powder
Winchester WAA12 Red wad
1⅜ oz. copper-plated shot
Pressure: 10,800 l.u.p.
Velocity: 1,480 f.p.s.

Federal 3″ plastic case (paper base)
Federal 209 primer
35.0 gr. SR-7625 powder
Federal 12S4 wad
1⅜ oz. shot
Pressure: 10,600 l.u.p.
Velocity: 1,375 f.p.s.

Winchester 3″ compression-formed case
Federal 209 primer
36.0 gr. SR-4756 powder
Winchester WAA12F114 wad
1⅜ oz. shot
Pressure: 10,800 l.u.p.
Velocity: 1,380 f.p.s.

Winchester 3″ compression-formed case
Federal 209 primer
34.0 gr. SR-4756 powder
Remington SP-12 wad
1½ oz. shot
Pressure: 10,900 l.u.p.
Velocity: 1,290 f.p.s.

Winchester 3″ compression-formed case
Winchester 209 primer
40.0 gr. Blue Dot powder
Remington SP-12 wad
1⅝ oz. shot
Pressure: 10,800 p.s.i.
Velocity: 1,300 f.p.s.

Federal 3″ plastic case (paper base)
Federal 209 primer
39.0 gr. Blue Dot powder
Winchester WAA12F114 wad
1⅝ oz. shot
Pressure: 9,900 p.s.i.
Velocity: 1,300 f.p.s.

Federal 3″ plastic case (paper base)
Federal 209 primer
33.0 gr. SR-4756 powder
Remington RP-12 wad
1¾ oz. shot
Pressure: 10,800 l.u.p.
Velocity: 1,180 f.p.s.

Federal 3″ plastic case (paper base)
Federal 209 primer
34.0 gr. Blue Dot powder
Remington RP-12 wad
1⅞ oz. shot
Pressure: 10,300 p.s.i.
Velocity: 1,160 f.p.s.

Winchester 3″ compression-formed case
CCI 109 primer
32.5 gr. Blue Dot powder
Remington RP-12 wad
1⅞ oz. shot
Pressure: 10,400 p.s.i.
Velocity: 1,165 f.p.s.

Remington 3″ Unibody plastic case
Federal 209 primer
29.0 gr. Blue Dot powder
Pacific Green Verelite wad
1⅞ oz. shot
Pressure: 10,600 p.s.i.
Velocity: 1,145 f.p.s.

THE 10-GAUGE MAGNUM

Handloading for the 10-gauge Magnum is a real money-saver. It also allows hunters to work up some lighter loads for those days when the birds are close and 2–2¼ ounces of shot aren't needed:

10-GAUGE
MAGNUM RELOADS

Federal 3½″ plastic case (paper base)
Federal 209 primer
29.5 gr. Hi-Skor 700-X powder
Remington SP-10 wad +
 ⅝ inch of filler
1½ oz. shot
Pressure: 9,900 l.u.p.
Velocity: 1,230 f.p.s.

Federal 3½″ plastic case (paper base)
Federal 209 primer
37.5 gr. Du Pont PB powder
Remington SP-10 wad +
 ⅜ inch of filler
1⅝ oz. shot
Pressure: 9,800 l.u.p.
Velocity: 1,295 f.p.s.

Federal 3½″ plastic case (paper base)
Federal 209 primer
41.0 gr. SR-7625 powder
Remington SP-10 wad +
 ¼ inch of filler
1⅞ oz. shot
Pressure: 9,700 l.u.p.
Velocity: 1,260 f.p.s.

Winchester 3½″ polyformed case
Federal 209 primer
36.0 gr. Du Pont PB powder
Remington SP-10 wad
2 oz. shot
Pressure: 10,000 l.u.p.
Velocity: 1,155 f.p.s.

Remington 3½" case (composition base)
CCI 109 primer
37.5 gr. SR-4756 powder
Remington SP-10 wad
2 oz. shot
Pressure: 9,000 l.u.p.
Velocity: 1,200 f.p.s.

Remington 3½" case (composition base)
CCI 109 primer
43.0 gr. SR-7625 powder
Pacific Versalite wad
2 oz. shot
Pressure: 10,000 l.u.p.
Velocity: 1,250 f.p.s.

Federal 3½" plastic case
Federal 209 primer
44.0 gr. SR-4756 powder
Remington SP-10 wad
2⅛ oz. shot
Pressure: 10,000 l.u.p.
Velocity: 1,230 f.p.s.

Federal 3½" plastic case (paper base)
CCI 109 primer
42.5 gr. SR-4756 powder
Pacific Versalite wad
2¼ oz. shot
Pressure: 10,000 l.u.p.
Velocity: 1,180 f.p.s.

Winchester 3½" polyformed case
Winchester 209 primer
30.5 gr. Hi-Skor 800-X powder
Remington SP-10 wad
2¼ oz. shot
Pressure: 10,000 l.u.p.
Velocity: 1,150 f.p.s.

Federal 3½" plastic case (paper base)
Federal 209 primer
37.5 gr. SR-4756 powder
Pacific Versalite wad
2³/₈ oz. shot
Pressure: 9,600 l.u.p.
Velocity: 1,150 f.p.s.

21
Handloads: Advanced Concepts

The reloads listed in the preceding chapter are mainly for close and intermediate ranges. With rare exceptions, they won't deliver the core densities needed for optimum long-range effectiveness.
As duck and goose hunting ranges go beyond 50–55 yards, advanced concepts must be worked into the loads. Such innovations require a little more time and money than reloads with plain shot charges, but better patterns producing clean, long-range kills make them worth it.

Advanced handloading subtleties designed to tighten patterns do so by (1) preserving pellet form, and (2) reducing pellet spin. Not every method does both, of course, but employing either one successfully is a stride in the right direction.

THE COMPRESSOR INSERT

Perhaps the easiest way to try for improved center densities is with a plastic shotcup insert called the Compressor. Manufactured by Bernie Ferri of Trinidad, Colorado, the Compressor insert is an injection-molded unit that is simply dropped into the empty shotcup before the pellets are added. It has a flat, round base sized for 12-gauge shotcups, and the essential part of it is a hollow, upright post that occupies the center of the shot charge.

The Compressor insert works like this: when the pressures of firing setback and bore travel squeeze upon the shot charge, the hollow, postlike upright gives interior pellets something soft to push in against so they don't mash against each other. To a certain degree the plastic pillar may also deny the abutting pellets a chance to deform by occupying the space into which the pellets would otherwise push. The result of providing inward relief through the shot charge's longitudinal axis is more pellets remaining in-the-round for maximum in-flight ballistics, direction, and concentration.

Exactly what can a Compressor do in heavy hunting loads with coarse pellets or buckshot? A variety of tests with handloads have proved to this writer that they can improve patterns by 10 to 15 percent and, equally important, will often contribute significantly greater core density. One such test involved a 32-inch-barreled Browning A-5 12-gauge Magnum and the following reload:

Federal 3″ plastic case (paper base)
Federal 209 primer
38.5 gr. Blue Dot powder
Remington RP-12 wad
1⅞ No. 2 Magnum shot
 (Lawrence high-antimony)

That is one grain of Blue Dot lighter than the maximum load listed in the *Hercules Reloaders' Guide* for 1,250 f.p.s. and 10,500 p.s.i. That particular load with just 38.5 grains of Blue Dot always chronographed near 1,250 f.p.s. from the 32-inch-barreled Browning, and I didn't bother to try it with the one extra allowable grain of powder.

For whatever reason, that particular Browning never did pattern well with 1⅞-ounce loads, and with this specific handload it averaged just 64– 67 percent even with hard, high-antimony shot. Its core densities were weak and promised little for long-range shooting.

When the Compressor insert was added, however, the patterning performance changed markedly. The average efficiency went from about 66 percent to 76 percent, which is the difference between weak improved modified and strong full choke. Moreover, the thrilling point was that Compressor-equipped reloads

delivered all of the additional pellets to the 15-inch-diameter core! This above all turned things around for the Browning, as the intense central thickening enhanced its long-range potential. Thus, the simple expedient of dropping a Compressor insert into the shotcup can work wonders for any given reload; however, each gun/load combo should still be tested for its individualistic nature.

The Compressor can be used with 10-gauge reloads as well, although it is a bit short. The situation can be remedied by slipping a segment of swizzle stick over the Compressor's upright, thus extending the relief hollow.

High-density granulated polyethylene is used to fill the spaces between pellets to prevent their deforming under setback pressures and to provide some fluidity as they pass through the forcing cone and choke constriction.

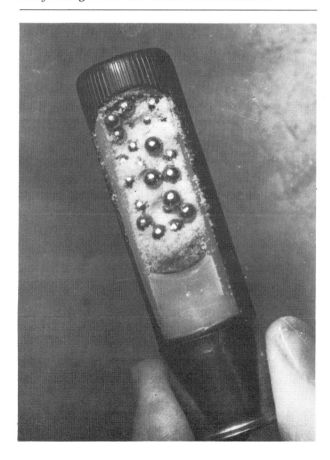

Buckshot loads also respond to the Compressor's presence, especially if the upright is extended by means of the slipover swizzle stick. The buckshot must be loaded singly if they are to pack properly, which requires some careful arranging. But in tests with both No. 00 and No. 4 buckshot, this writer has gotten both increased pattern percentages and more symmetrical distributions using Compressors. Even with the soft buckshot *sans* antimony, 100 percent patterns have appeared. On the other hand, the same reloads with the same soft buckshot did only 50–70 percent when Compressors were omitted.

The results of pressure testing conducted by leading laboratories has indicated that Compressors do not cause increased chamber pressures; therefore, they can be added to favorite handloads without any downward powder adjustments. Because Compressors do take up space, however, some modification of the wad column may be necessary. This generally means going to the next smaller wad in the same family of plastic units.

Compressors are new on the reloading market and may not be distributed widely. Further information can be had from the company: Ferri & Associates, Inc., P.O. Box 769, Trinidad, Colorado 81082.

BUFFERED SHOT CHARGES

It is a moot question as to who made buffered shot charges popular, the commercial loading industry or handloaders? Some writers delved into the subject before Remington and Winchester brought out their buckshot and hunting loads with coarse

---

Comparative patterns showing how the Compressor insert can enhance the center density of patterns for improved long-range density. The pattern on the right was fired with a 1⁷/₈-ounce reload without the Compressor and registered only 41 core hits; the pattern on the left was made with the same gun and reload, except that the reload hosted the Compressor insert, and it put 64 pellets into the core without weakening the annular ring significantly.

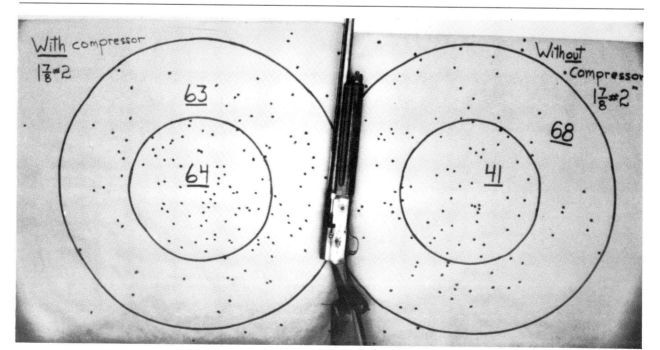

pellets bedded in grex, but most hunters were oblivious to those sophisticated articles and didn't catch up with pellet-bedding until commercial loads of that persuasion began showing up on dealers' shelves. Regardless of who influenced the trend toward buffered shot charges; however, the practice is now widely known among handloading hunters, some of whom approach it in a dangerous, helter-skelter fashion, while others shy away from it for fear of accidentally assembling over-pressured loads.

The first point to be made about buffered handloads is that they should not be indiscriminately assembled by stuffing a granulated material into any reload that happens to be a favorite. Buffering material does cause higher pressures, and, if a given pet reload were already generating maximum chamber pressures for that particjlar gauge, adding buffer would certainly produce excess pressures.

The safest way to handload buffered shotshells is by sticking with published, lab-tested data. Not very much of this is available. However, one upper Midwest shotgun supply company has been built around specialty concepts, and it has made reloading data available for this book. The company is Ballistic Products, Inc., and is headed by Dave Fackler, whose initial foray into this field was a plastic 10-gauge wad known as the Pattern Driver. Ballistic Products has extended its line to include additional innovative wads for buffered 12-gauge reloads as well. Most of the buffered 10- and 12-gauge reloads listed in this chapter involve the use of Ballistic Products (BP) wads and their high-density #47 Buffer.

The Ballistic Products two-piece wad column fits a corrugated shotcup atop an overpowder gas-sealing cup. The little rim on the overpowder cup creates an air cushion effect between the two components.

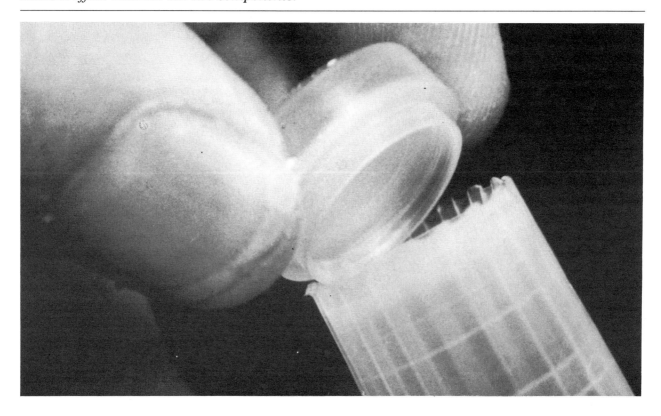

A special mix, #47 Buffer is very fine, and it packs snuggly into those voids between pellets to prevent their deformation on firing setback and during the squeeze through the forcing cone and choke constriction. It performs beautifully with the larger shot sizes, which leave substantial room between pellets.

Caution: do not, under any circumstances, substitute such kitchen items as flour, cream of wheat, or corn meal for specified and specialized buffers. They have different compression factors and can increase chamber pressures significantly. Kitchen flour was once given rave notices in magazines as a pellet buffer, but it can "cake" under setback pressures and will harden if it becomes moist. It is not unusual for chamber pressures to jump by 2,500 to 3,000 p.s.i. when flour is added indiscriminately. The few extra dollars involved in obtaining the right buffer will not work a hardship on anyone who can afford to go hunting. A half-pound jar of #47 Buffer costs about $3.

10-GAUGE BUFFERED RELOADS

The Ballistic Products wad used in the following reloads is a long, spacious, heavily walled unit known as the Pattern Driver (BPD). It's designed to hold a normal shot charge and buffer mixture, however, the addition of filler wads is necessary for some lighter loads. These are stipulated in each recipe. The wads come unslit but should *not* be left that way. Unslit wads can flip immediately after exiting the muzzle and trap shot inside, thus becoming a veritable solid, sluglike projectile. The handloader must slit each wad himself, the number and length of the slits depending on the intended range:

- For long-range waterfowling, slit each wad with only two opposing cuts extending from the mouth to near the heavy base.

- For intermediate range, each BPD wad should be slit three times, with cuts running only two thirds of the way down.

- For close-range work, it is advisable to slit the BPD wad four times, carrying each cut to the base of the wad. If a special wad-slitting tool isn't handy, a tin snips works well.

Some of the buffered 10-gauge Magnum loads shown have lighter shot charges than hunters have equated with the giant 10-bore in modern times. Along with greater velocity, such lighter loads pattern exceptionally well when buffered and launched through the Iron Monster. For example, it isn't unusual for a 1¾-ounce buffered reload to pattern better than a 2- or 2¼-ounce load with naked shot. Here, again, it isn't a matter of how much you start with, but rather how much is left at the target.

To keep chamber pressures down by expediting payload slippage, some of the following reloads will require powdered graphite or motor mica on the wad's exterior. This reduced friction between the wad, case wall, and bore produces smooth ejecta movement and provides adequate early combustion area for expanding powder gases. Either powdered graphite or motor mica will do. Ballistic Products supplies both, as does your local automotive supply store:

Federal 3½″ plastic case (paper base)
Winchester 209 primer
50.0 gr. Blue Dot powder
BPD wad + ½ inch filler in cup
1¾ oz. shot
Buffer: about 18 grains #47 mix
Pressure: 10,500 p.s.i.
Velocity: 1,300 f.p.s.
(Dust outside of BPD wad with graphite)

Winchester 3½" polyformed case
Winchester 209 primer
43.0 gr. SR-4756 powder
BPD wad + ¼ inch 20-ga. filler
1¾ oz. shot
Buffer: 20 grains #47 mix
Pressure: 9,000 l.u.p.
Velocity: 1,280 f.p.s.
(Dust outside of BPD wad with graphite)

Remington 3½" SP case (composition base)
CCI 157 primer
43.0 gr. SR-4756 powder
BPD wad + ¼ inch 20-ga. filler
2 oz. shot
Buffer: 20 grains #47 mix
Pressure: 9,800 l.u.p.
Velocity: 1,230 f.p.s.
(Dust outside of BPD wad with graphite
or motor mica)

Federal 3½" plastic case(paper base)
Winchester 209 primer
43.0 gr. Blue Dot powder
BPD wad + ¼ inch 20-ga. filler
2 oz. shot
Buffer: 20 grains #47 mix
Pressure: 11,000 p.s.i.
Velocity: 1,250 f.p.s.
(Dust outside of BPD wad with graphite
or motor mica)

12-GAUGE BUFFERED RELOADS

The Ballistic Products wad used in these 12-gauge buffered handloads is a two-piece assembly. The overpowder cup is known as the BPGS, (Ballistic Products Gas Seal); the upper shotcup segment is labeled the BP-12, and, when fitted atop the BPGS, it leaves a narrow air cushion between them for cushion-

The Ballistic Products 10-gauge Magnum Pattern Driver wads are huge plastic containers and deliver excellent performance from guns such as this high-grade sidelock 10-bore of European manufacture. (Photo by Gerald F. Moran)

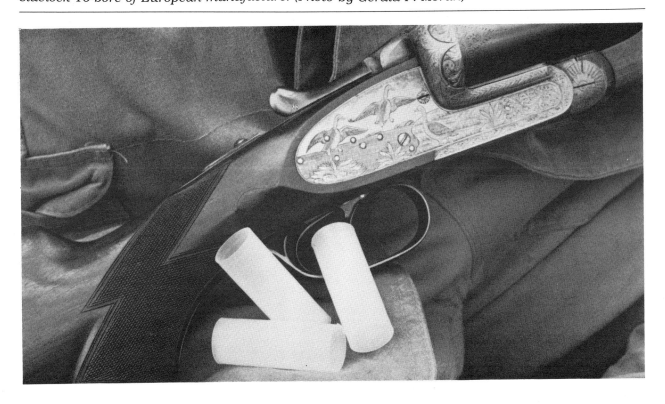

ing. Like the 10-gauge Pattern Driver wad, the BP-12 shotcup comes unslit and must be cut by the handloader according to distances and the results of test patterns. The BP-12 is a spacious cup and, for some shot charges, requires a 20-gauge filler to be added. One additional feature of the BP-12 shotcup is its longitudinal ribs which, by exposing less surface to the interior case and barrel walls, help lower the friction factor for lower pressures.

Some of the "custom" buffered reloads specified here have relatively light shot charges, but 1¼ to 1½ ounces can be dynamite at surprising distances when they hold 90 to 100 percent patterns:

Winchester 2¾″ AA target case
Winchester 209 primer
26.0 gr. SR-7625 powder
BPGS + BP-12 + ⅛ inch 20-ga. felt filler
1¼ oz. shot
Buffer: fill spaces between shot with #47 mix
Pressure: 10,300 l.u.p.
Velocity: 1,230 f.p.s.

Remington 2¾″ Unibody case
Winchester 209 primer
27.0 gr. Hi-Skor 800-X powder
BPGS + BP-12 + ¼ inch 20-ga. felt filler
1¼ oz. shot
Buffer: fill spaces between shot with #47 mix
Pressure: 9,800 l.u.p.
Velocity: 1,350 f.p.s.

Remington 2¾″ Unibody case
Winchester 209 primer
25.0 gr. Hi-Skor 800-X powder
BPGS + BP-12 + ⅛ inch 20-ga. felt filler
1⅜ oz. shot
Buffer: fill spaces between shot with #47 mix
Pressure: 10,500 l.u.p.
Velocity: 1,300 f.p.s.

Winchester 2¾″ AA target case
Winchester 209 primer
23.5 gr. Hi-Skor 800-X powder
BPGS + BP-12
1½ oz. shot
Buffer: fill spaces between shot with #47 mix
Pressure: 9,900 l.u.p.
Velocity: 1,225 f.p.s.

(3-INCH)
Federal 3″ plastic-base case
Federal 209 primer
35.0 gr. Blue Dot powder
BPGS + BP-12 + ¼ inch 20-ga. felt filler
1⅝ oz. shot
Buffer: fill spaces between shot with #47 mix
Pressure: 9,500 p.s.i.
Velocity: 1,200 f.p.s.

Winchester 3″ compression-formed case
CCI 109 primer
31.0 gr. SR-4756 powder
BPGS + BP-12 + ¼ inch 20-ga. felt filler
1⅝ oz. shot
Buffer: 23 grains #47 mix
Pressure: 10,000 l.u.p.
Velocity: 1,230 f.p.s.

Federal 3″ plastic-base case
Federal 209 primer
31.0 gr. Blue Dot powder
BPGS + BP-12 + ⅛ inch 20-ga. felt filler
1⅞ oz. shot
Buffer: fill spaces between shot with #47 mix
Pressure: 10,600 p.s.i.
Velocity: 1,120 f.p.s. (at 35°F)

Federal 3″ paper-base case
Winchester 209 primer
31.0 gr. SR-4756 powder
BPGS + BP-12
1⅞ oz. shot
Buffer: fill spaces between shot with #47 mix
Pressure: 10,500 l.u.p.
Velocity: 1,150 f.p.s.

HIGH-VELOCITY BUFFERED LOADS

Some hunters like the idea of launching pellets at ultra-high velocities to reduce forward allowances and to increase pellet on-target energy. Getting the combination of ultra-high velocity and pellet buffering to jibe, however, is a difficult ballistics chore, requiring relatively light shot charges to keep pressure levels on the safe side. But Ballistic Products has had experimental work done on the concept, and through their courtesy the following reloads are offered:

Mixture #47 is a high-density buffering agent that fills the spaces between pellets to force them to retain their best aero-dynamic shape. (Photo by Gerald F. Moran)

Federal 3½" 10-gauge Magnum
  case (paper base)
Federal 209 primer
50.0 gr. SR-4756 powder
BPD wad + ¾ inch 20-ga. felt filler
1½ oz. shot
Buffer: fill spaces between shot with #47 mix
Pressure: 10,000 l.u.p.
Velocity: 1,450 f.p.s.

Winchester 3½" 10-gauge polyformed case
Winchester 209 primer
57.0 gr. 571 Ball powder
BPD wad + ¾ inch 20-ga. felt filler
1⅝ oz. shot
Buffer: fill spaces between shot with #47 mix
Pressure: 10,300 l.u.p.
Velocity: 1,430 f.p.s.

Federal 3″ 12-gauge plastic-base hull
Winchester 209 primer
40.0 gr. SR-4756 powder
BPGS + BP-12 + ¼ inch 20-ga. felt filler
1¼ oz. shot
Buffer: fill spaces between shot with #47 mix
Pressure: 9,800 l.u.p.
Velocity: 1,510 f.p.s. (!)

Federal 3″ 12-gauge paper-base hull
Winchester 209 primer
32.0 gr. Du Pont PB powder
BPGS + BP-12 + ¼ inch 20-ga. felt filler
1⅜ oz. shot
Buffer: fill spaces between shot with #47 mix
Pressure: 10,500 l.u.p.
Velocity: 1,350 f.p.s.
(A very good cold-weather load)

BEDDED BUCKSHOT RELOADS

In areas where it is legal, No. 4 buckshot
is a popular load for geese. It is also employed
by obnoxious skybusters who clutter the
autumn air with useless gunfire, and I hesi-
tated to include buckshot data because I do
not want to add any impetus to such indiscriminate blasting and crippling. However, for
those hunters who can use them effectively,
here are a couple of bedded buckshot reloads
that hold tighter patterns for ultra-long shots:

Winchester 3½″ 10-gauge polyformed case
Winchester 209 primer
41.0 gr. Blue Dot powder
Remington SP-10 wad
41 pellets No. 4 buckshot bedded in 25 grains
  of #47 mix or Tru-Square #520 buffer
Use a thin, waxy overshot wad
Pressure: 9,500 p.s.i.
Velocity: 1,165 f.p.s.

Federal 2¾″ 12-gauge Hi-Power
  case (paper base)
Winchester 209 primer
27.5 gr. SR-7625 powder
Winchester WAA12 Red wad
27 pellets No. 4 buckshot bedded in
  18 grains of #47 mix or Tru-Square #520
Use a thin, waxy overshot wad
Pressure: 10,500 l.u.p.
Velocity: 1,300 f.p.s.

ADDING THE BUFFER

Pellet buffering media should not be added
in heaps and thick layers. As we learned
earlier in the chapter about ammunition advances, buffering materials serve mainly to fill
the space between pellets so that there is no
room for deformation. Building thick layers
between pellets takes up too much space for
a good crimp. It is acceptable for pellets to be
touching *if* the natural spaces around them
are filled by high-density buffer that compacts
and fills the void under setback forces.

The best way to accomplish such loading
is by putting a portion of the buffer atop the
total shot charge and vibrating it into place
by holding the brass rim against an electric
shaver or something similar. Let the buffer
trickle down into place. Tapping the case head
to settle the media isn't the best alternative,
as that makes the pellets jump around to produce constantly changing structure which
may leave voids. If a vibrator isn't handy, one
alternative is loading the shot and buffer by
increments, ladling in the buffer and jiggling
the hull to fill voids between the freshly
dropped pellets.

Finally, some hull types will require an
overshot wad to prevent the buffer from trick-
ling out at the center of the crimp. A thin
wafer of wax paper will do. Such wafers have
no disruptive influence on patterns.

22
A Positive Approach to Steel Shot

He grumbled all the way up the slippery embankment, kicked his boots against the pickup's front tire to loosen the mud, and cased his open-actioned pumpgun in a huff. "Darned steel shot can't stop anything," he complained. "I was leading and swinging, but those ducks never flinched. Pellets must have bounced right off. That steel's bad stuff!" Then he pitched the gun behind the seat and took off in a cloud of dust.

Comments like that were universally sounded when steel shot was first mandated for certain waterfowling zones, and they continue as new zones fall under the same restrictions — use steel shot or don't hunt waterfowl. And a lot of hunters have done just that: they quit duck hunting because of the steel shot requirement. Some dropped out because they wouldn't run steel through their guns for fear of damaging the bore, others became frustrated with their lack of success, and still others refused to pay the high price of steel loads. But this is not to lament their leaving. The sport of waterfowling may be better off without those of marginal interest, and their exit leaves more room for the truly dedicated sportsmen who enjoy the sport for something other than the supposedly cheap meat it puts on the table. A few extra dollars, plus the need to learn something new about steel-pellet ammo, won't detract from the enthusiastic waterfowler's pleasures.

Some hunters may still ask why use steel shot? Its use is an attempt to halt the lead poisoning that plagues waterfowl and other birds in some heavily hunted areas. For over a hundred years biologists have known that waterfowl die — sometimes in massive numbers — of lead poisoning contracted by ingesting spent lead shot scattered about by hunters. And the problem has expanded. Eagles have been found dead or dying of lead poisoning caused by black shot imbedded in ducks they've eaten. In England, the lead poisoning problem extends into fishing; the swans of the Thames River are decreasing in number, dying off because they pick up and ingest lead sinkers snagged and left by anglers. Thus, the same metal, lead, which has caused environmental problems when used in paint and gasoline, is harmful to waterfowl.

Some hunters doubt the severity of the lead poisoning situation. "If so many ducks are dying of lead poisoning, why don't we find them?" they'll ask. One reply takes the form of another question: why don't we also find the other birds — song, game, and predatory — that die of natural causes? The fact is, most sportsmen don't tramp out to the marshes and reed-rimmed potholes where birds die except during a few days of the hunting season, just as they don't search out woodlots and hedges for song birds that drop there of natural causes at the end of their short life cycles. Moreover, massive die-offs have been documented; state departments of natural resources can provide that data. Just a few years ago, for instance, thousands of Canada geese wintering in south central Wisconsin died of lead poisoning. The birds pick up the lead pellets as they would gravel for their

---

Some of the more common loadings of steel shot, left to right: the Federal 3-inch 20-gauge with 1 ounce of pellets; the standard 12-gauge 2¾-inch Remington round; Winchester's 3-inch 12-gauge load; and Federal's 3½-inch Magnum 10 with 1⅝ ounces of shot.

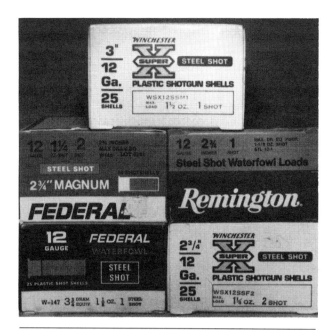

A number of ammunition manufacturers now offer steel shot loads.

crops. Lead poisoning is an accumulative type of poisoning, and if a sufficient number of pellets have been ingested, the bird dies.

Therefore, although some hunters and hunter groups argue against steel shot, steel pellets (or some other form of nontoxic metal) will gradually be mandated for more and more areas by federal decree. The powerful National Wildlife Federation, which has always backed hunting as a game management tool, has editorialized against lead shot, and various other ecology groups have done the same. The handwriting is on the wall. Intelligent hunters with foresight and a concern for conservation practices and the environment will read that handwriting and, for the benefit of future hunting, learn all they can about the qualities, characteristics, and use of steel shot.

THE PELLETS COMPARED

There is a world of difference between steel and lead shot in the way they perform.

The only real similarity is that they are both spherical and have the same diameters for their size numbers. A No. 2 steel pellet, for instance, has the same 0.15-inch diameter as a No. 2 lead pellet; No. 4 steel runs akin to lead 4s at 0.13 inch; and steel BBs match the 0.18-inch diameter of lead BBs. (*Do not* confuse steel BBs with air rifle shot! Air rifle shot has a 0.175-inch diameter and is considerably harder than steel shot. Guns can be damaged by the use of steel air rifle shot in shotshells.) But aside from the basic similarities in shape and size, steel loads differ markedly from lead loads.

How hard is steel shot? Measured by the Diamond Pyramid Hardness (DPH) test, lead shot seldom exceeds 30 DPH, but steel shotgun pellets run about 90 DPH. By way of comparison, ball bearings average about 270 DPH while air rifle shot goes 150 DPH. Thus, it is indeed a "soft" steel which is nevertheless substantially harder than the normal lead shot, and the 90 DPH rating makes it hard enough to withstand the forces of firing setback and bore travel without deforming. The reason why it is kept rather soft as steels go is to avoid damage to gun bores; anything harder than 90 DPH could be troublesome, and those who handload steel shot must be certain to learn the DPH hardness rating of their pellets. Don't reload with any steel shot harder than 90 DPH.

Steel shot is made in the same way that ball bearings are made; small chunks of steel wire are placed between two huge, hard roller plates and are then rolled into shape. To form the various sizes of steel pellets, the chunks are snipped to different sizes and the roller plates are set for different clearances.

Because steel has less density than lead, steel pellets of any given size are lighter than lead ones. This means that (1) there are more steel pellets per ounce than there are lead ones for each size, and (2) that steel shot must be driven faster than lead if it is to overcome air drag and carry penetrating energy downrange. Here are the respective counts per ounce by industry standards:

Shot Size	Steel	Lead
BB	72	50
2	125	87
4	192	135
6	315	225

There are no black lead No. 1s available at this time, but steel 1s run 103 per ounce. The increased number of steel pellets per ounce helps sweeten patterns with lighter charges. A 1¼-ounce load of steel 2s will count about 156, whereas a 1½-ounce magnum load of lead 2s only packs about 132 pellets. Moreover, a 1½-ounce load of lead BBs has only 75 pellets, while a 1¼-ounce charge of steel BBs tops that at 90. Such figures indicate that steel pellets are about 25 to 30 percent lighter than lead pellets of the same diameter.

To accommodate these greater numbers of steel shot, the loads require shotcups with additional capacity; the extra space was obtained by eliminating the cushioning section. Technically speaking, wads without cushioning sections aren't ideally suited to perfect interior ballistics, because wad compressibility is useful in soaking up initial gas expansion to help keep pressures down. Teamed with the ultra-slow-burning propellants employed in steel loads, however, the industry was able to eliminate the cushioning segment. Unlike the standard plastic wads made for lead shot, which are injection molded of flexible, low-density polyethylene, the wads fitted to steel shot loads are molded of a stiff, high-density polyethylene, and they have thick, tapering walls. This wad strength was needed to keep steel pellets from perforating the plastic under setback and bore-travel pressures, as pellets that poke through the shotcup's petals will score the bore.

As stated, velocity is a factor in effective steel loads. Air drag slows light, less-dense objects faster than it slows heavier objects of higher density. Even if lead and steel pellets have the same size and shape, plus the same muzzle velocity, the steel ones will slow down sooner. The answer, of course, is starting steel shot faster for greater energy. Unfortunately, there are limitations dictated by current powders and pressure standards. When the loading industry developed the current lines of steel shot loads, they had to balance the various wad/pressure/velocity/load-weight elements, and not all manufacturers came to the same conclusions. Remington, for example, opted for sheer speed with the lighter payloads, assuming that the higher steel shot counts would give adequate pattern density. Remington subsequently stoked its 1⅛-ounce standard-length 12-gauge steel load to 1,365 f.p.s. and gave virtually the same speed to its 1¼-ounce 3-inch 12-gauge steel round. Winchester, on the other hand, chose heavier shot charges at less velocity. The 1½-ounce Winchester 3-inch 12-gauge steel load does only about 1,200 f.p.s., while the 1¼-ounce standard-length 12-gauge steel load reaches about 1,275 f.p.s. Recently, however, Winchester expanded its steel shot line to include 1⅛-ounce 12-gauge loads of steel shot at speeds over 1,300 f.p.s. to compete with the others. It does seem that, with steel pellets on waterfowl, there is no substitute for velocity when the appropriate size is used.

Federal Cartridge Corporation has been the most active in turning out new steel loads, producing them in 10 and 20 gauge as well as the popular 12 gauge. Except for a couple of 12-gauge loads, Federal has also chosen velocity over sheer shot mass. The 1⅝-ounce 10-gauge Magnum load of steel clocks 1,350 f.p.s., and the 3-inch 20-gauge 1-ouncer leaves

Steel shot has its range limitations on geese. This Canada was taken with Remington's 3-inch 12-gauge load of 1¼ ounces of No. 1 shot at about 35 yards. The Lab is somewhat camera shy.

at a brisk 1,330 f.p.s. Perhaps the fastest commercial shotshell around today is Federal's ¾-ounce steel loading for the standard-length 20, which generates 1,425 f.p.s.!

In 12 gauge, they make a 1⅛-ounce steel load that rivals Remington's at 1,365 f.p.s. In the heavier 12-gauge loads, however, Federal has backed off somewhat. Their 1⅜-ounce 3-inch load does about 1,210 f.p.s. from a 30-inch 12-gauge barrel, and the 1¼-ounce 12-gauge standard-length steel magnum load turns in 1,275 f.p.s. These velocities may change as new powders become available, but this is how they stack up at press time.

THE RETAINED VELOCITY PROBLEM

Despite the high muzzle velocities of some commercial loads, the laws of aerodynamics and fluid mechanics still apply. Steel pellets shed velocity faster than lead ones of the same size and shape; about all higher velocities do is extend the range a little. Indeed, steel shot is *not* meant for long-range shooting. The fastest commercial load with steel BBs is hardly more than a 50-yard proposition.

Obviously, the rapidity of velocity loss has a bearing on forward allowances and penetrating energy, and it invites the questions: how far can we shoot and expect to kill waterfowl cleanly with steel? And what difference does it make, if any, in forward allowance?

When comparing forward allowance values for steel shot with those of lead shot, we find a minor complication arising. For although steel shot loses its velocity faster than lead shot, the high muzzle velocities *and* excellent retained shape of steel pellets actually makes steel shot slightly faster at short range. Another element in the forward

Because steel shot is hard and doesn't deform, it tends to hold high center densities, which makes it tough for unpracticed wingshots to hit consistently. This is especially true at close range, as this 90 percent pattern at 30 yards illustrates. You have to be right on target to score with such a pattern.

The wads used with steel shot must perforce be tough, high-density plastic to prevent damage to the bore.

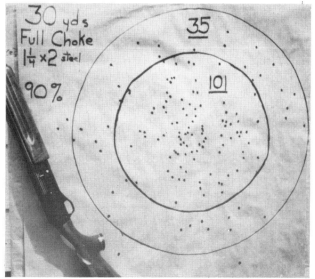

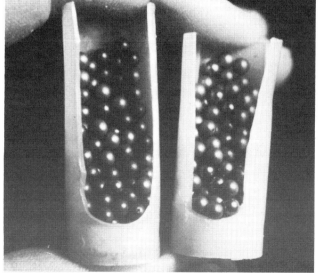

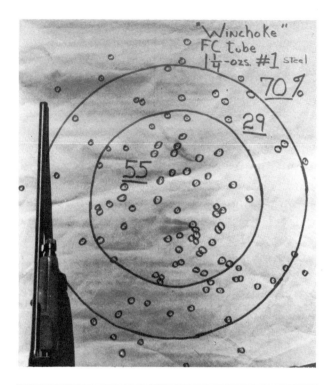

Even at longer ranges, steel shot loads generally continue to throw high center densities.

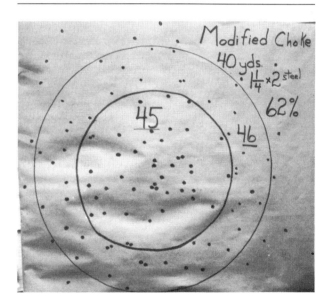

The writer did not find that modified chokes and improved cylinder bores invariably patterned tighter than full chokes with steel.

allowance equation is a load's speed out the barrel, and in this respect most steel loads beat commercial lead loads; consequently, that's another possible adjustment in one's timing and leading; for a load that's out the muzzle quickly requires less apparent lead than one that exits slower.

Basically, steel loads are slightly faster to the mark inside 30 yards than are commercial lead shot loads. Hunters who haven't delved into the exterior ballistics of steel shot loads, and who have heard bland remarks about steel shot slowing down faster than lead shot, often overreact by measuring off longer forward allowances whenever they experience a series of misses on easy shots — which is the reverse of what should be done. If any alteration in a formerly successful sight picture is tried with steel shot inside 30 yards, the modification should be on the short side. These are not drastic lead changes; they may amount to only inches when calculated. But increasing the forward allowance throws the pattern well ahead of a close-range target. One flaw here is that hunters frequently overestimate range, and when they slap a 40-yard lead on a bird only 30 yards away, the speed of steel shot exacerbates the problem. They miss well ahead of the target.

At 35 – 40 yards, steelshot slows down and requires about the same forward allowance as lead shot. When the range increases beyond 45 yards, the hunter must understand that steel is slowing abruptly and that forward allowances must, in turn, be lengthened.

Hunters who don't believe that steel shot is fast over short ranges will change their mind when they try steel loads at skeet. Shooters report halving their normal leads with steel. Forward allowances learned with target loads of No. 9 lead shot are far too long, sending steel patterns well ahead of the target. Indeed, one problem with steel is that most people talk about it but don't practice with it to learn what's going on.

THE HARDNESS FACTOR

The main reason why steel shot retains velocity so well inside 30–35 yards is because of its retained shape. Steel is hard and doesn't deform under setback and bore-travel pressures; hence, steel shot retains its optimum aerodynamic shape. This same hardness gives clean-cutting penetration when the energy/velocity values are still adequately high.

What does that mean in the way of pellet energy and steel shot selection? Hunters encountering steel shot for the first time usually stick with the same pellet sizes they use in lead loads — which is wrong! Because steel shot is lighter than lead shot, a hunter must select a steel pellet *two sizes larger* than his lead spheres if he wishes a similar energy level at 40 yards. Steel No. 4s have about the same energy as lead No. 6s; steel No. 2s have about the same authority as lead No. 4s; and steel BBs flirt with the energy of lead No. 2s. But these comparisons, one must remember, are for about 40 yards. Thereafter, lead retains its energy better. As a rule-of-thumb calculation, Federal's high-speed 10-gauge Magnum load of steel BBs is marginal beyond 45–50 yards on geese. Steel 4s fired at 1,365 f.p.s. have about 2.75 foot-pounds of energy left at 40 yards, which is submarginal on geese and barely adequate on big ducks. Steel 2s have

---

Muzzle velocity, pellet shape, and air resistance play roles in the exterior ballistics of steel shot, Steel pellets start faster than lead and, because of retained aerodynamic form, need a bit less forward allowance at 30–35 yards or so. Around 35–40 yards, however, air drag slows the lighter steel pellets faster than it does lead shot, and the forward allowances are about the same. Beyond 40–45 yards, steel shot slows faster than lead shot, and one must increase his forward allowance.

AIMING POINT

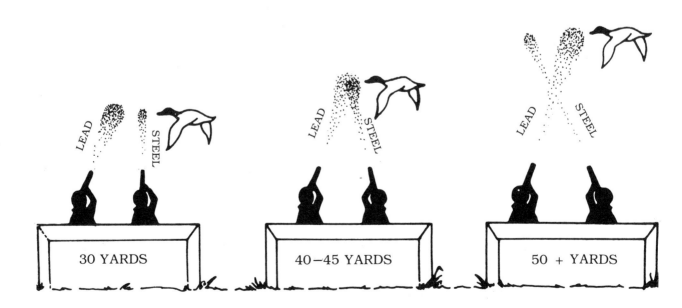

a calculated energy of 4.50 to 4.75 foot-pounds at 40 yards, but that fades rapidly as air drag takes control thereafter. The influence of cold weather can also detract from the load's velocity, thus lowering energy as well.

All things considered, magnum loads of steel don't extend one's effective range very far. The velocity and energy of steel pellets from a 10-gauge Magnum load of BBs or 2s will wear off as rapidly as they do from 12- or 20-gauge loads. What heavier magnum charges of steel shot contribute is mainly added pattern density with the heavier shot sizes that retain velocity better than steel 4s. If a hunter can handle Ithaca's Mag-10, it can contribute to clean kills by throwing 1⅝ ounces of steel 2s or BBs, thus giving the hunter more chances to find the vital area of a bird. But when it comes to added range, forget it. The pattern is there, but the power dissipates.

Therefore, *steel shot simply isn't a long-range proposition.* It starts out fast but slows abruptly at the start of intermediate waterfowling ranges. Hunters who curse steel for not folding birds up high are really expressing their own ignorance. Steel shot brings with it a more limited set of parameters than we are used to with lead shot. Skybusting is a waste of money with steel shot; a hunter would be far wiser to hold his fire on distant birds and spend his dollars on summertime skeet so that his technique improves.

Remington once made a steel shot version of its Model 3200 over-under with extra-thick muzzle walls, a precaution soon found to be unnecessary. These mallards were taken along Maryland's Eastern Shore with steel No. 2s.

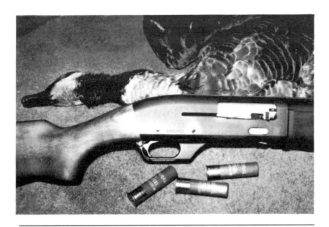

The 10-gauge Magnum's role in steel shot usage is putting more heavy pellets into the pattern. Magnum loads do not really extend the range of steel shot because the pellets slow down after 40–45 yards and lose penetrating power.

In general, steel 4s are best suited to ducks inside 30 yards, and these pellets work nicely with modified chokes. The best all-round duck pellet in steel is the No. 2, especially if a hunter can limit himself to 35-yard shots. Steel 1s are favored with a full choke for heavy ducks and geese to 40– 45 yards. Theoretically, steel BBs should be good for geese, but my patterning has come up with erratic results, some guns varying wildly from improved cylinder- to full-choke performances on successive shots with loads from the same box of steel. The steel 6s now available are not good waterfowl loads except for 20–25 yards over decoys from an open-bored gun, but even then steel 4s are preferable. Steel No. 6s were made in response to dove shooters and rail hunters who hunt in steel shot zones.

SHOT STRING LENGTH

Aside from the sudden speed and abrupt deceleration of steel shot, there are two other reasons why hunters may be having such difficulty scoring with it. One reason is shot string length; the other, tight patterning. We'll consider the shot string first.

Because steel pellets remain in-the-round, they tend to have identical exterior velocities. In other words, they fly in a bunch. Test patterns fired against patterning sheets attached to vehicles moving at waterfowl speeds show that "tails" don't appear as happens with loads of deformation-prone lead shot. Patterns on those moving sheets came away looking pretty much as they did on stationary sheets from the same gun and load. Guesstimates put a steel load's in-flight shot string at about one third or one quarter the length of a load of chilled shot.

Thus, steel shot loads leave few trailing pellets to pick up the bird if the main mass misses ahead. I have a hunch this has frustrated many hunters, because millions of birds have been dropped by trailing pellets from lead loads triggered by hunters who overestimated both range and lead. Bluntly stated, the short shot strings of steel loads put a premium on improved pointing and, especially, timing. If the pattern isn't almost

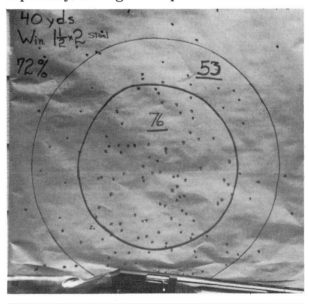

A common pattern with steel shot loads. The more densely perforated inner circle is 20 inches in diameter, which explains why many shooters miss with steel; the effective pellet concentration is too narrow for their skill.

precisely at the required point of interception when the bird gets there; it's a clean miss. Sloppy pointing, swinging, and timing won't score. Consequently, a hunter must work with just a two-dimensional pattern (height and width); gone is the luxury of a third dimension, depth.

PATTERNING CHARACTERISTICS OF STEEL

Along with the short shot string, the patterning characteristics of steel shot also frustrate hunters by holding extremely snug clusters. This is another result of hard pellets; there are no fliers around, and there is a definite propensity toward high center densities as the spherical pellets fly true.

Patterns from full-choked guns are too tight for the average hunter at ranges inside 35 yards. Steel loads commonly shoot 80 to 90 percent into a 30-inch circle at 40 yards from bona fide full-choked guns, while those same barrels only do 65–70 percent with black shot. And a careful study of those patterns printed by full chokes with steel loads will disclose that the effective pattern is frequently no wider than 25 inches at 40 yards. There will be some steel pellets in the annular

---

Federal now markets steel shot loads of No. 6s, marginal for close, decoying ducks and mostly meant for rail and dove hunters who roam non-toxic shot zones.

ring, of course, but they present patchy conditions that feather, wing-break, or cripple rather than kill cleanly. If such concentrations are only 2 feet wide at 40 yards, consider how small they are at 20–30 yards where a lot of shooting is done. A 15-inch-diameter spread is normal for a full choke with steel loads at 20–25 paces. Egotism aside, few hunters have the ability to slap those small patterns on speeding ducks with any regularity.

For many hunters, a modified choke is better with steel loads. There will still be a tendency for high center densities, but there is also a better chance for wider patterns inside 40 yards with more pellets in the annular ring. The crippling that occurs with steel shot can, in large measure, be traced to the weak fringe areas of small patterns launched by full-choked guns; the hunter misses with the dense core, nipping the target with only an outside pellet or two. A few added pellets in the annular ring of a pattern can reduce the number of cripples by supplying the density needed to find a target's vital area.

Popular mythology holds that steel shot will give tight, full-choke patterns even from modified chokes. My own patterning doesn't support that contention. There are *some* modified chokes that will deliver full-choke densities with *some* steel loads; however, a tremendous number of modified chokes will indeed throw modified percentages with steel. Their efforts will run between 60 and 64 percent. I have found that modified chokes give full-choke patterns primarily when fed Winchester steel loads, which are loaded to a lower velocity level than Federal and Remington steel shot ammo. Sometimes a Federal 3-inch 12-gauge 1⅜-ounce steel load will also tighten up in a modified choke, but don't bet on it. Each gun/load combo must still be checked individually.

Some armchair experts have opined that open chokes — skeet and improved cylinder — are excellent with steel shot because their reduced muzzle constriction lets the payload pass smoothly. This hasn't appeared on my patterning sheets, either. The open bores have universally spread their steel loads around much as they do with lead shot. It appears that skeet and improved cylinder chokes should be held inside 25 yards, and certainly inside 30 yards, when their patterns are filled by 1⅛ or 1¼ ounces of steel 4s. If the range increases, skeet and improved cylinder patterns become very patchy and prone to crippling.

Thus, full-choked guns are often too-tight patterning for the average duck hunter with steel loads. He hits mainly with the crippling fringes of his patterns, if he hits at all, and the missed or crippled birds leave him disgusted. Steel shot immediately becomes a convenient scapegoat, even though it will kill cleanly whenever a hunter centers his birds inside effective ranges.

Although No. 2 steel serves well on ducks, I tend to believe No. 1 steel is the best all-round number. Its heavier quality gives better knockdown and anchoring performances with one- or two-pellet hits, whereas one or two No. 4 or No. 2 steel pellets can leave crippled birds to get away. I have had especially good luck with the Remington 3-inch 1¼-ounce load of steel No. 1s on both ducks and geese. The load produces a dense, killing pattern from my modified choke at a full 40 yards.

Winchester offers a 12-gauge high-velocity round with 1¹/₈ ounces of shot (left), and a 2¾-inch 20-gauge load with ¾ ounce (right).

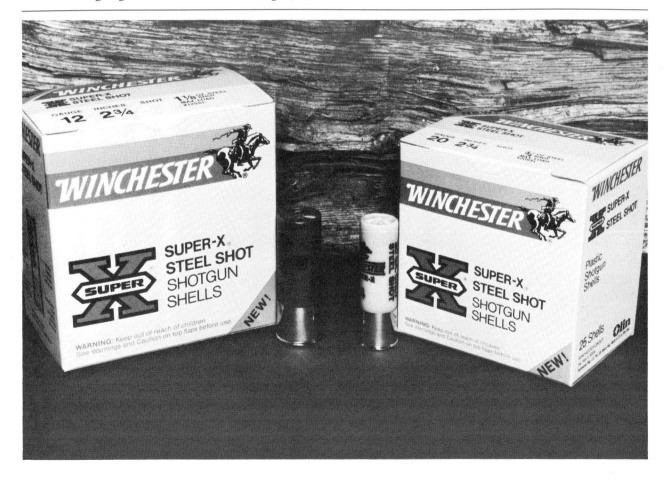

STEEL LOADS AND GEESE

Canada geese are a special case. They are the big game of wingshooting, difficult to drop even with lead shot. Part of the reason, of course, is the same as already mentioned: unpracticed shooters who don't center birds. Fringe hits with steel are rarely effective on honkers. And when the steel pellets fail to register en masse, the probability of crippling is heightened. Indeed, steel shot that retains the 2-foot-pound energy requirement for ducks frequently falls short of the 3-foot-pound blow needed on geese.

At this point in the steel shot game, BBs or No. 1s are the top choices for geese. But, being steel, they do lose penetrating power quickly beyond 40 yards; and in the best interests of our sport, we need to discipline ourselves not to shoot beyond 35 yards at such tough targets. If a goose can "carry a lot of lead," it can in fact carry a great deal more steel!

Some guns do not pattern steel BBs very well. Those big, bulky spheres have shown themselves to be erratic in my tests. The 32-inch-barreled Browning A-5 mentioned earlier in this book vacillated from 57 to 75 percent in trial patterning with various makes of steel BBs. Shells from the same box would print 60 percent with one round and either fall to 57 percent or vault to 70 percent with the next. That being the case, a hunter doesn't know whether his next shot will give a weak modified-choke or a mediocre full-choke pattern. Thus, hunters are advised to pattern with several shells before concluding that steel BBs are performing riflelike from their pet guns.

When a goose is hit by steel, a hunter should keep his head down and throw in another load or two as the bird falls. Too many hunters will drop their gun and raise their head immediately upon seeing a goose flinch or buckle, thinking it's all over. It isn't. Geese can catch themselves and plane away to be lost. Others have been hit and dropped, only to escape into thick marsh cover before the hunter arrives. A few more pellets in the vital area will simplify retrieving. So stick with the bird and keep shooting. One or two extra shells spent on a falling bird are nothing compared to the expense of the rest of the trip, and they'll help ensure success. In fact, this follow-up shooting is equally good with lead shot when there's any doubt about the impact of the initial hit.

It will undoubtedly take hunters, as a group, a long time to learn and to appreciate the differences between steel and lead shot. Not all waterfowlers have an academic interest in shotgun performance; they merely grab a gun and go hunting, totally oblivious to the finer points. Therefore, we'll continually hear uninformed people and bum shots complain about how weak and ineffective steel loads are. But the problem really doesn't rest with the concept or the factory loads. It's caused by hunters who don't judge range properly, who fire steel loads at targets well beyond the effective range of steel pellets, and who don't have the ability to hit with small patterns and short shot strings. Despite all those past, present, and impending complaints; however, if you center a duck or goose within the effective range of a steel load, the results will be as positive as they are with any load of lead shot.

23
Reloading with Steel Shot

Commercially loaded steel shotshells, as we know them today, have had a revolutionary impact on waterfowling. The steel BBs, 1s, 2s, 4s, and 6s now available to us in factory loads have made long-range shooting a thing of the past. Instead of giving us tight patterns and high energy for long-range gunning, they limit us to about 40–45 yards. And anyone who has read the price tags on factory-loaded shotshells stuffed with steel shot has also drawn another conslusion: they're expensive! Because of limited production, compared to lead-loaded shotshells, the ammunition companies charge more per box. Thus, any compulsory use of steel shot will continue to be a costly, short-range affair — unless one learns the techniques of handloading steel.

Handloading steel shot — a subject that was virtually taboo until 1984 — will certainly reduce the cost of steel loads. And by applying some innovative components and subtleties, a hunter may also be able to extend his clean-killing range beyond that of the commercial steel loads covered in the preceding chapter.

Before anyone recklessly plunges into steel shot reloading; however, let me emphasize that the introduction of steel pellets sets up a new set of complexities and parameters. *It definitely is not the same as reloading with lead shot!* The misapplication of components and data commonly employed with relative safety when lead shot is involved can have disastrous results in a shotgun firing steel pellets! Before getting into the sources for steel shot reloading components and load development, let's review the theory and practice of reloading with steel shot as compared to lead shot.

PELLET PITFALLS AND PROBLEMS

The complexities of steel shot reloading begin with, and center on, pellet hardness. As already mentioned in chapter 22 relative to patterning, steel pellets don't deform like lead ones. They won't compress under safe, standard shotgun pressures. Thus, the basis for reloading steel safely is to use such components and powder charges that will start steel loads slowly so that they flow as fluidly as possible from chamber to bore without wedging tightly in the chamber or forcing cone when subjected to the sudden acceleration (setback) of intensifying powder gas. For whereas lead shot will compress, deform, and move forward without becoming a dangerous obstruction to gas pressures, steel shot will do no such thing! Given increasing gas pressure at its base and either the unopened crimp's restraint or the funnel-like forcing cone's narrowed passage up front, a charge of steel shot can potentially wedge tightly together and exert an outward circumferential pressure which bears heavily on the shot-cup and case wall. Should the gas pressures mount high enough, the noncompressible steel shot could cause a blockage in the chamber/cone area. And, obviously, if the ejecta doesn't move forward to give the ever-expanding powder gases continuously greater expansion area, the mounting gases would invariably seek an avenue of escape other than the bore and rupture the case head to cause gun damage or a full burst in the breech/chamber region.

Since steel shot is rigid and won't compress like lead, special wads and slow-burning powders are needed for safe loads and uniform ballistics in steel loads. The wads must be tough, high-density plastic to prevent perforation by steel shot under setback and bore travel forces. They must also enclose the entire shot charge and have considerable capacity because, steel pellets of any given size be-

New components, conversion kits for reloading presses, and manuals detailing the use of each manufacturer's steel shot equipment are now available to help handloading hunters make the switch from lead shot to steel shot safely and intelligently.

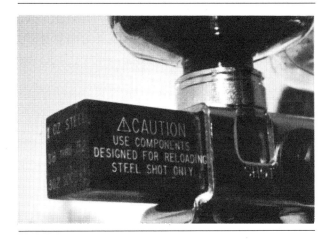

Handloaders must use a different charging bar and bushings for steel shot than for lead shot. This MEC steel shot bar is black and carries a cautionary message, plus load information on the end.

ing lighter than those of lead, more case space is needed for any set charge weight. These shotcups will protect the bore walls, and, despite some wedging by pellets, they are generally sturdy enough to prevent harmful perforation. The unperforated sides of steel shot wads are in effect self-lubricating full length to expedite slippage.

Normal wads common to lead shot loads are unacceptable for steel-stuffed shotshells. Wads made for lead shot are soft, low-density items that perforate easily. They would not only allow bore scratching, but might also permit enough direct steel shot contact with case walls or forcing cone to create a blockage. In other words, under setback forces the steel pellets would wedge tightly, perforate the soft

shotcup petals, and bear circumferentially against the hull and/or forcing cone incline. This obstacle to powder gas expansion would then create excess chamber pressures and could lead to a burst. Therefore, never use anything but strong, high-density wads made specifically for steel reloads. In many instances, in fact, wads made for lead shot will not have the capacity for full steel charges due to their cushioning section, and the excess pellets will spill out. This is a strong clue, but there's no excuse for mistaking one wad for the other.

Wads specially made for handloading steel shot frequently come unslit. *Always slit them before using!* Some cockeyed theories have it that unslit wads will throw tighter patterns because they hold the pellets together longer after muzzle exit, but, in reality, the theory is erroneous. Unslit wads, in fact, can be counterproductive with steel as well as with lead. The best patterns with steel come when wads drop away quickly to leave the shot charge unaffected, and this necessitates that the shotcup have some slits for their air-brake effect. Likewise, unslit wads will normally flip over with steel loads, as well as with

---

The MEC steel shot conversion kit includes a new plastic bottle for steel pellets.

Note the wider mouth on the bottle used when loading steel shot (left) compared with the standard bottle (right). The larger opening is needed to allow easier flow of steel shot pellets.

lead shot, as the heavier base portion retains more velocity and passes the lighter open end, and this flipping can upset patterns and/or trap some pellets inside. In the latter instance, the trapped pellets supply weight and energy to make the wad fly dangerously like a slug! I'd hate to be a hunter on the other side of a pond when such a pellet-laden wad whistled down! Thus, always slit shotcups according to the manufacturer's instructions. If there are no instructions, make three to four slits.

Steel shot wads should have extremely fine slits so that, under a shot load and the pressures of surging gases, the slits will not open sufficiently for pellets to press through to the case and bore walls. There are some special cutting tools now available for such work. Slit size is another reason why the soft,

low-density wads designed for lead shot shouldn't be used with steel shot: the petal slits or divisions in lead-shot wads are often wide for convenience in injection molding.

With lead shot it makes no real difference if pellets do somehow snuggle into a shotcup slit and touch the case or bore, as they will do no harm. Steel shot, on the other hand, can ruin a bore quickly if they should perchance penetrate a shotcup slit.

Powders for steel shot must always be ultra-slow-burning types. The idea is to get the charge of steel pellets moving slowly at first to minimize wedging. This is best done with a slow pressure rise. If the fast-burning powders used with skeet and trap loads were burned behind loads of steel shot, the quick pressure applied to the shot charge would cause maximum wedging which, in reality, could turn the charge into a virtual solid steel mass incapable of compressing adequately for safe passage into and through the forcing cone and bore. There have been reports in which unthinking reloaders have blown up shotguns by putting steel shot atop a fast-burning powder like Red Dot while using a wad intended solely for lead shot.

Powders for steel shot reloads must be of the slow-burning type such as Blue Dot and HS-7.

Wads used with steel shot have much thicker walls than those for lead shot. This photo compares the Supersonic steel shot wad (left) with a standard Winchester WAA12 wad (right).

Of the currently obtainable propellants, the ones that come closest to the requirements for steel shot reloads are Du Pont SR-4756, Hercules Blue Dot, Hodgdon HS-7, and Winchester 571 Ball. _Again, however, readers are cautioned to employ these or any other powders only with exact data developed specifically for steel shot loads._ The noncompressible nature of steel shot, along with the hard plastic wads which do not have cushioning sections, create pressures that are unlike those of lead shot loads.

If ever accurate and uniform powder charging were needed in shotshell reloading, it is in the assembly of steel shot handloads. Overcharging with powder will run up chamber pressures faster with steel shot than it will with lead, all other things being equal. Reckless, accidental, or indiscriminate increases of the powder charge are _never_ right, of course, but with steel shot it reaches disaster stages much sooner. If, by chance, a slight overcharge of powder is used with lead shot, there is a marginal possibility of escaping gas damage or a burst because the lead

shot will compress and move ahead to give the excess gases expansion room. This does not happen with steel shot, as noted earlier, meaning that chamber pressures will magnify quickly!

In my early work with steel shot, I scaled each powder charge, and those reloads gave me the most uniform results I've had thus far with steel handloads. That doesn't mean one can't reload from a charging bar or powder measure; it just means one must be very sure of the load he's dropping, which brings us to a discussion of the basic equipment and accessories for reloading with steel shot and the correct components.

EQUIPMENT AND ACCESSORIES

Press-type reloading equipment used for lead shot must be modified when steel shot is loaded. These hard pellets, which are normally large hunting sizes, do not flow smoothly from hopper to hull the way lead No. 7½s and No. 8s do. Hunters who have reloaded with No. 2 shot know how those bulky

Steel shot wads are, in reality, plastic buckets for optimum capacity and bore protection. Shown here, left to right, are the Supersonic 10-gauge Magnum wad, the Ballistic Products 10-gauge Pattern Driver, the Non-Toxic Components 12-gauge, and a conventional Winchester WAA12 lead shot wad for comparison.

Supersonic steel shot loadings are assembled with a special steel shot buffer and graphited lube supplied by U-Load.

pellets jam, shear, and bridge as they go from the hopper to the bushing and through the drop tube — but they haven't seen anything yet! Steel pellets flow even worse, and for improved pellet flow a larger-necked hopper (plastic bottle), a wider drop tube, and a different charging bar are needed. As this chapter is being written, Mayville Engineering Company, more popularly known as MEC, is the only manufacturer thus far with a conversion kit on the market; however, other companies will no doubt follow with conversion kits for their presses, too.

The MEC conversion kit consists of three parts: one is a new plastic bottle, or hopper, with a larger hole in the neck. This is necessary because the steel setup does not have a grommet to prevent shot shearing, and the wider bottle neck was needed to prevent pellet-jamming between the bottle neck and the charging bar. Secondly, MEC has designed a new drop tube with a special shape that will eliminate, or at least greatly reduce, the tendency that large pellets have of bridging in the drop tube. The third MEC item is a wad ram tube with a straight inside diameter rather than a taper, the purpose

again being to alleviate bridging and facilitate flow.

Along with this steel shot conversion kit, handloaders will need special charging bars for steel shot. One reason, of course, is that, because steel is lighter than lead, a given weight of steel shot requires more space than the same weight of lead. For example, a charging bar that throws about 1⅜ ounces of lead shot *may* handle no more than a mere ounce of steel shot. I wrote "may" because there are all sorts of variables that deny any linear conversion from lead to steel; hence, reloaders must *not* equate bushings made for lead shot with steel shot.

MEC has begun making charging bars designed for steel shot. These are black (as opposed to the Normal MEC red for lead) and are given a rubber insert that prevents shearing and jamming. Equally important, however, is the fact that steel shot charging bars are drilled for specific sizes of steel shot. The MEC line, for instance, includes two different bars each for ⅞-, 1-, and 1⅛-ounce charges, and the handloader must be alert to the fact that the purpose of two different bars in each weight class is based on different pellet sizes. In the

Looking like tiny beads, Supersonic steel shot buffer is fine and helps improve the fluidity with which the massive shot charge moves through the bore and choke constriction for tight patterns.

The new drop tube developed by MEC for better hopper-to-hull reloading with hard, bulky steel pellets A ball-point pen is shown for size comparison.

⅞-ounce MEC bars, one bar (30207814) is drilled for steel shot sizes No. 1 through No. 4, while a second ⅞-ounce bar (30207856) is cut for steel shot sizes No. 5 and No. 6. This need for two different bars, depending on pellet diameter, exists because bulky No. 1s have more air space between them than smaller steel No. 6s; therefore, larger bushing diameters are needed for the heavier steel pellets while lesser diameters are needed for the smaller pellets. (The same is actually true for lead shot, especially in the larger sizes, but most reloaders sloppily ignore the variation and drop all shot sizes wrongly from the same bushing.)

In the remainder of MEC's steel shot charging bar line, the 1-ounce bars show one unit (30210036) drilled for an ounce of steel shot sizes No. 3 through No. 6, whereas a companion 1-ouncer (302100BB2) is made for BBs through No. 2s. In the 1⅛-ounce category, one MEC bar (30211846) handles No. 4s through No. 6s, and another (302118BB2) handles BBs through No. 3s.

All MEC steel shot bars have a polyurethane insert in the shot hole, are clearly marked on their ends as to bar number and shot size/capacity, and have provision for replaceable powder bushings so that different propellants can be employed. When running steel shot through a reloading press, the drop tube assembly should not be pressed deeply into the hull when the charge is dropped; for that only causes the pellets to pile up and bridge at the base of the ram tube when they can't drop free. Instead, the press handle should be held so that the rammer tube is *just* inside the case mouth, leaving room for the pellets to fall free and not clog the tube. Moreover, charging bars should be brought across slowly so the pellets do not drop in a mass but rather trickle down in a thin stream which is less likely to bridge in the drop tube.

If a handloader wishes to charge from a conventional press, he must employ these specialized steel shot accessories for smoothness and safety. For when a charge bar jams with lead shot, added force can free the

---

For greater energy beyond 45 yards, Supersonic steel buckshot and BB sizes are offered by the pouch from U-Load. A steel pellet must normally be two or three sizes larger than a lead pellet to give approximately the same downrange energy performance.

assembly by shearing the soft lead shot, which generally isn't possible with steel. Steel pellets simply won't shear under the pressure applied to charging bars, and when a jam occurs it could cause damage to the press and bar. For extra protection to the shot cavity, MEC has put a polyurethane insert into each shot hole.

Unless a handloader expects to scale all his powder and shot charges, such an appropriate steel shot conversion kit and special charging bars are necessary to expedite the smoothest movement of steel pellets from hopper to hull.

COMPONENT SUPPLIERS

Handloading with steel shot requires hulls with optimum capacity. This tends to negate the popular plastics such as the Win-chester compression-formed (AA-type), and Peters blue target cases, because their tapered interiors reduce capacity. The most likely candidates for steel shot reloads are the Federal field-style Hi-Power cases and Gold Medal target cases, the Remington SP cases, and Winchester polyformed cases. Equally good, if not better, are those hulls made specifically for Federal, Remington-Peters, and Winchester factory-loaded steel shot ammunition. These cases have been designed with a cylindrical (nontapered) interior to accept the heavy loads of slow-burning powder and the long, heavy wads. For the handloader, obtaining these hulls will normally mean saving and scrounging. Luckily, there are always enough hunters who don't reload to leave empties scattered about the firing lines for those who do.

As this is being written, there are three

Steel shot wads generally come unslit, and the reloader must slit them for proper functioning. Cutting tools, such as the four-bladed one shown here, are available from the various component suppliers. This one is made by Supersonic and has a pilot segment plus a tapered upper portion to fit the drop tube of a reloading press for easy up-down cutting.

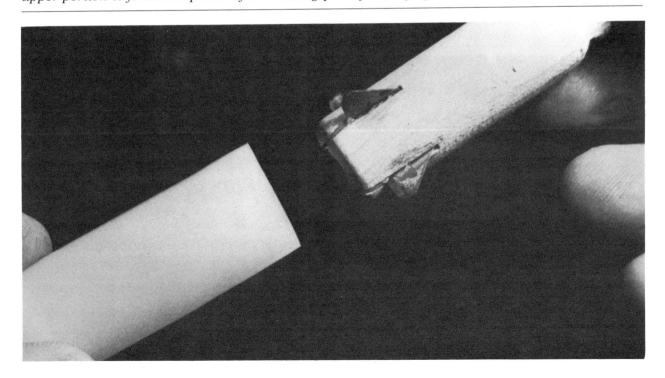

leading sources for special steel shot wads: (1) U-Load, Inc., P.O. Box 443-177, Eden Prairie, Minnesota 55344; (2) Non-Toxic Components, Inc., P.O. Box 4202, Portland, Oregon 97208; and (3) Ballistic Products, Inc.. Let's cover their products in reverse order.

Ballistic Products supplies a 10- and a 12-gauge shotcup for steel shot known as the TUFF wad. The 10-gauge unit is cataloged as the TUFF-BPD, while the 12-gauge is called the TUBB-BP12. The 10-gauge wad works alone, but the 12-gauge TUFF-BP12 is used in combination with the BPGS overpowder cup discussed earlier in chapter 21. Both wads have longitudinal venting which reduces friction and tends to lower pressures. These TUFF wads have different pressure-building characteristics than the Pattern Driver and BP-12 wads also made by Ballistic Products, and must be used only with data supplied by the company. They publish a handbook about reloading with their steel shot components. After a customer buys the book (about $5) they will sell him their line of steel shot and wads after a liability waiver is signed.

The Oregon-based company, Non-Toxic Components, came onto the scene in the autumn of 1984 with kits intended to make steel shot reloading easier for a typical handloading hunter. The kits included NTC's own wad design, a complete manual of instructions, suggested data, and a quantity of its own steel shot.

Readers should write directly to the company for complete, up-to-date information on NTC products.

For purposes of illustration, this photo shows the cutter being used manually. The blades make straight, even cuts which are more desirable than random slits made with a knife or other sharp instrument. Wads not cut evenly and with straight lines can fly off course on exit and disrupt patterns.

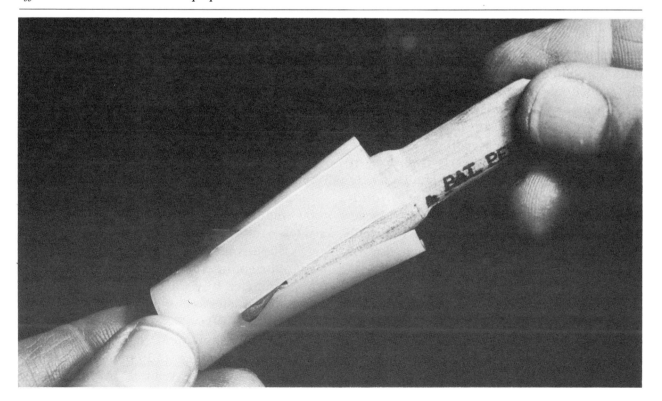

AN ENERGY/PATTERNING BREAKTHROUGH

The steel shot reloading components *and* concepts advanced by U-Load can be considered a breakthrough in delivering greater on-target energy to birds, especially geese, that are beyond the normal 35- to 45-yard ranges deemed reasonable for most hitherto conventional steel shot ammo. Originally developed by experimenter Don Vizecky, and marketed through U-Load under the trade name Supersonic, this concept is predicated on getting ultra-tight patterns with pellets larger than the standard steel BBs which, at this writing, is the largest steel pellet offered in factory loads and by other steel shot sources. Instead of stopping with steel BBs, Vizecky, a dedicated goose hunter, began working with his own buckshot-sized pellets rolled of "soft" steel for greater long-range impact.

To make the significantly larger buckshot-sized steel pellets pattern tightly (in chapter 22 I said steel BBs pattern very poorly and erratically), Vizecky worked with different buffering materials to obtain the same fluidity found in lead shot loads with buffering. His selection is a hard, spherical material (which looks to this writer like expandable polystyrene) that performs to perfection with bulky steel pellets for exceedingly snug long-range patterns. The buffer is available in 1-pound packages from U-Load, as is Vizecky's instruction book, *Steel Handloaders' Manual.* Don't plunge into steel load buffering without first reading the manual!

Vizecky has designed his own line of Supersonic wads, which are more cylindrical inside than most other such cups, but they are equally tough, and U-Load offers wad cutters for slitting them with 3, 4, or 6 elements. These wad cutters are designed to fit into the wad ram of a reloading press for straight-down cutting, although they can also be applied by hand. One nice feature about the cutter is that it has a gauge-sized pilot to keep it aligned in the wad.

To help alleviate pressure due to wad friction, Vizecky incorporates a graphite lube mixed into the buffer. When loaded, some of this lubricated buffer will seep through the slits in the wad under firing pressure (and perhaps crimping pressure) to reduce friction. This apparently makes possible higher velocities with less chance of running dangerous or erratic chamber pressures.

The important aspect of Vizecky's experiments, however, is his stabilizing of buckshot-sized steel pellets to produce dense patterns *plus* higher per-pellet energy for cleaner kills at over 50 yards. Included in the Supersonic line are sizes ranging from BB + to No. 0 buck, and the developer claims that tight patterns of said No. 0 steel buckshot can kill out to 80 yards or more! That's something no waterfowler ever thought he'd hear about steel loads, because, based upon factory ammunition with nothing heavier than BBs, steel is a short-range proposition, as I argued in chapter 22. With these specialized reloads using steel buckshot sizes in a lubricated buffer, however, a significant breakthrough has been scored.

The steel buckshot being distributed by U-Load is *not* the same diameter as lead buckshot bearing the same designation. This is somewhat unfortunate as it will mean reloaders who don't read carefully will be confused and will make incorrect selections. Thus far there are six Supersonic steel buckshot sizes.

Supersonic No. BB + steel shot is larger than the commercial steel BBs. Measured on a micrometer, it averages 0.187 inch to 0.1875 inch in diameter as compared to just 0.18 inch for standard BBs.

The next step up is Supersonic No. BBB steel which averages 0.219 inch in diameter, making it a close relative of No. F lead buckshot (0.22 inch). With a muzzle velocity around 1,300 f.p.s. or a mite higher, steel BBBs are rated as 70-yard pellets. From what I have seen of it purely in patterning work, it appears to be an excellent choice for pattern density and energy out to at least 55 yards.

There is a Supersonic No. BBBB steel ball, but I have not tried this size.

Supersonic No. 4 steel buckshot averages 0.250 inch in diameter, or about that of No. 3 lead buckshot. Given tight patterns and a velocity of about 1,300 f.p.s., No. 4 steel buckshot seems a good choice for the 10-gauge Magnum and some 3-inch 12-gauge loads for shots out to 60 yards.

Number 1 Supersonic steel buckshot measures 0.279 inch, which brings it mighty close to the No. 1 lead buckball at 0.30 inch. And the No. 0 Supersonic steel buckshot runs 0.3095 inch, which about splits the difference between No. 0 and No. 00 lead buckshot.

The graphited buffer supplied by U-Load helps stabilize charges of massive buckballs for unbelievably tight patterns! Previously, I noted that the open-choked barrels didn't handle steel shot very well, generally throwing low-density clusters.

When we get to buffered buckshot rounds, however, it's another matter. With Supersonic components loaded according to instructions, the bedded steel buckshot loads will often throw exceedingly tight patterns from improved cylinder and modified chokes. That is not to say that such high-density patterns are assured; each shotgun is still an individual case. But the potential for tight patterns with the more open chokes is there, as compared to steel loads *sans* buffer. In fact, full choke will frequently be an indifferent performer with buffered steel buckshot loads as the narrow choke constriction appears to have an adverse effect on such huge pellets. To begin, try Supersonic steel buckshot concepts with modified choke and experiment with improved cylinder also.

The same 12-gauge Supersonic wad is used in both 3- and 2¾-inch hulls. It must be trimmed by an eighth of an inch for the standard-length hull, an easy task when the special wad trimmer is employed.

The following load data are printed here through the courtesy of U-Load, which has had the material checked by three different laboratories. You will immediately note that the reloading technique is involved. The bulky buckshot are not dropped in via a charging bar; they are counted out and stacked according to instructions. To balance the load with interior hull capacity, the recommendations may call for a given number of undershot and/or overshot wads, both of which are supplied by U-Load. A specific weight of graphited buffer is called for, and handloaders should follow the weight suggestion to fill the shotcup properly without going overboard and encountering pressure problems. Loads seem to perform best with as deep a crimp as possible; and finished crimps should be coated with clear fingernail polish to prevent any seepage of the fine buffer. From this writer's point of view, crisp, once-fired hulls give the most uniform results on a shot-to-shot basis. Following are some recipes that have given excellent patterning results:

SUPERSONIC 10-GAUGE MAGNUM RELOADS

Federal 3½" plastic case (paper base)
Winchester 209 primer
41.0 gr. Blue Dot powder
Supersonic #1000 wad (slit) +
   one undershot wad
90 pellets of Supersonic No. BB + steel
40 grains of Supersonic graphited buffer
Two 10-ga. overshot wads
6-point crimp, sealed
Pressure: 10,300 l.u.p.
Velocity: 1,291 f.p.s.

Federal 3½″ plastic case (paper base)
Winchester 209 primer
41.0 gr. Blue Dot powder
Supersonic #1000 wad (slit) +
   two undershot wads
55 pellets of Supersonic No. BBB steel
   stacked 7 pellets per layer
40 grains of Supersonic graphited buffer
Two 10-ga. overshot wads
6-point crimp, sealed
Pressure: 9,400 l.u.p.
Velocity: 1,288 f.p.s.

Remington 3½″ plastic case (paper base)
CCI 157 primer
44.0 gr. Hodgdon HS-7 powder
Supersonic #1000 wad (slit) +
   three undershot wads
48 pellets of Supersonic No. BBB steel
   stacked 7 pellets per layer
40 grains of Supersonic graphited buffer
6-point crimp, sealed
Pressure: 10,500 l.u.p.
Velocity: 1,335 f.p.s.

A close-up of the Supersonic overshot wad plus some of the graphited buffer on the outside of the wad to reduce friction, which in turn helps to lower interior pressures.

A reload using Supersonic graphited buffer to bed 24 balls of No. 4 steel buckshot over 33.0 grains of HS-7 powder. The hull is a Gold Medal; the wad is a Supersonic trimmed to fit the standard-length case.

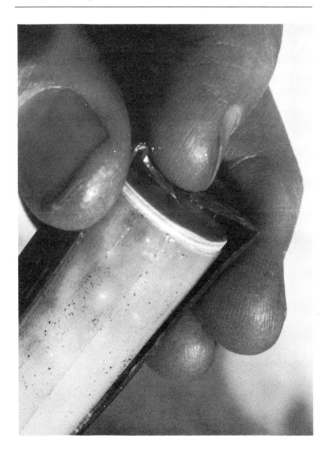

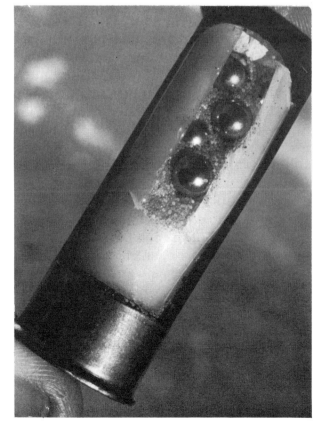

Remington 3½″ plastic case (paper base)
CCI 157 primer
43.0 gr. Hodgdon HS-7 powder
Supersonic #1000 wad (slit) +
  three undershot wads
24 pellets of Supersonic No. 1 buck steel
  stacked 4 pellets per layer
45 grains of Supersonic graphited buffer
One 10-ga. overshot wad
6-point crimp, sealed
Pressure: 10,300 l.u.p.
Velocity: 1,290 f.p.s.

SUPERSONIC 12-GAUGE MAGNUM RELOADS

Federal 3″ plastic case (plastic base)
Winchester 209 primer
32.0 gr. Blue Dot powder
Supersonic #1200 wad (slit)

70 pellets of Supersonic No. BB + steel
35 grains of Supersonic graphited buffer
One 12-ga. overshot wad
6-point crimp, sealed
Pressure: 10,300 l.u.p.
Velocity: 1,294 f.p.s.

The new MEC steel shot conversion kit includes a cylindrical and wider wad ram to eliminate bridging of bulky steel pellets.

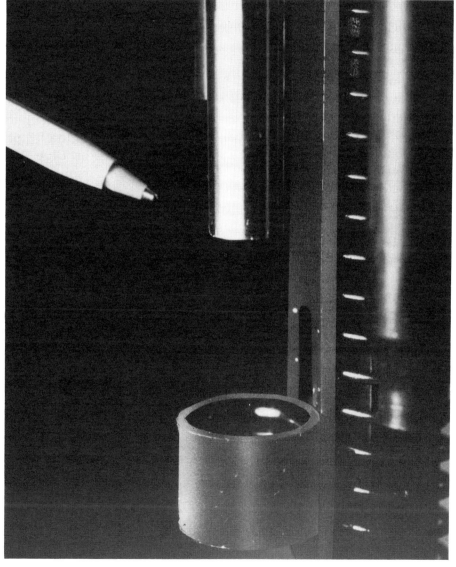

Federal 3″ plastic case (plastic base)
Winchester 209 primer
33.0 gr. Blue Dot powder
Supersonic #1200 wad (slit)
28 pellets of Supersonic No. 4 buck steel
   stacked 4 pellets per layer
40 grains of Supersonic graphited buffer
Two 12-ga. overshot wads
6-point crimp, sealed
Pressure: 10,100 l.u.p.
Velocity: 1,346 f.p.s.

SUPERSONIC STANDARD 12-GAUGE RELOADS

Federal Gold Medal (2¾″) plastic case
Winchester 209 primer
32.0 gr. Hodgdon HS-7 powder
Supersonic #1200 wad trimmed ³⁄₁₆″
40 pellets of Supersonic No. BBB steel
   stacked 5 pellets per layer
30 grains of Supersonic graphited buffer
One 12-ga. overshot wad
8-point crimp, sealed
Pressure: 10,700 l.u.p.
Velocity: 1,299 f.p.s.

Federal Gold Medal (2¾″) plastic case
Winchester 209 primer
33.0 gr. Hodgdon HS-7 powder
Supersonic #1200 wad trimmed ³⁄₁₆″
24 pellets of Supersonic No. 4 buck steel
   stacked 4 pellets per layer
35 grains of Supersonic graphited buffer
One 12-ga. overshot wad
8-point crimp, sealed
Pressure: 10,400 l.u.p.
Velocity: 1,333 f.p.s.

Federal 2¾″ field-style plastic case
   (plastic base)
Winchester 209 primer
33.0 gr. Blue Dot powder
Supersonic #1200 wad trimmed ³⁄₁₆″
40 pellets of Supersonic No. BBB steel
   stacked 5 pellets to a layer

30 grains of Supersonic graphited buffer
One 12-ga. overshot wad
6-point crimp, sealed
Pressure: 10,100 l.u.p.
Velocity: 1,358 f.p.s.

Supersonic leads the way in making steel buckshot reloads perform beautifully for long-range waterfowling, and also offers data for the finer sizes of shot to be used on ducks and close-range geese. Some of these reloads follow. Since I feel that the No. 1 steel pellet is the best all-round shot size for waterfowl, this data emphasizes the Supersonic No. 1 pellet.

SUPERSONIC 10-GAUGE MAGNUM RELOAD

Remington 10-ga. 3½″ plastic case
   (paper base)
Remington 57 primer (Star)
44.0 gr. Blue Dot powder
Supersonic #1000 wad (slit) + one
   undershot wad
148 Supersonic No. 1 steel pellets
40 grains of Supersonic graphited buffer
One Supersonic overshot card
6-point crimp, sealed
Preasure: 9,800 l.u.p. (approximate)
Velocity: 1,338 f.p.s. (nominal)

SUPERSONIC 3-INCH 12-GAUGE MAGNUM RELOAD

Federal 12-ga. 3″ plastic field case
   (plastic base)
Winchester 209 primer
32.0 gr. Blue Dot powder
Supersonic #1200 wad (slit)
124 Supersonic No. 1 steel pellets
30 grains of Supersonic graphited buffer
One Supersonic overshot card
6-point crimp, sealed
Preasure: 10,200 l.u.p. (approximate)
Velocity: 1,288 f.p.s. (nominal)

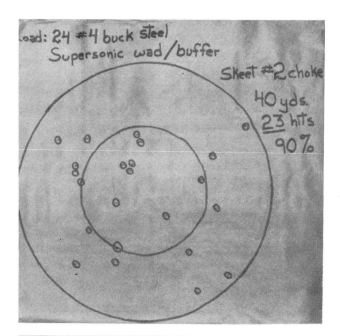

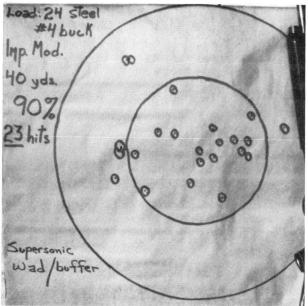

Buffered steel buckshot reloads patterned very well for the author from open-bored guns. This 90 percent pattern was made with a No. 2 Skeet tube at 40 yards. Only one ball of the loaded 24 failed to group.

Here's an example of exceptionally tight center density with No. 4 steel buckshot. Fired through an improved modified choke, the total spread at 40 yards is a little more than 21 inches.

SUPERSONIC STANDARD-LENGTH 12-GAUGE RELOAD

Federal 12-ga. 2¾″ plastic field case
  (plastic base)
Winchester 209 primer
33.0 gr. Blue Dot powder
Supersonic #1200 wad (slit) trimmed ³/₁₆″
104 Supersonic No. 1 steel pellets
30 grains of Supersonic graphited buffer
One Supersonic overshot card
6-point crimp, sealed
Preasure: 10,100 l.u.p. (appoximate)
Velosity: 1,361 f.p.s. (nominal)

The future will undoubtedly bring more data from U-Load, as innovator Don Vizecky continues to work with his materials. Some ultra-high-velocity 1- and 1⅛-ounce loads are in the offing; they team the 3-inch 12-gauge Magnum hull with these lighter payloads for searing speeds which, if patterns hold tight, will drive goose-folding energies to heights previously undreamed of. Inventive handloaders are leading the way to making steel loads considerably more effective. We cannot only live with steel shot, but by applying some ingenuity and understanding we will soon be making it equal to the typical wingshot's skill with a shotgun.

Because high-density steel patterns will have a short shot string, however, there will always be a lot of missing, which hunters will blame on the loads rather than their lack of precision. When those short, energy-laden shot strings of steel buckballs get to the target, though, the job will be done very cleanly. It was just a matter of time until new concepts arrived, and it is now the hunter's responsibility to realize how different steel is from lead and to make certain of his gun/load combo's performance before complaining.

24
The Psychology and Practice of Decoying

A typical hunter will buy a dozen or so decoys, spread them at random in front of a makeshift blind, and sit back to await the results — which in most cases are quite meager. More than a few modern hunters of said ilk have spent full days without having a single bird work their spread even though several flocks may have passed within easy sight of the decoys. The reason for such failures, of course, is that there's much more to attracting birds than tossing out a few decoys. First, there's the psychology of decoying; secondly, there's the practical aspect of setting them properly.

From a purely psychological standpoint, there are few reasons why flying waterfowl should be expected to plop enthusiastically into any and all decoy spreads offered by hunters. For although waterfowl tend to be gregarious, the birds in flight are hardly naive creatures winging about lost and lonely. With certain exceptions, ducks and geese have definite flight plans and destinations. Birds that leave the marsh every morning know in which stubble field they'll feed. Later, those leaving the stubble or other feeding areas make a beeline back to the safety of the marsh. And if there is flighting during the midday hours, the birds have undoubtedly fed and are mainly exercising their wild instincts. In either case, there is no special reason for them to swoop down and visit every duck in sight. Indeed, there is nothing more natural than a duck or goose flying over other ducks and geese. Simple spreads of just a few decoys indiscriminately set can be expected to fail. Moreover, since waterfowl begin seeing decoys as soon as they start their southward migration, one can assume that the flocks quickly learn to be skeptical of setups even if that knowledge comes to them by sheer rote.

The main exception to this cautiousness may be when fresh migrants reach a stopover marsh or refuge on their way south; then the new arrivals will search for feeding areas, and they might be attracted to a good spread of decoys in a likely feeding or resting location. This is one reason why it pays to be out hunting when a weather front moves toward your area, because waterfowl often migrate ahead of approaching bad weather and will decoy easier at the end of a long flight into strange surroundings. Another exception is the lone goose, which will accept many invitations to drop into decoys because it lacks a leader. Wedges of geese with leaders have an experienced "brain" to guide them, and they are less readily drawn into a spread of decoys. As a rule of thumb, the greater the hunting pressure and/or the more familiar the birds are with a given area, the harder it is to bring them into the decoys no matter how realistic the setup and the calling.

Before one can begin to use decoys successfully, he must accept the fact that ducks and geese aren't dummies cavorting about in the sky looking for buddies with which to frolic. Attracting their attention and getting them to come within effective shotgun range requires realism, action, and innovation. After all, waterfowl that have been nonchalantly flying over all sorts of other waterfowl virtually every day see nothing especially exciting about another dozen "birds" on a pond or in a grain field. To them, such sights are routine.

The secret to successful decoying today pivots on decoy size, decoy numbers, and decoy action. Couple those with expert calling and you've got a chance, despite competi-

DIVING DUCKS FROM SHORE BLIND OR BOAT

The common fishhook rig shown here provides an open invitation for birds to land upwind into the unoccupied area left in the hooklike gap. The tail string of decoys should always stretch downwind into open water and if there is a switch in wind direction during the hunt, the spread should be changed accordingly for optimum effectiveness. A grassed-over duck boat would be an advantage if this happens, since it can be repositioned easily if need be; a blind is stationary.

WIND ⟶

tion from other hunters, and despite birds that have been under hunting pressure all the way along their migration route.

Many hunters today find that the so-called magnum decoys produce more action than standard-sized blocks, be it on ducks or geese. The best explanation for this is simply that magnum-sized decoys are more easily seen. Some goose hunters have carried that to an extreme, and in some areas they employ goose decoys large enough to accommodate a hunter. Don't laugh. The method works well enough to have been written up in some leading outdoor journals. Traditionalists may scoff at such gimmicks, arguing that the Indians of James Bay bring in geese with only scattered pieces of white cloth draped on bushes; however, those Indians are operating virtually on the birds' breeding ground when

the flights are still inexperienced in the tricky ways of man. For hunters just getting into decoying, or for frustrated waterfowlers who can't draw birds over the blocks, an investment in magnum-sized decoys is recommended for large marshes, big lakes or sounds, and grain fields.

Some experienced hunters may debate the use of magnum-sized mallard blocks in flooded timber, but birds looking **down** through tree crowns can spot a big decoy easier than a small one. About the only way to determine their overall effectiveness is by trying the larger decoys in your particular hunting situation.

The number of decoys in a spread can be a critical factor. Like schooling fish, waterfowl instinctively follow the concept of finding safety in numbers. In other words, the more the

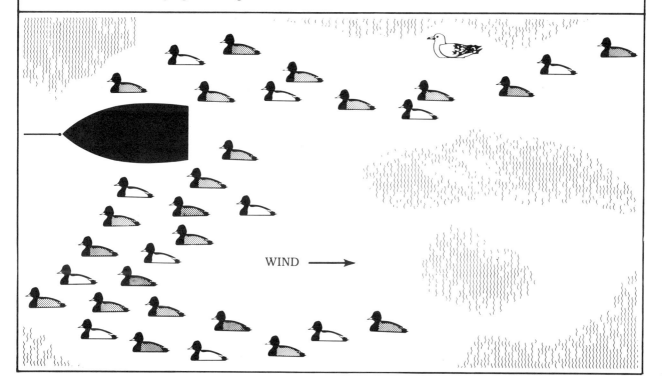

DIVING DUCKS FROM OPEN WATER BLIND OR BOAT

To the novice, this spread with a boat or blind among the decoys seems like nonsense. However, divers flying low, as they usually do, will work over and into just such a setup, a variation of the fishhook concept. Of course, the hunters should remain low and motionless in the boat. A seagull confidence decoy will help. The large, mostly white gull block also adds to the spread's visibility. In rough weather, with the boat rocking, this is challenging shooting.

WIND ⟶

merrier. Thus, massive decoy spreads will almost always do better than paltry ones, which is why the weekend hunter is often frustrated and experiences long waits between shots as he sits beside his dozen or so fakes. From on high, a passing duck or goose may see several similar setups; and if it comes in at all, it'll go to the one that offers or intrigues it the most. Intrigue being absent, the drawing force is numbers — a bird trusts a hundred ducks far more than it trusts just a dozen. Sheer decoy count, then, will lure birds that overfly lesser spreads. Today, one hundred duck decoys is a nice starting number for spreads that stand out against those of other hunters; they win in the competition for the birds' attention, and they tend to overcome the birds' sense of caution.

Of course, a population explosion of decoys outside your blind isn't going to bring in everything like a magnet. I have some friends who lug a thousand goose silhouettes and decoys to North Dakota each fall, and still see many flights pass up their spread. It's the nature of waterfowl to overfly other waterfowl, and one must expect that to happen. Generally, however, massive layouts of decoys do improve your chances.

INNOVATIONS

A group of decoys can look extremely lifeless and uninviting to waterfowl passing overhead, and the only way to change that is to include some extreme realism and action. In the old days, it was legal to use live birds as decoys — Judas ducks, they were called — and that technique worked beautifully. Using

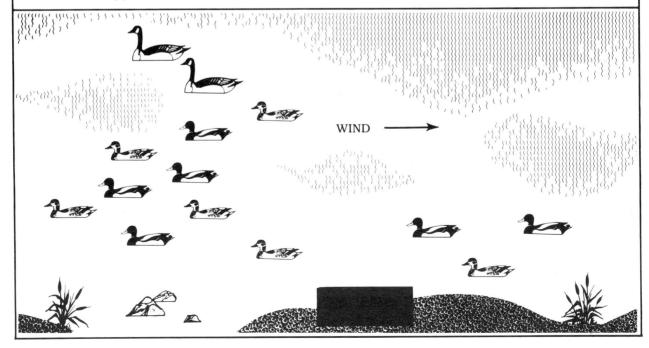

J-RIG FOR PUDDLE DUCKS FROM SHORE BLIND OR BOAT

This is another application of the fishhook or J-rig spread, but it has variations for puddle ducks like mallards and teal. Fewer decoys are needed, but the J-shape is retained. The bulk of the spread is upwind from the boat or blind, because puddlers tend to land near the tail of the spread. However, leave more space between decoys when rigging for puddlers than when setting up for divers, as puddlers will sometimes drop right into the main mass. Therefore, it is also wise to keep the main body of blocks within easy range of the blind or boat. This is probably the most commonly used layout for puddlers when hunting from shore. It will work on lakes, ponds, marshes, and rivers.

WIND ⟶

domesticated live decoys has been against the law for decades and today a hunter must think up mechanical and innovative things to make his spread stand out and to make birds *want* to visit.

Adding action to a decoy layout is something that hunters have been doing lately. In Texas, for instance, the gunning guides have been flying kites over the blocks to simulate birds pitching in. Another method devised to give the impression of geese dropping into a spread of decoys has been developed in the Chesapeake Bay area, where imaginative waterfowlers have begun waving black flags from their pits. Sometimes they use a big

black flag attached to a long pole, which is a ploy to get the attention of distant birds, but when birds work closer they wave a pair of smaller black flags in semaphore fashion. Experience tends to indicate that flag waving works best on freshly arrived birds, and that geese will quickly become leery of flags and ignore them. But it's always worth a try. Those birds that are lured by flag waving seem to pay no attention to a human among the decoys at a distance.

Activating floating decoys is another way to attract both ducks and geese. Decoys can be made to move and cause ripples by means of a long string from the blind to the blocks.

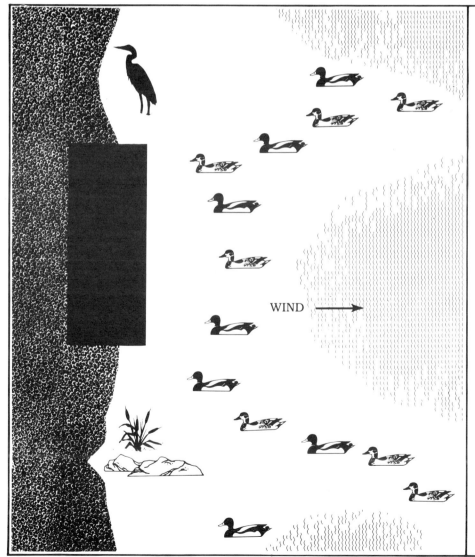

WIND →

PUDDLE DUCKS FROM SHORE BLIND WITH OFFSHORE WIND

The formation here encourages incoming birds to land in the open space in front of the blind. The spread should retain a sort of J-shape rather than a U-shape, with one string slightly longer than the other. Skill and experience are needed to make this setup productive, as incoming birds look directly at the blind and can spot unnatural clutter or foreign objects. Be sure to police up any empty shells, paper, and so forth in the vicinity. A confidence decoy helps with this situation, be it a heron, crow, or pair of goose blocks. If you use a crow, put it in a tree or on a pole some distance down the shoreline.

Monofilament fishing line works best for this because it is nearly invisible, but any dark line will suffice.

Some manufacturers provide decoys made specifically for animation. These include the tail section of a mallard or pintail to simulate a puddler feeding. Also, if you search hunting supply catalogs carefully, you can find some decoys designed to be self-activating via a battery-powered drive system.

Hunters also can create ripples and rings in the water by other physical means; guides who work the pin oaks of Arkansas and other flooded timber do so by sloshing the water with their booted legs. Hunters with foresight often take stones into the blinds with them and toss some among the decoys to make waves when birds swing by curiously.

Another trick among decoy experts is the so-called ''confidence'' set. This is the use of a decoy other than a duck or goose, and it can take the form of a sea gull, crow, grebe, or other water or shore bird. More than one type of confidence decoy can be used, but the layout should always look natural and not overdone.

In theory, the presence of some other species of bird makes the waterfowl feel confident that the decoy spread is the real thing. This is especially true if the other species is crafty or skittish by nature and likely to spook at the first sight of a man or some other potential danger. A great blue heron, for example, will flush if a human or coyote approaches, and a sharp-eyed old crow will let out a squawk at anything it doesn't like. The ducks know that a crow won't hang if any hunters are nearby.

In some respects, the use of a crow as a confidence-builder is the easiest way for many

---

PUDDLE DUCKS AND DIVERS FROM SHORE

This combination scheme works well where both divers and puddlers ply the same area. There are really two strings of blocks tailing out. The puddlers are expected to come down the slot and land behind the main body of those decoys because puddlers are, in general, reluctant to swing over divers. The space left between the two groups invites divers to pitch in. Note the space between the rearmost puddler ''guide'' decoys and the main body of puddlers, which leaves open water in front of the blind. Again, the addition of a confidence decoy or two doesn't hurt.

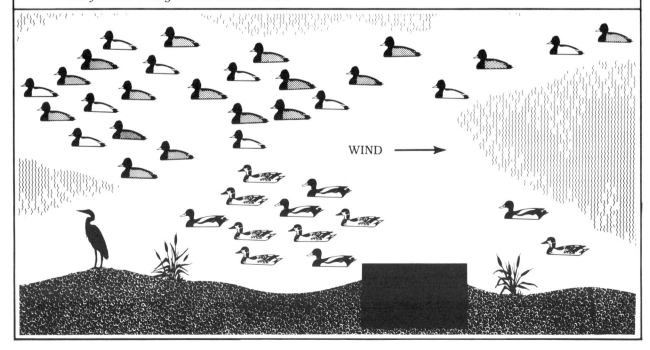

WIND ⟶

hunters to add another dimension to their setup. Crow decoys are readily obtained, and they can be placed very prominently in a tree or on a pole so that they can be seen from afar. Crows and mallards aren't exactly feathered friends, of course, and it is best to locate the crow decoy well away from the immediate landing/action zone. A tall tree some distance behind the blind or off to either side will work better than if the crow decoy is placed close to the duck or goose decoys.

The availability of confidence decoys is improving as the method becomes more widely known and practiced, and a perusal of outdoor catalogs will help hunters find other types of decoys made for this purpose.

A variation of the confidence concept is using a spread of Canada goose decoys to draw ducks into stubble. This can work unbelievably well on mallards because they seem to respect the wariness of geese. If the big birds find a safe place to feed or rest and congregate en masse, the mallards throw caution to the winds. We chanced upon this characteristic of greenheads in Canada, and it has since worked for me stateside. One good place to use the trick is in the stubble fields surrounding big marshes and refuges where mallards and geese mix on the resting grounds and make morning and evening feeding flights. In an area where flighting was heavy, but where ducks simply wouldn't work

PUDDLE DUCKS AND DIVERS IN OPEN WATER

Here is a good pattern for a floating or a stake blind. Use plenty of decoys to attract attention, and have the divers in a version of the J-rig to one side and the puddlers on the other side. The puddler duck decoys will be set approximately like those of the shoreline rig. Place a couple of seagull confidence blocks downwind. Some hunters will actually place a standing gull decoy on the bow of the boat itself for added "confidence." The birds know that no "gull" will land on a boat with people in it.

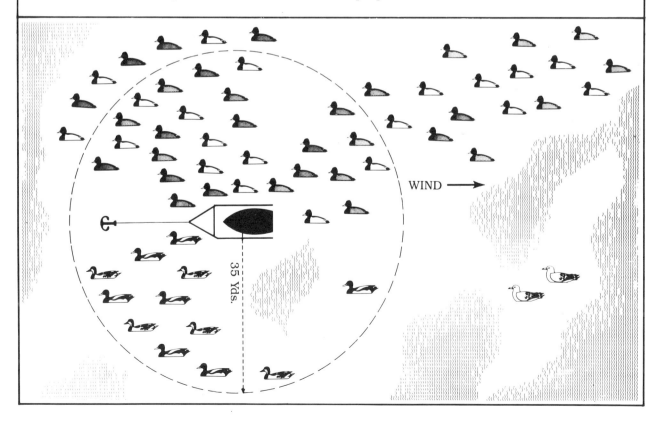

WIND →

35 Yds.

to duck decoys, I was able to get some shooting inside 40 yards by setting out goose decoys instead of mallard blocks.

Finally, you can use live decoys supplied by nature. If a less desirable bird, such as a ruddy duck, coot, old squaw, or bufflehead drops into the spread, don't shoot or otherwise spook it. Let the visitor swim around, thus making the setup much more lifelike and providing some movement in the blocks.

GUNS AND LOADS

Although decoys supposedly bring birds closer for easier shooting, today's ducks don't invariably cup their wings and slant to the blocks. Heavy hunting pressure has given many waterfowl a kind of "street savvy," and they often won't pitch into the most realistic spread even when it is presided over by an expert caller. Therefore, don't assume that all

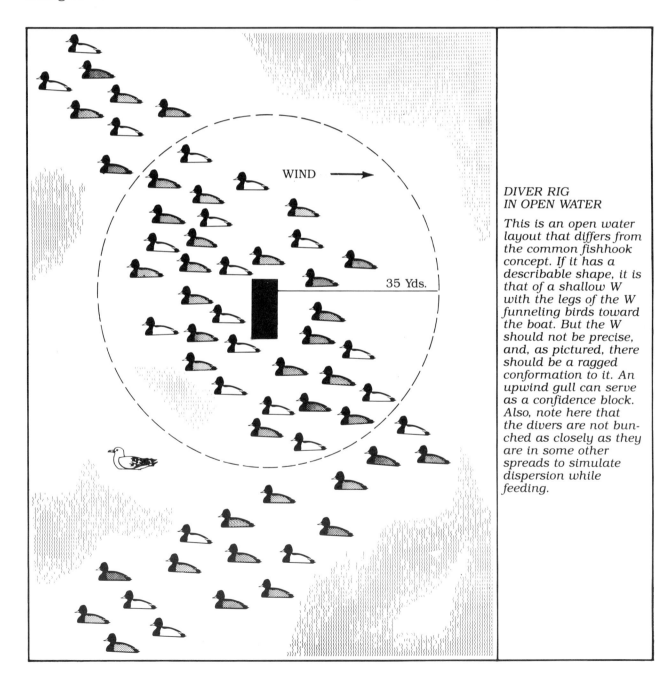

DIVER RIG IN OPEN WATER

This is an open water layout that differs from the common fishhook concept. If it has a describable shape, it is that of a shallow W with the legs of the W funneling birds toward the boat. But the W should not be precise, and, as pictured, there should be a ragged conformation to it. An upwind gull can serve as a confidence block. Also, note here that the divers are not bunched as closely as they are in some other spreads to simulate dispersion while feeding.

WIND →

35 Yds.

shots over decoys will be easy. The theory of using an open-bored gun and lighter loads of smaller pellets is applicable only when the birds *do indeed* break formation and drop in to offer slow, close-range shots.

These days, decoys frequently do little more than hold the birds' attention for a couple of passes, and if the hunter wants any shooting, he's forced to take them on the closest swing which can still be 30- to 40-yard shooting. Open-bored guns and light loads don't deliver perfectly under such conditions, and a modified choke isn't too tight even when one is enthusiastic about decoying and calling. Nor are No. 5s out of the picture. The combination of modified choke and 1¼ ounces of hard 5s is an excellent selection with decoys, as it can handle a full 45 yards if needed. When the gun is a repeater, some 1⅜- or 1½-ounce magnum loads of 5s are also good back-up insurance in the magazine.

With steel shot, No. 4s are about the lightest pellet one should consider, even with an open-bored gun. Since there are more steel pellets of a given size per ounce than there are lead pellets, steel 4s still give adequate coverage from an improved cylinder or skeet bore while providing penetrating power at reasonable distances. However, if any passing shots are to be taken, steel 2s and 1s are preferred.

Thus, the hunter who can discipline himself to wait for close shots can get by with lighter loads and a more open choke, but those who take chances on birds that circle but make no obvious move to drop in must compensate for the added range with tighter chokes and heavier pellets and shot charges.

SELECTING DECOYS

An old saying tells us "all that glitters is not gold," and we can apply the same idea to waterfowl decoys. For although many species of ducks and geese are brightly colored, they don't glitter sparkle, glint, and shine like some

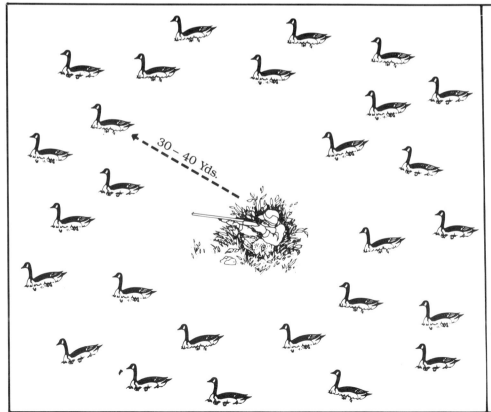

FIELD SET FOR DUCKS OR GEESE

The basic pattern is a random feeding distribution of decoys circling the hidden hunter. Shell-type decoys and silhouettes are made for this kind of field shooting. Decoys should be kept within 30–40 yards of the blind or pit, as arriving birds tend to land on the fringe of the spread. Position the birds facing or quartering into the wind, especially if it is strong, because birds don't like to have their feathers ruffled by wind blowing "against the grain."

30 – 40 Yds.

of the glossy decoys on the market. One is inclined to believe that some decoy makers fashion their products to lure unsophisticated hunters rather than wary waterfowl, and such products are best utilized as decorative items for the den. Effective decoys tend to be drab and to absorb light, not reflect it. Instead of splitting a purchase of decoys between drakes and hens, it is wise to include more hens for their darker coloration regardless of the species in question. If your present decoys do have a flashy finish, use some method to rough them up and eliminate the shine, or repaint them using special decoy paints available from a number of suppliers.

The least expensive decoys today are made of plastic, and they are popular with many hunters because of their lower cost per dozen. Modern molding techniques produce some very realistic replicas with careful wing and feather detailing, but one must wonder just how vital those minor lines are to a duck

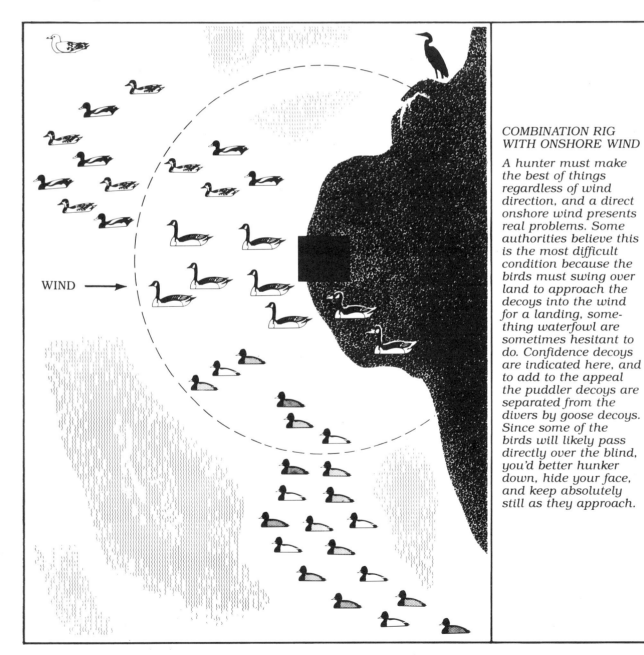

COMBINATION RIG WITH ONSHORE WIND

A hunter must make the best of things regardless of wind direction, and a direct onshore wind presents real problems. Some authorities believe this is the most difficult condition because the birds must swing over land to approach the decoys into the wind for a landing, something waterfowl are sometimes hesitant to do. Confidence decoys are indicated here, and to add to the appeal the puddler decoys are separated from the divers by goose decoys. Since some of the birds will likely pass directly over the blind, you'd better hunker down, hide your face, and keep absolutely still as they approach.

in the distance. Here, again, the features may be more attractive to the hunter than the hunted. However, on the positive side, such plastic molded decoys are durable, relatively tough, and very easy to maintain.

There are two types of plastic decoys. One type has a hollow body, while the other type is filled with polyurethane foam. The type with a polyurethane core is virtually unsinkable. A hollow plastic decoy, on the other hand, will tilt and look unnatural if it somehow springs a leak.

Dyed-in-the-wool waterfowlers, purists, and traditionalists opt for wooden or cork decoys. In addition to the nostalgic and aesthetic appeal of wooden decoys, carving and painting them is considered a true American art form. Decoy shows are held in various parts of the country, and interest is especially keen in the Chesapeake Bay region. Antique decoys that can be traced to the great old carvers command lofty price tags running into hundreds of dollars per block.

Unfortunately, wood is not the perfect material for decoys. It demands annual maintenance (painting and patching), and it is prone to soaking up water and possibly splitting when it dries out in storage. Moreover, a bag of wooden decoys is quite heavy when compared to the light plastics. Only a handful of sources offers wooden gunning blocks today.

Cork decoys ride the waves in buoyant, lifelike manner, but they are quite expensive when priced against molded plastic ones. Also, the nature of cork eliminates the possibility of carving in fine detail, but their lifelike floating qualities more than make up for the lack of feather and wing detail. By the time a duck notices the absence of feather veins and wing lines, it's too late. Cork-bodied decoys are available in magnum sizes and in a variety of species.

Whenever possible, select decoys with moveable heads. There are commercially obtainable cork and plastic models with this desirable feature. Birds on the water will often have their heads turned variously, including to the rear when preening. Using different head positions in a spread of decoys lends to its overall realism.

One doesn't really need full sets of decoys for land and water respectively. Floating decoys can be used for field gunning, but they will have to be braced upright due to the keel. Such bracing can be done with corn cobs, clumps of dirt, or twigs. If the ground is workable, a slot can be dug to accept the keel and added dirt can be pressed into place for a secure hold. Most field hunters use silhouettes and decoy shells because they are relatively inexpensive and lightweight. Many waterfowlers use homemade goose silhouettes, which needn't be fancy.

For the hunter facing a long walk, or for the hunter who works in flooded timber with small openings, there are collapsible rubber decoys that carry easily in the game pocket of one's hunting coat. These are self-inflating; they pop into shape as you toss them on the water. Such collapsible rubber decoys are best suited to sheltered, relatively calm waters.

When massive decoy spreads are made up of different types of decoys, keep them grouped according to size and material. Such grouping presents a more uniform layout to the birds, whereas having a couple of large cork decoys amidst smaller plastic ones gives a curious, unnatural appearance that could be a detriment under certain conditions. When a wind is blowing, for example, large blocks will ride differently than lighter ones.

Once the decoys have been selected and rigged, the next step is setting them in a natural manner *and* in such ways as to arouse the birds' curiosity and draw them into position for a close-range shot.

25
Good Calling Will Work – Sometimes

Have you ever been on a crowded duck marsh when practically every hunter there thought he was an expert caller, but the sounds were more like those of a New Year's Eve party? The mismanaged call reeds hummed, buzzed, crackled, and tooted like those in cheap party horns, producing totally unlifelike noises. Whenever a duck hove into sight, everyone tried to call louder than his neighbor, apparently hopeful that the birds, like teenagers buying rock records, wanted sheer volume. The score for such days, if it were kept, would show that no ducks decoyed and that few, if any, even bothered to circle. The amateur antics scared every bird away before it could get remotely interested in joining the decoys.

That situation is certainly common these days as hunting areas shrivel while the number of hunters grows or remains the same. Poor callers perforce gather where everyone else hunts, thus cluttering the air with sound waves that repulse birds. And nobody gets shooting.

Conditions such as this have caused beginners, along with inexperienced and casual hunters, to believe that calling doesn't work; that the stories of greenhead mallards and sprig with flashing wings being lured to the blocks are just figments of some magazine writer's imagination. They've never seen it happen.

But ducks and geese still do slant to the decoys at the behest of a good caller. They may circle warily, but they can be coaxed in. It's a classic part of waterfowling that's still with us. The birds haven't changed.

What has changed is the skill of the caller and the conditions under which he operates. Just as many hunters don't practice with their shotguns during the offseason, neither do they work on the basics and fine points of waterfowl calling. At the end of a season, the calls are set aside with the oiled guns, and they aren't resurrected until the next opening day. So, too, do many hunters buy their first call the evening before opening day and, without any expert advice or conscientious practice, proceed to make a mockery of the art.

THE BASICS OF DUCK CALLING

What a waterfowl hunter must realize is that game calls are *definitely not* mere horns made to be blown with the same steady breath release used with party horns. Game calls, after all, are nothing more than vibrating reeds set inside resonance chambers, and they don't automatically give off mallard music. The secrets of successful duck calling are twofold. First, the breath release must be controlled in a certain way for lifelike sounds. Secondly, specific calls must be applied to different situations. Random and reckless squawking, heard all too often these days, is hardly effective calling. Indeed, it is a moot question as to whether it is true calling at all, and may best be described as pure noise.

Calling can still bring in ducks and geeses, but overall hunting conditions must be favorable — and the caller must sound like a duck, not a New Year's Eve reveler.

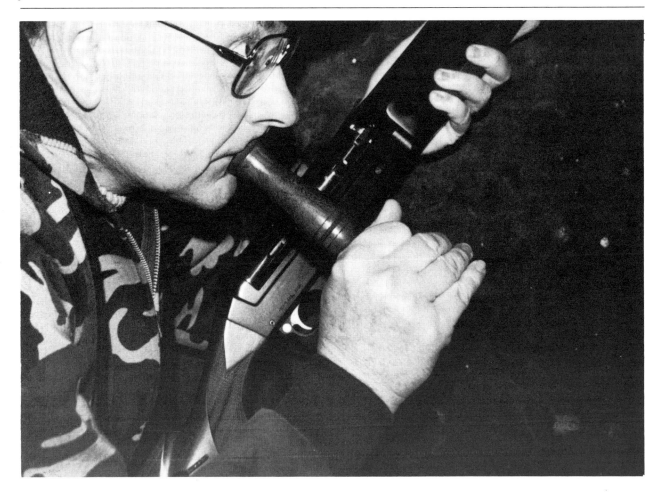

For the purposes of this chapter, we'll center mainly on the mallard call. It is the most versatile and the most popular, for the mallard is widely distributed and most other species will come to a mallard call and decoy spread.

The hardest part of using a call for a beginner is getting a true lifelike sound. This is because they insist upon blowing from the mouth, perhaps even from puffy cheeks, which sets an impossible foundation for both the basics and finesse points.

We'll begin with the grip. Place the barrel between your thumb and index finger at the point where the barrel joins the call's bulbous keg. This leaves three fingers free to be flexed cuplike around the barrel's opening for sound manipulation. The call is set tightly against the upper lip, with that upper lip covering half the opening. Keep the call in that position by hand pressure, and make all movements with the lower jaw.

Now we come to forming the lifelike "quack." Keep your tongue still, blow from the diaphragm or stomach area, and say "kak" into that call while forcing air from deep down. This technique is in keeping with what music teachers instruct young singers, namely, to sing from the diaphragm. The mouth, tongue, teeth and other articulators only help shape the sounds, they don't originate them. So, too, in mallard calling. The call starts deep down. You can stubbornly insist upon blowing from the mouth, but no truly good or great caller has ever done so. They not only follow the fundamentals of blowing from the depths, but they are the ones who developed the technique.

Producing a true, controlled, lifelike sound takes a lot of practice. It is not

The reward for good calling: birds sweeping the blocks and offering close-range shots. The teal shown here will respond to mallard talk, as will most other species of puddle ducks.

Take 'em when they break over the blocks.

something one picks up overnight by tooting into his first cheap call. That's the difference between a dedicated hunter and a Saturday morning also-ran: the dedicated hunter/caller knows it won't come easily, and he puts time and money into the skill. Thus, the nonexpert must work at calling, realizing that the pressure he builds up in the call is of paramount importance, and he can only learn to regulate that by serious, critical practice. A "that's good enough" attitude won't suffice. The sounds must be perfect for consistency on wild birds.

Saying "kak" into a duck call may not seem correct to many who have never taken an in-depth look or listened to expert calling. But it does reproduce the mallard's normal sound. Anyone who spends time listening to wild mallards — *something a caller must do* — should notice that they don't make a slow, lazy, slurring, sloshy "quack" of the sort inexpert callers produce. The mallard's voice, if it can be called that, is brisk and crisp and brassy, given to the "k" sound more than the "c" or "q" sound. Moreover, duck talk is considerably faster than most typical hunters realize, and each individual "kak" should be broken off sharply, not dragged out. Paying attention at the local zoo's duck pond will help any beginner appreciate the speed and brassy chatter of mallards. The biggest mistake made by many modern hunters is that they never listen to what they are trying to copy, which explains their ineptitude.

There are three calls based on the "kak." The first is the long-range hailing call, known also as the highball. Its purpose is to attract distant birds. The caller uses considerable

---

For optimum effectiveness today, a caller's best work is done with the largest spread of decoys possible. Small spreads of decoys on heavily hunted marshes seldom attract wary birds looking for plenty of company.

Interested, but still swinging wide, this flock presents a challenge to the caller who must cajole them into range.

force to project the call, and the best sequence seems to be a series of five distinct "kaks" beginning with a long one followed by progressively shorter ones, such as: "ka-kaaaaak! kaaaak! kaaaak! kaak! kak!" Keep each call well defined. Don't slur them or run them together, but don't waste time between them. Listen to real ducks to get the idea. Put the emphasis on the first notes and use a slightly descending volume on the final three.

Blasting a highball call directly at flying ducks is courting disappointment. Instead of inviting the birds and arousing their curiosity, such blasts will scare them. A highball is useful when birds are 200 yards or more away. Angle the call downward and let the sound spill along the water or stubble in a natural manner. A direct skyward call can help the ducks pinpoint the caller and recognize a phony setup for what it is.

When ducks are within 200 yards, but passing while paying no attention to the decoy spread, a variation of the highball call is used. Termed the welcome call, it is much like the highball except that it has significantly less volume. For experimentation, three "kaks" can be employed instead of five. Keep it friendly and soft. This is where finesse comes in. Manipulate the sound by cupping the fingers toward the end of some notes to muffle them. It is important, however, to stay crisp even though the volume is reduced, and continue to grunt up the air from well down. Don't get sloppy and start to think "quack" instead of "kak." That's not a Halloween horn!

What if the birds make a swing or start to depart? Those are normal occurrences. Don't panic or give up. Birds must feel totally at ease in an area before they drop in without a pass, and gunfire puts them on guard. This is where skill enters the game. You've got to coax them by finesse. Continued quacking won't do, so keep it plain. Now it's time for the comeback call, which is a long string of emotional, pleading "kaks" intended to turn the outgoers. Again, don't blast directly at the birds; point the call downward. Be emotional. Send the notes rapidly and urgently. Make the call say, "Hey, you guys, come back here. We need you. The food's good!" If two or more callers can get in on this pleading, so much the better. The problem is finding two good callers to occupy the blind at the same time, and a faulty sound by anyone can send the birds out of sight. Don't worry about five- or three-"kak" sentences. Just let 'em rattle. The note of urgency and pleading is more important.

When ducks are working close, the so-called feeding chuckle is necessary. It is made by saying "ticket" into the call while still bringing air up from the diaphragm. Listening to contented mallards on a farm pond or at a nearby park lagoon will help you get the idea. This chuckle goes on like machine-gun fire, and to duplicate it the hunter must flip his tongue rapidly, crisply, and continuously. Thus, whereas the tongue is left out of the highball, welcome, and comeback calls, it is brought into the feeding chuckle and becomes an integral part of the call as one goes from the first syllable of "ticket" to the second.

One important point relative to the feeding chuckle is that it can become too mechanical. Hunters deliver it without expression. But the key is making it sound real, meaning that the hunter must inject a calm, contented feeling. Botching the feeding chuckle spells disaster, because it's the final phase of the calling sequence. If you can't convince working birds that your decoys are feeding contentedly and feeling safe, you'll soon be repeating the comeback call — often in vain. Heavy hunting will frequently render the comeback call worthless, and when the birds keep swinging a sharp hunter will be ready to take them on the closest swing. Even the most expert feeding chuckle will fail when the marshes are filled with hunters. Therefore, don't anticipate birds to cup their wings and glide in; sometimes, a swing over the blocks is the best chance you'll get. Recognize the situation and take your shots as they come.

An effective calling combination for on-coming birds is the feeding chuckle with some soft, playful quacking mixed in. Anyone who watches mallards on water knows there is some quacking intermingled with the chuckle. But guard against making the quacks sound argumentative, for other birds know that mallard drakes can be quarrelsome, and they'll avoid potential disputes.

Random calling is a dubious practice except on foggy days. Then the sounds will attract birds that are moving but have no definite destination. Even in hunted areas, they'll drop lower on days of limited visibility and seem more interested. Otherwise, random calling into birdless skies does little good.

A trained ear will immediately note that much calling is done too slowly. Mallards don't have southern drawls. They are swift talkers

Although special calls are available for various species — wood ducks, pintails, and widgeon, for example — the mallard call will still attract attention because the mallard is so widespread.

and would probably make exceptional hucksters as humans. Their quacks and chuckles rattle along, perhaps twice as fast as most hunters call. Once lifelike sounds are developed, then, a hunter must practice speeding them up.

Mallards make raspy, brassy sounds, and the calls should duplicate that natural timbre. Don't buy a call unless you can try it, and insist upon a natural sound (provided, of course, that your own blowing technique can produce one). Many calls are inherently far better than they sound in the hands of poor callers. A single-reed call suffices for most open hunt-

ing, but a double-reed is recommended for enticing them into flooded woodland.

There is such a thing as too much calling. The more you call, the greater will be your chance of error. Likewise, flocks of mallards don't always raise the roof. They feed quietly, chuckling, and extensive calling is unnatural. You might like to hear yourself tooting, but excessive calling does not fit into the natural scene. After you've learned to control the call, learn to control yourself.

Another helpful point is keeping your face down while calling. Angling the call skyward not only produces an unnaturally strong and

---

A good caller can bring geese right over the blind.

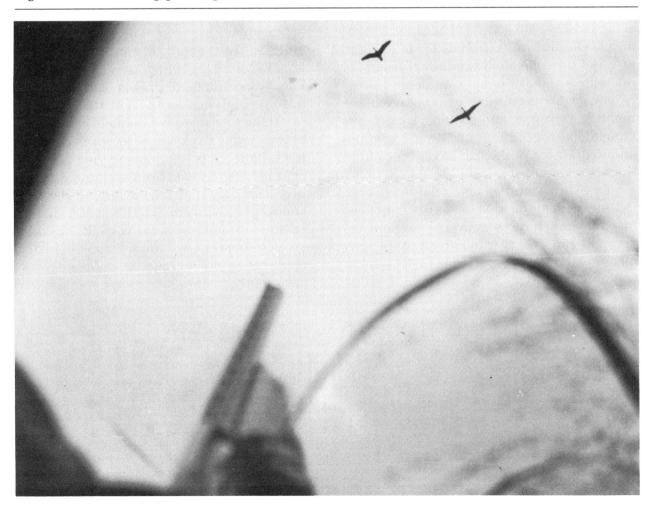

direct blast, but it can also expose one's face, and the shine on a hunter's face will invariably scare the birds. Wear a long-billed cap, keep your face down, and watch the birds by rolling your eyes upward. Try to be in the blind or in shade when calling. Birds do spot hunters by zeroing in on the sound, but they have difficulty pinpointing shaded figures.

WHERE TO CALL

Does it pay to improve one's calling for today's crowded conditions? It does — and it doesn't. If one's hunting is done solely on crowded waters during busy weekends, there is scant advantage in even the most expert calling. The birds are simply too spooky; they won't respond. Under such conditions the most successful hunting technique is to use massive decoy spreads and just a modicum of expert calling. And even then it probably isn't the calling that turns the trick, but is instead the vast number of decoys. How many decoys are we talking about? A hundred will be fine for starters! Weekend hunters with just a dozen or so aren't even in the ball game except for occasional singles or small flocks that do nothing more than overfly the spread. Ducks understand that there is safety in numbers, and under hunting pressure they may be drawn to the tremendous spreads if they react at all.

For optimum success in calling these days, it's best to gun on a private hunting area where the birds can work without being fired upon or cajoled by other hunters. When that sort of situation is available, calling will help.

Although calling may not pay off on a widespread, day-in, day-out basis, there's always the matter of self-satisfaction, of perfecting — or at least improving — a personal outdoor skill. It's fun being good at something, to stand well above the typical horn blowers and terrible squawkers who frequent our duck marshes and refuge lines. As a skill, good calling is akin to championship shooting and to expert dog training. Not one out of a hundred duck hunters is a truly good caller. Perhaps, then, the first secret of becoming a better duck caller is accepting a personal weakness and backing up to start again rather than merely practicing one's old mistakes. Forget the notion that calls are blown like horns. Grunt up those "kaks" and "tickets" from your stomach. Make the abdomen draw tight like it does at the end of a long whistle. Develop a feel for pitch, tone, articulation, volume, and even emotions. That's the difference between hooting with a New Year's Eve horn and luring wary ducks into your spread.

26
Potholes
and Jump Shooting

Decoy spreads on lakes and marshes can do a brisk business on opening weekends and misty mornings. Ditto for those blustery days at the tag end of a season when snow squalls and nor'easters boom across the bay.

But there are a lot more days each season when conventional sit-and-wait hunting nets naught. Strings of red-winged blackbirds flitter by on their way south; mosquitoes still buzz; and there isn't a cloud in the breezeless sky. Bluebird days, they're called, a time when hunters need plenty of hot, black coffee to keep them awake *just in case* something happens (but normally never does).

Experienced hunters know better than to expect action in a classic blind-and-decoy setup on those balmy springlike days. The birds, be they ducks or geese, seldom move when life is easy. That's where potholing, alias jump shooting, comes in. When the ducks don't move, the hunter must. The only thing predictable about a decoy spread on a bluebird day is inactivity. If you want some action, you've got to stir it up.

In many regions, potholing and jump shooting are forgotten sports. Hunters congregate at the marshes and reed-rimmed lakes where they fight for limited space and then try to blow duck calls louder than everybody else. The resulting cacophony scares every duck and goose, leaving the skies empty. And if the hunters can't squeeze into such madcap situations, they turn against the sport and either quit or go home to sulk.

For the hunter who has just a trace of adventurous spirit stirring in his blood, however, some excellent hunting can still be had via shank's mare. Ducks spooked off the big waters go somewhere,

There is no easier chance in all of wingshooting as that given by a jumping mallard as it vaults off reed-clustered openings of marshland or potholes.

and it isn't always south. They learn to work the smaller — much smaller — waters associated with uplands and agriculture, and they hang around for weeks after they've abandoned the larger lakes and marshes.

Before one can become an accomplished potholer or jump-shooter, he should acquire a thorough knowledge of the surrounding countryside, the characteristics of local duck flight patterns, and develop some physical endurance. Important, too, is equipment, but we'll get to that later.

Today, much potholing and jump shooting focuses on mallards, teal, and wood ducks.

Mallards and teal have somewhat different characteristics than wood ducks, favoring the more open areas around farmlands and natural flatlands. This is especially true for teal, which seldom pitch into wooded areas. Their forte is fast flying, and open spaces are best for that. It's seldom that teal are jumped from woodlot ponds. Look for them on drainage ditches, irrigation systems, farm ponds away from standing timber, and flooded spots around corn or grain stubble.

Mallards will upon occasion pitch into wooded potholes, but, except for the flooded oak country of Arkansas, such spots seem to be secondary choices for greenheads. Like teal, mallards enjoy the more open areas where takeoffs and landings are easier. Some of the greatest jump shooting is done on mallards by hunters on swamp skis. It's not the easiest method as it demands lots of high knee action, but mallards relish the small open spaces tucked far back into dense stands of cattails; and the hunter who can probe there not only finds some good shooting, but he's also away from the crowd and gets some of the easiest shots in all of wing-gunning. There's no pushover like a fat greenhead clawing for air at a steep angle. Swing with his bill,

go up with him to compensate for the rising angle, and follow through. He should be lying where he fell, perfectly centered. The shooting in most other forms of potholing or jump shooting is generally considerably tougher.

But when we get to the wood duck — ah, that's a different story. His name tells it all. The bird is at home in the woods. He's a tricky, shifty flier that can thread his way through tree crowns with the skill and artistry of a ruffed grouse. And a woodie may just be doing it with greater speed than a partridge can muster or a woodcock can dream about. Wind

Slipping along the fringes of potholes and streams may be more work than sitting in a blind, but it's the only way to get some action on bluebird days.

and surroundings mean little, if anything. Even on blustery days they'll drop full flaps, tumble through a canopy of oak crowns, and touch down lightly on a pool of water no larger than your bathtub. They handle their departure with the same grace, ease, and speed. Make no mistake about it — woodies can fly.

One secret to finding woodies is knowing that they love acorns. They'll feed heavily on them if a fresh crop is handy. True, wood ducks use duck weed and other marsh-grown foods, and they will drop into corn. One of the best, and fastest, duck shoots I've had in recent years came in a half-picked corn field where I was anticipating mallards and geese. The woodies came from nearby ponds just as the first streak of pink tinged the eastern horizon. Later in the season I bagged a couple more in the same vicinity, and their midday crops were bulging with corn. However, when the day is hot and sultry, or when they've been hassled around marshes and corn fields, wood ducks will feed contentedly on acorns in shady woodland ponds. Few hunters bother to check out these wet upland patches, and, once settled, the wood ducks have no compulsion to leave.

If ever a duck was made for hunters who

A drake wood duck collected from a shallow depression between two oak-covered hillsides. Woodies like to feed on acorns here. The gun is a Weatherby Model Ninety-Two.

like to prowl, it is the woodie. We're lucky to have wood ducks to hunt, for at one time they were endangered. They were totally protected in both the United States and Canada from 1918 to 1941. Their plight wasn't solely due to market hunting, although that practice certainly contributed to their decline in numbers. Habitat destruction was a definite factor: lumbering interests removed the hollow trees in which woodies nest, and the birds didn't bring off broods. By stopping all hunting for wood ducks and by providing them with man-made nesting boxes, conservationists brought back the species until now it is healthy and huntable. In many respects it is a classic comeback, showing what conservation efforts can do.

Walking through the hardwoods helter-skelter isn't the way to pothole woodies and occasional mallards, of course. That can be a long, hard pull. The shortcut to potholing wood ducks is taken by remembering the lay of the land. They might drop in where only a depression between hills holds rain; a true pond or pothole isn't needed. Note such depressions while you're hunting squirrels,

Blue-winged teal making a quick getaway. A gun on the order of an upland piece is suggested for jump shooting because fast gun handling is important here.

America's most beautiful duck is also the one most suited to jump shooting — the woodie.

grouse, or rabbits and come back during the duck season when bluebird days silence the marshes. But remember to sneak up quietly on the potential hideouts; stop a long distance off and watch carefully. If ducks are there, plan a stalk. Obviously, this type of hunting depends on conditions. Dry seasons may negate the possibility of finding woodies spread through the uplands, while wet years may provide tremendous sport and widespread opportunities.

Beaver ponds make excellent resting and feeding places for wood ducks, teal, and mallards. In heavily forested areas, such sites are naturals for all three species.

Decoys set on woodland ponds and other lesser waters aren't very productive unless other hunters move the birds around, such as on opening day. Ducks that find smaller waters to their liking aren't inclined to charge, and decoys draw mainly in the early moments of shooting light or in the last half hour before quitting time. These birds remain settled for most of the daylight hours; consequently, they won't fly enough to see a decoy spread. The only possible exception can be on stormy days

Swinging on woodies that jumped from a small stand of rain water in a hardwood grove where they were resting and looking for acorns. Note that the shooter's check is tight on the comb of the stock.

For a potholer who hunts where lead shot can still be used, Remington's Lightweight 20-gauge Magnum can get the job done, and it's easy to carry on long walks to isolated pools.

when high winds prompt midday flighting. Otherwise, the game is one of the hunter making his own luck by scouting the countryside.

GUNS AND LOADS FOR POTHOLING

Although potholing and jump shooting are equated with the uplands, the shooting isn't the same type of close-range stuff one gets on ruffed grouse, pheasants, and woodcock. Open-bored guns, small bores, and light loads are not recommended. Ducks are tougher than most upland species, thanks to their thick layer of down plus heavy muscles and bones, and they are spooky and will jump before the hunter gets close. The goal of getting within few yards of the birds is seldom realized; ducks on small ponds are constantly alert, and the first misstep by a hunter will send them off. For these reasons, a jump-shooter's patterns begin where the grouse hunter's leave off, namely, at modified choke. A solid modified cluster of 60–64 percent is about minimal for jump shooting. If the gun is a double-barrel, its second tube should be a full choke throwing an honest 70 percent pattern or better.

Pumpguns and autoloaders with modified barrels can be excellent potholing guns. A certain amount of patterning versatility can be had from them if the hunter is careful about load selection and implementation. Some modified chokes will do full-choke

percentages with selected magnum loads, and if such loads are put into the magazine as second and third rounds, the gun will deliver modified patterns on the first shot and follow up with full-choke densities.

Extra-full-choke patterns can be a blessing when birds jump well out and fly straight away. Such a target exposes very little of its vital area to the gun, and the shot string must concentrate enough pellets of sufficient energy to supply both multiple hits and deep penetration. A duck flying away from the hunter represents a vital area no bigger than a clay target, and to reach that area the pellets must drive through down and backbone or through down and viscera. For this kind of shooting, patterns of 75 percent or better come in handy; however, they are a definite handicap on shots inside 40–45 yards. For most hunters with a modicum of stalking ability, patterns of 60 to 75 percent are about right.

Shotguns for potholing and jump shooting split the difference between the feathery styles used on upland game and the heavyweights lugged into blinds. They should be lively for fast handling on surprise flushes, yet heavy enough to absorb some of the recoil from high-velocity or magnum loads. Doubles with 28-inch barrels bored M&F are fine, be they over-unders or side-by-sides. Browning's 12-gauge B-SS and Winchester's Model 23 fit the description nicely. As for less expensive guns, there's always the Stevens Model 311 and the current Savage Fox Model B. Browning's field-grade Citori is deservedly popular and points well with 28-inch tubes while still being readily portable. Ruger's Red Label 12 gauge serves well on waterfowl, too, as does the Weatherby Orion.

Among repeaters, Ithaca's field-grade Model 37 with a 12-gauge, 28-inch barrel bored modified or full will get the job done, as will Remington's Sportsman 12 or 870. The Mossberg Model 500 with a 28-inch barrel also serves well. Weatherby's Model Eighty-Two autoloader gave me a full season of potholing successes with a 28-inch barrel in place and the choke tubes used judiciously. Remington's Model 1100 12-gauge is about the best pointing autoloader ever designed for use on flushing birds, but is topping out on weight for a jump-shooter's gun at 8–8½ pounds. Stick to the 28-inch barrel for an 1100, as the 30-inch barrel can make the gun unwieldy for quick pointing.

Whenever possible, a carrying strap should be attached to the potholing smoothbore for easier transportation between potholes and ditches. Any gun — single-shot, bolt-action, double, pump, or auto — can be fitted with the proper swivels by Michael's (Uncle Mike's), P.O. Box 13010, Portland,

Swivels are available for all modern shotguns. This one fits the popular Remington Model 1100 autoloader.

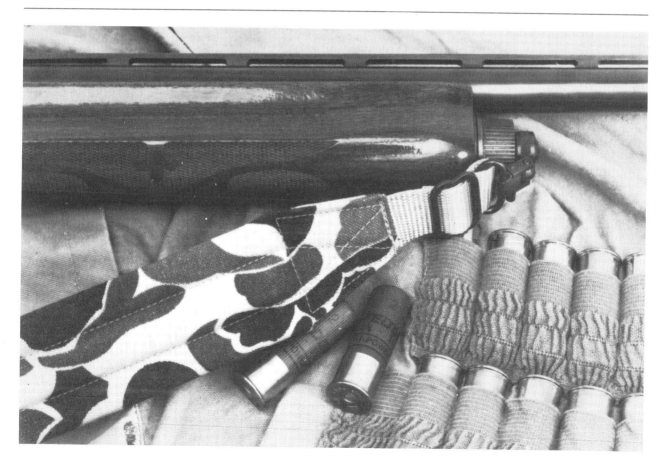

When ducks frustrate the hunter and retriever alike by not working the big water,
that's the time to start moving. If the ducks don't move, you must.
(Photo by Gerald F. Moran)

Oregon 97213. Local dealers generally carry the line, but a color folder will be sent detailing the complete line if requested.

Load selection is important to potholing because much of the shooting is at outgoing targets which expose less of the vital area to the pattern than do passing or overhead birds. Moreover, the velocity of a pellet is reduced by the speed of the outgoing bird; and, however slight that reduction may be, it can have consequences if the range and velocity are marginal. Thus, potholing loads should deliver dense patterns of potent pellets to anchor the birds where they fall.

The lightest lead pellet suggested is the hard No. 5 in 1¼- to 1½-ounce loads. These are perfectly suited to the modified choke for ranges of 40 yards, and they are ideal for the 3-inch 20 for a combination of density and penetration. Number 5s are also good in the full-choked potholing gun out to 40 yards, as their greater density is an advantage. On overhead and passing shots, No. 5s can perform perfectly out to 50 yards because more of the target's vital area is exposed; however, on outgoing birds that range is reduced somewhat due to the need for optimum penetration.

When ranges begin to exceed 40 yards, full-choke patterns of No. 4s come into play. Fours are not this writer's favorite pellet, but, when teamed with a full choke that will hold them tightly for multiple hits at long range, they do add a degree of penetrating energy for 40- to 50-yard shooting. Buffered magnums with copper-plated 4s are recommended.

In many respects, the shots one gets in jump shooting are like those of the trap range — rising outgoers with the vital area becoming proportionately smaller relative to the spreading shot charge. Summertime practice at trapshooting can help immensely.

A carrying sling comes highly recommended for potholing, as there can be a lot of distance between potential hot spots. A game carrier is useful, too.

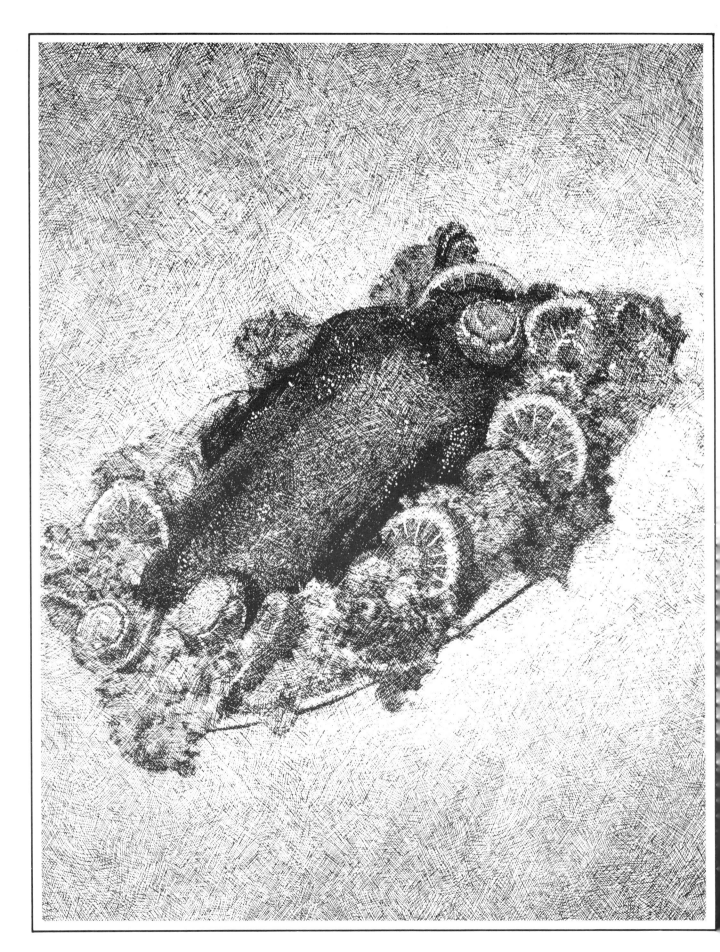

27
From Gunner
to Gourmet

"I sure love duck hunting," the man said, "but I hate to eat them. They taste horrible!"

His wife added, "I don't mind cooking pheasants or grouse, because they always come out of the oven tasting good, and I can get some satisfaction from that. But wild ducks turn me off. No matter what recipe I try, they still have that wild, liverlike flavor and marshy, fishy cooking odors. The Lord knows I've tried, but I can't find any recipe to improve their taste. I hate to waste ducks, but. . ."

These same comments are made time and again by ardent duck hunters and their families; people who don't like a strong, wild flavor cannot enjoy ducks *au naturel.* It is mainly for those whose olfactory senses and taste buds disapprove of waterfowl flavors that this chapter is being written. Others, who can abide the wild flavor and cooking odors without grimacing, need little help; for them, recipes abound. Their main problem is avoiding drying out the bird during cooking. This can be countered in three ways: by steeping, using sauces, and by stewing.

In a household where the wild flavor of waterfowl (ducks in particular) is acceptable, the most common method of preparation is roasting in an oven, or pan frying like domestic birds. Leaving a wild duck to roast invites dry, stringy results; no amount of basting will moisten the bird throughout. Unless such birds are served with a sauce, the meal becomes a chewy chore and requires substantial amounts of water or wine to wash it down. I'll get to sauces in a moment. First, however, there's an interesting way to enhance the meat via soaking in the basting liquids or a specially prepared formula.

With his bird safely in hand, the hunter may be wondering how it's going to taste on the table. It's a fact of waterfowling life that many hunters don't like the taste of ducks and geese, unless some pre-cooking preparations are observed.

To improve the moisture of roast duck and goose, time the cooking so that the bird will be done about an hour before serving. Carve the bird in the roaster (if possible) as soon as the meat is finished. If you can't carve the bird in the roaster, do it on a cutting board but don't let the meat cool. Slice the breast but leave the wings and legs whole. Discard the skeleton and return the meat to the basting fluid in the roasting pan, immersing the pieces as much as possible. You can add some spices at this time if desired. If the liquid isn't deep enough to cover the pieces, at least coat both sides of the slices and appendages by working them into the liquid on a long fork. Then return the roaster to the still-warm oven to steep until mealtime. Turn the meat after the first half hour.

A minimum of an hour's steeping time in basting juices will generally find the slices being penetrated by the juices to make the meat more succulent. The slices can be probed with a fork while steeping to ensure more penetration by the juices. The best way to serve is directly from the roasterr so that as much of the moisture as possible remains in contact with the slices. Most sportsmen who are not put off by the cooking odor or table flavors of wild ducks readily admit that steeping the slices makes each meal more enjoyable because of easier chewing.

The steeping time can be longer than one hour, but the important point here is using ample basting fluids initially during the roasting period so that the pieces will be covered during steeping.

Sauces can also enhance the dish when ducks and geese are cooked *au naturel*, meaning without any pre-cooking manipulation (parboiling, poaching, marinating) to alter their table flavor. One must always remember that a sauce differs from a gravy, however. A gravy is made from the ingredients derived from the meat itself. For instance, chicken gravy is made from the giblets and pan drippings of the chicken being cooked. Sauces, on the other hand, are made from stock and other ingredients not common to the bird being prepared. Prior to the widespread use of refrigeration, sauces were developed to cover up the taste of leftover meats that had lost their freshness. Today, sauces serve a different purpose, being used instead to influence flavor and to instill moisture. However, in the case of wild ducks and geese, sauces can also be used legitimately to cover up those flavors some people find peculiar. Following is a very easy sauce to prepare, plus a couple of variations:

¼ cup of butter or margarine
2 tablespoons of flour
1 tablespoon of cornstarch
1 cup of light cream (cold)
1 can (approx. 10 oz.) of chicken stock
Salt
Black pepper

Use a medium-sized saucepan, preferably with a heavy bottom. Begin by melting the butter or margarine over moderate heat until it starts to foam.

In a separate bowl, blend the flour and cornstarch into the light cream. Then pour this mixture into the foaming butter, always stirring, until the sauce has thickened. Reduce the heat so that scorching doesn't occur.

When the sauce is thick and consistent, stir in the chicken stock and simmer over low heat for about 6 to 7 minutes. Season the mixture with salt and pepper after cooking, and strain it through a sieve into a

---

Skin the bird and open any wound channels to permit the flow of blood and other fluids during poaching and parboiling. Make many more perforations with a long, sharp fork before and during the poaching/parboiling session.

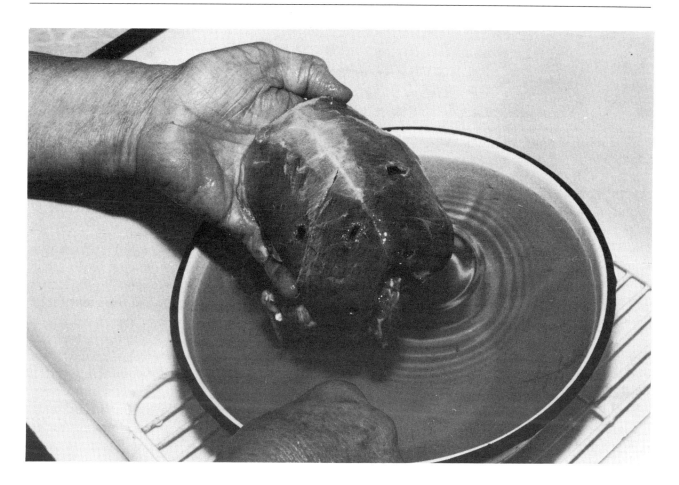

Have a small strainer handy to remove the brownish froth that floats to the surface.

serving bowl. Keep the sauce warm until the meal is served, and spoon on according to personal tastes.

This sauce can be thought of as basic, subject to some embellishment. Some people may wish to use white pepper, because it is a white sauce. For use with ducks, it is enhanced by the inclusion of 1 tablespoon of anchovy paste and 1 tablespoon of capers that have been rinsed under cold, running water to eliminate the chemical taste from jar liquids. Both the paste and the capers will be added during the early cooking, of course.

For those who enjoy a zestier flavor, 1 or 2 tablespoons of French mustard and 1 tablespoon of curry powder can be stirred in instead of the anchovy paste and capers. Or, rather than use table salt, one can sprinkle in celery salt.

The point is that sauces can lend greater enjoyment to the meal when the basic meat is potentially dry and suspect on flavor. Recipe books reveal many ideas, and the creation of sauces is open to innovation.

Stewing is a method generally used for tough meats, and it works well with fowl that have a tendency to be dry and stringy after normal cooking (roasting, pan frying). Stewing works especially well with the diver ducks, but don't hesitate to stew puddlers, either, if they hint of marshy, liverlike flavor.

To prepare a duck for stewing, the breast

should be skinned and cut into bite-size pieces. This also can be done to the meat on the legs and wings. Such cutting will expose more area to the tenderizing and flavor-influencing effect of the stewing mixture.

Before stewing a duck, marinating is suggested. Marinate the bite-size pieces in either buttermilk or your choice of red wine for at least 24 hours in either a glass bowl or a suitable crock. Do not use aluminum containers, as they often lend a trace of metal flavor. Prior to removing the duck meat from the marinade, assemble these ingredients for the stew, which is based on about 1½ pounds of meat:

½ pound of bacon, sliced
1 large onion, chopped coarsely
1 medium carrot, sliced finely
½ teaspoon of garlic powder
2 large stalks of celery, diced
½ teaspooon of dried basil
¼ cup of red wine
¼ cup of water

Begin by taking the meat from the marinade and drying off the excess liquid. Set these pieces aside briefly while starting the stew in a large, relatively deep skillet by frying the bacon until it is crisp. Then remove the bacon, add the onion, garlic, celery, car-

More poking with a fork, together with a long cut down the breastbone, will help release distasteful fluids.

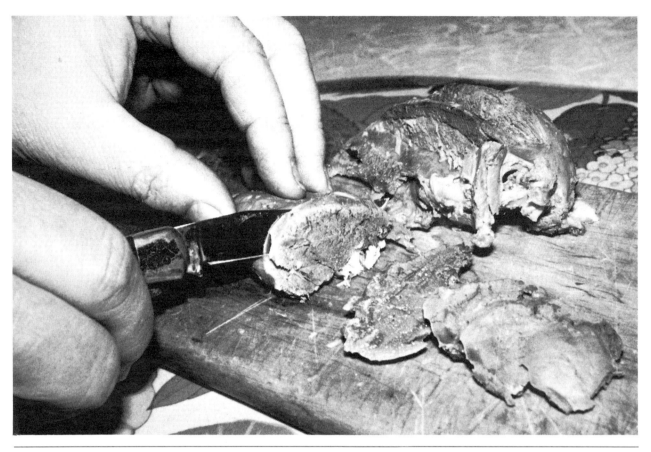

After poaching or parboiling, the breast meat is first filleted and then sliced into tiny steaks.

rot, and basil and cook over low heat until the onion is soft. Introduce the meat and increase the heat slightly to cook quickly. Turn the pieces, but sparingly. When the bite-size pieces appear to have been penetrated thoroughly by heat, pour in the wine and water and cook over moderate heat for 20 minutes. The amount of wine can be reduced according to individual preference, but probably should not be increased. When finished, this stew can be served atop buttered toast or either white rice or steamed wild rice. As a variation, the vegetables can be left chunky.

The many recipe books available carry tremendous numbers of other recipes for sauces and stews. Don't be afraid to try some different ones. The joy of discovery is a big part of the fun of cooking.

THE FLAVOR/FLUID CONNECTION

So much for those who can enjoy (or tolerate) the natural cooking odors and flavors of wild duck. My experience has been that considerably more people find wild duck offensive and distasteful. Some writers and city chefs continually parrot the old line that ducks of the year and puddle ducks that feed on grain and corn have a better flavor, but in over thirty-five years of hunting I haven't found that to be true., Puddle ducks may feed in corn and grain fields, but after feeding they return to the marshes and swamps where they guzzle duckweed and other aquatic vegetation. Nor do preparations such as a simple soaking in cold water remove the offensive wild flavors or eliminate the objectionable cooking odors. Indeed, those who are the slightest bit sensitive to peculiar or robust fowl odors and flavors will turn away from a table of duck *au naturel* — and I happen to be one of them.

Sporting ethics tell us that everything we bag should be utilized on the table or not hunted. Anything less is a sheer waste of a natural resource. In that vein, I have experimented with methods which, in large measure, reduce and eliminate the wild odors and flavors. These include poaching, parboiling, and marinating.

Essentially, a waterfowl's offensive cooking and table character *come from its body fluids*, and the problem will persist as long as the fluids remain imbedded. Soaking whole birds, basting, inundating with wine, and using sauces will not remove those fluids, but will, as mentioned earlier, merely cover up some of their extremes. All is not lost, however. Ducks can be retrieved in the kitchen as well as in the marsh.

The wild, offensive flavors can be virtually eliminated by (1) drawing out the dastardly fluids, and (2) influencing the meats in a new flavor direction by marinating them. The process may sound involved, but it isn't, and it takes one to the early stages of gourmet cooking with a purpose and without drudgery. The ends will indeed justify the means.

The key to this method is poaching or parboiling. The bird can be either plucked or

The final marinade containing sliced onions, celery, bay leaves, and black pepper in chablis.

Mallard mini-steaks browned and sauteed in beef broth served atop rice. Top with a sauce, and the offensive "wild" flavor is completely gone.

skinned: the main difference is that a skinned bird will release more of the fluids that will be drawn out by the heated salt water. Moreover, it isn't necessary to keep the birds whole; they can be disjointed and poached or parboiled as breasts, legs, and wings. If the birds are to be roasted, leaving them whole works fine, provided a large boiling pot is available.

In poaching, the water is kept at a temperature just below boiling. Parboiling, on the other hand, is done with a rolling boil. In general, poaching is adequate for geese because geese often do not have the same offensive flavors as ducks because they feed less, if at all, on aquatic vegetation. With some mallards and wood ducks, though, poaching will work provided the meat is well-perforated.

If frozen, allow the meat to thaw completely so that all blood and fluids will flow freely from the start. With a long-tined fork, stab the breast and upper legs deeply and frequently. These perforations will serve as exits for the escaping blood and fluids.

Use at least one heaping tablespoon of salt per quart of water, and fill the pot with enough water to cover the meat, plus a little more. Heat the water.

Have a small strainer and cup ready as the purification begins. The blood and fluids will appear on the surface as reddish-brown froth, and they will have to be skimmed off. Adjust the heat to prevent a sudden boiling that could send foam over the top. Dropping back a few degrees won't hurt the process as long as the basic temperature remains near the boiling point.

A good poaching or parboiling session will take about 12 to 15 minutes. Two or three times during this session, remove the meat, one part at a time, and perforate again. Work the fork sideways slightly to open the holes for more efficient draining. Although repeated perforations may appear to be excessive, they are necessary and, fortunately, they do not have an adverse affect on the finished meat. Expansion from heat tends to close them, which is why additional perforations are recommended at intervals throughout the 12- to 15-minute period.

The meat should not be lifted out of the water when ready. There will be a scummy film on the water, and lifting the pieces will only coat them with the scum as they are raised. Instead, place the pot under a faucet and let cold water run into the mixture and float the film away. Finish by rinsing the meat under a strong flow from the kitchen faucet.

After a 15-minute parboiling session, the meat on many ducks, especially the smaller ones, may be cooked well enough for eating. However, they are rather dry and stringy and totally lacking in flavor at this point.

Whole birds can now be roasted, the taste being influenced by various spices, vegetables, and basting liquids. Of course, the roasting time must be adjusted downward because of the amount of heat already absorbed by the meat. Use a moderate oven (300 °– 325°) and baste often. This technique of putting a poached or parboiled duck into an oven brings an amazing tenderness to otherwise tough, stringy flesh.

Birds that have been sectioned can also be pan fried immediately, the same time adjustments being necessary.

But for further improvements in flavor, consider marinating.

MARINADES

The best marinating technique for our purposes exposes the most meat to the wine and spices. A whole duck, or an entire breast or leg, is too big and solid to absorb much of the marinade liquid. The secret is cutting the breast and legs into bite-size pieces before marinating. Leg meat will have to be trimmed according to the smaller muscles. An excellent method of exposing breast meat to the marinade is filleting the meat from the breastbone and slicing it laterally to make mini-steaks, just as one would steak the backstrap of venison. Cut the mini-steaks about three eights of an inch thick. When browned later, heat can get through these mini-steaks more easily than it can penetrate the full breast.

Marinades can be assembled in a deep crock, or glass or stainless bowl. (Avoid aluminum, which tends to leave a metallic hint.) They can be as simple as a mere wine bath, or they can be garnished with spices. For simplicity plus flavor enhancement, a combination of wine, black pepper, sliced carrots, onions, and celery is recommended. Begin with a layer of sliced onions, carrots, and celery, then place the first layer of meat atop that vegetable base. Sprinkle liberally with black pepper, then repeat the layer-building procedure. Three vegetable layers are generally sufficient for most waterfowl marinades. Cap with a heavy sprinkling of pepper before adding wine.

Which wine? There is tremendous leeway. Traditionally, fowl have been associated with the white wines, and a sturdy Rhine or authoritative chablis will do. However, a dry sherry will also appeal to some diners. A cheap Rhine or chablis contributes nothing, however. Moreover, since waterfowl meats are dark, a red wine isn't entirely taboo. A port can be effective. Some wine producers now market a white port that deserves attention. Personal taste should be your guide. Trying different wines is part of the fun.

In any case, the wine should cover the meat. Pour it on the layered vegetables and meat. Then cover the bowl with plastic wrapping and let it stand for at least 48 hours at a temperature of 40°–45° or in the refrigerator. Turn the meat once every 12 hours to stir the mixture and to bring new wine molecules into contact with the meat.

At the end of the marinating period, the vegetables can be saved for use in the final dish, if desired, or discarded.

COOKING FOR FLAVOR AND SUCCULENCE

After the marinating period, waterfowl meat can be cooked about any way one wishes. If the meat has been chunked or sliced, however, it lends itself best to stews and pan frying.

An important point is that a careless, unimaginative cook can still ruin much of the preparatory work. For although most of the unsavory flavors and odors will have been removed and replaced by the poaching, par-boiling, or marinating, heat and an indifferent attitude can render the mini-steaks tough and tasteless. The best approach is one that seals

in the new flavor of wine seasoning and increases the succulence. In this hunter's humble opinion, that means browning in a frying pan and finishing in a stew or stewlike medium. The method works like this:

Strain the marinade, separating vegetables and meat. In a deep frying pan of generous proportions, preferably one of the Teflon-lined or Silverstone-types, pour in a light layer of unsaturated oil, and heat. Add a fresh, medium-size onion either sliced or chopped. When the onion begins to sizzle and dance, begin adding the chunks or slices of waterfowl meat. Adjust the heat to minimize spatter, and brown the meat on all sides. Browning seals in the juices and should be done at the highest temperature possible without getting one's fork-wielding hand prickled by red-hot spray. Once all the meat has been browned, it can either be left in the frying pan (if it is large enough) or moved to a deeper stew pot or Dutch oven.

The next step is adding vegetables and seasoning. Add your choice of black pepper, salt, celery salt, poultry seasoning — whatever. Then put in either the vegetables from the marinade, or freshly sliced or chunked carrots, celery, and onion in amounts deemed sufficient for your table and taste.

Then comes the final step, the one that brings moisture and further flavor: pour in a can of soup or bouillon, such as cream of mushroom soup, cream of celery soup, cream of onion soup, or beef bouillon. Incidentally, I have found most commercial chicken bouillon rather weak for this purpose. Beef bouillon exerts itself more fully, even though seemingly being out of place. Sophisticated chefs may cringe at the thought, but who cares? It all tastes pretty good to those of us who hunt and cook quantities of wild game instead of merely reading books written by big-city chefs.

Pour in the soup or bouillon, adding water as needed. Cover the mixture after stirring and let cook for 20 to 30 minutes over medium heat. Stir occasionally to prevent sticking; add some water if and when the mixture cooks down. Finish while there is still some sauce in the pan. Check for seasoning. Serve over buttered toast or wild rice. For speed, minute rice will do fine.

The above steps will work with all waterfowl — mud hens through puddlers, geese, and brant — transforming a common "fish duck" into a thoroughly enjoyable meal. In fact, mud hens, alias coots, can be turned into meals that rival those featuring corn-fed mallards when their unsavory body fluids have been drawn out by poaching or parboiling. Geese generally have less obnoxious flavors and/or cooking odors, and poaching (meaning the use of hot water just below the boiling point) is generally adequate, provided the bird has been skinned and its breast

muscles perforated deeply to free the imbedded fluids.

To summarize, the classic error made by hunters and cooks is trying to handle waterfowl like domestic birds. It can't be done. They are birds of not only a different feather, but also of a different fluid. And if those fluids remain in the meat, the results will always offend many people regardless of the cooking and seasoning method. The offending fluids must be drawn off by parboiling or poaching before any improvement can take place, and tangy marinades tend to replace those lost fluids with wine seasoning and to temper whatever potentially offensive flavors are left. Heating the mini-steaks in a medium that protects against dryness, while adding to the meal's overall attractiveness, completes the procedure. While the method does take time, it also works wonders.

The methods presented here are applicable to all waterfowl, such as this drake redhead and even coots and sea ducks.

Epilogue

He brought in the mallard, the black Lab did, and when he shook himself no corner of the blind was safe from the spray of icy water. He was alert and excited, watching every move the hunters made and scanning the leadened skies, waiting for more retrieves. Perhaps later he would curl up on a scrap of burlap in the blind and sleep when the action slowed down, which was fine with his master, who also found the blind a relaxing sanctuary. It was all part of the sport — the Lab escaped confrontations with the neighborhood kids and cats; the hunter escaped from the work-a-day world. And whether the action was fast and furious as birds moved on a weather front, or whether things were dead calm on a bluebird afternoon, it made little difference. They were duck hunting.

More than one hunter has felt that way, of course. The same must be true of retrievers who always seem to sense the season and the next day's hunt. The fun of waterfowling is just being there — seeing, hearing, smelling, freezing, experiencing the thrill of autumn and early winter. Those are the things of which memories are made. They keep the hunter sane when the boss screams and overtime piles up. They are the reason retrievers can tolerate pesty kids, and cats that stalk food dishes.

Despite the scientific bent of the preceding pages, all the advanced equipment and concepts of modern waterfowling run secondary to the pleasures of the sport itself. The best guns and loads, the biggest decoys, the most lifelike calls, and all the practicing one can do with guns and calls and dogs somehow do not generate the electricity that builds and crackles when they are all put together in a marsh blind, a stubble field pit, a layout boat, or during a jump shoot. Then they play like a symphonic crescendo.

Today, we must keep things in proper perspective. The days of market and meat hunting are over. No one who can afford to go hunting is going to starve if he doesn't bag the limit. The total outdoor experience is the pure pleasure of waterfowling, and it has an ethical basis that stresses clean kills, good sportsmanship, and a deep concern for conservation. Utilizing on the table all the game we take is another tenet of that ethic. If the game is not to be eaten, why harvest it? Hunting merely to kill isn't sport — it's slaughter.

Our dwindling wetlands, along with gradual and periodic dips in overall waterfowl populations, cannot support indiscriminate hunting and killing. Two things that technology cannot provide for hunters, unfortunately, are self-discipline and common sense. Therefore, we must hope that modern hunters will use advanced equipment and concepts to improve their sport — not destroy it.

Index